Ethnicity, Gender, and Diversity

Ethnicity, Gender, and Diversity

Law and Justice on TV

Edited by
Peter Robson and Jennifer L. Schulz

LEXINGTON BOOKS
Lanham • Boulder • New York • London

Published by Lexington Books
An imprint of The Rowman & Littlefield Publishing Group, Inc.
4501 Forbes Boulevard, Suite 200, Lanham, Maryland 20706
www.rowman.com

6 Tinworth Street, London SE11 5AL, United Kingdom

British Library Cataloguing in Publication Information Available

The hardback edition of this book was previously catalogued by the Library of Congress as follows:

Library of Congress Cataloging-in-Publication Data

Names: Robson, Peter, 1947- editor. | Schulz, Jennifer L. editor.
Title: Ethnicity, gender, and diversity : law and justice on tv / edited by Peter Robson and Jennifer L. Schulz.
Description: Lanham : Lexington Books, 2019. | Includes bibliographical references and index.
Identifiers: LCCN 2018047709 (print) | LCCN 2018049907 (ebook) | ISBN 9781498572910 (electronic) | ISBN 9781498572903 (cloth) | ISBN 9781498572927 (pbk)
Subjects: LCSH: Justice, Administration of on television. | Law on television. | Ethnicity on television. | Sex role on television | Minorities on television
Classification: LCC PN1992.8.J87 (ebook) | LCC PN1992.8.J87 E84 2019 (print) | DDC 791.45/6554—dc23
LC record available at https://lccn.loc.gov/2018047709

To Elliott, with love. —JLS
For Linda, the inspiration who named me. —PR

Contents

Chapter 1

Introduction

Ethnicity, Gender, and Diversity on TV in Context

Peter Robson and Jennifer L. Schulz

Scholarship in the field of law and popular culture is paradoxical. It is, on the one hand, highly international. We watch, it seems, the same films and see the same television series whether we are in North America, Europe, or Australia, and so we write about them for international audiences. The context, however, is a significantly local affair. Our legal systems are markedly different, whether it be approaches—common law to codes, or personnel—elected judges to professional civil servants. Our educational practices are also quite distinctive. Thus, the role of the media in shaping perceptions of law and justice are determined by different local histories.[1]

The approach one takes to uncovering the nature of law and how it operates depends crucially on the questions one wants answered. These in turn depend on who is making the inquiries, in what circumstances, and in what broader social context. The concern of many has been to uncover how it is that the legal system, which promises so much in terms of equal treatment by law, so consistently does not deliver equality. Our legal systems operate in the interests of the few against the interests of the many and are allowed to do so with no or minimal social conflict. It is to answer questions like this that scholars have asked questions not just about the impact of particular rules, but more importantly, about what contribution is made by the way law is represented in books, films, and on television. This is the most recent approach found in many law schools. It is linked, however, with issues that have fascinated scholars since the beginning of modern legal education and scholarship.

MODERN LEGAL SCHOLARSHIP

In Britain, law faculties were in existence for many centuries but it was not until the nineteenth century when they took on any role in the actual preparation of students for practice. Legal education as distinct from in-house professional training for lawyers by the profession has only existed in the United Kingdom since the 1870s.[2] In the United States, the separation of the academy and the profession has led to qualification through State Bar exams and a profession with a wide range of business and political connections.[3] In Europe, with its civil law system, the systems for training for the various branches of the profession have varied.[4] When British universities started to take undergraduates and offer courses in law from the 1870s there were two approaches. One was to offer a degree in the style we are familiar with today from the United States—the postgraduate law degree. This British law degree focused on the details of the operation of the legal system and was geared toward teaching professional practical subjects to graduates who had commenced working in the legal profession. These young men—and they were, by order of the courts,[5] all men—already had a university degree, usually in some Arts subject, so they were in some sense "educated." The law degree focused on those areas of practice that were central to the working life of the lawyer. These part-time law degrees were undertaken at the beginning of the day, at lunchtime, and at dinner time to enable British law students to combine their study with full-time work as trainee lawyers. The second approach, which many lawyers opted for, was the in-house training route. Here, would-be lawyers completed a period of service in legal firms as articled clerks or apprentices, while taking examinations set by local legal professional societies. It was in this second context of focused professional training that legal education as a distinct degree for students immediately out of school in the United Kingdom commenced on a broad scale. In North America, law students do not go to law school straight from school; they already have a first university degree. In Canada, law school graduates go on to complete a period of articles followed by a bar exam, while American law graduates immediately take the exam. In Europe and beyond the variable goals have similarly been contested and this remains an ongoing issue.[6]

In the 1960s when higher education expanded, the full-time law degree dominated and addressed the crucial issue of balance between professional training and university education.[7] It was recognized that would-be lawyers need to reflect on the nature of law and its relationship with justice, and this featured heavily in all the debates on the nature and function of the law degree. A consensus emerged that there was more to a university law degree than merely providing training for the profession, which was recognized in the inclusion of more "esoteric" subjects like jurisprudence. These would allow the formation of fully rounded lawyers for the future, capable of disputation and contemplation above the narrow details of the common law, statutory codes, and the dangerous view that "the law is the law." The aim was to produce the kind of lawyer whom the distinguished lawyer and internationally recognized novelist, Sir Walter Scott spoke of when he distinguished between the lawyer as "a mechanic, a mere working mason" and one with some knowledge of history or literature who might call him or herself "an architect."[8]

Now, in the 2000s, we are even more cognizant of the role that context, culture, and circumstances play in the operation of law and justice. According to MacNeil and Hutchings, one of the most remarkable developments in common law jurisprudence in the 2000s is its shift away from "critique" to "culture."[9] The focus on culture includes both textual sources and interpretative method, and thus Cultural Legal Studies refuses strict disciplinary boundaries and embraces new, interdisciplinary connections. In fact, Rosemary Coombe argues that "the relationship between law and culture should not be defined."[10] Instead, "an ongoing and mutual rupturing—the undoing of one term by the other—may be a more productive figuration than the image of relationship or joinder."[11] Within cultural legal studies there is an expanding scholarship focused on popular culture, and especially on images of law and lawyers. In 1986, Anthony Chase noted what he described as the failure of legal scholars to recognize and embrace the images of law and lawyers in popular culture as legitimate subjects of scholarly study.[12] He wanted to encourage the study of the quotidian experience of law and lawyers,[13] and use popular culture as a bridge to legal culture.[14] Law and popular culture, as a field of study in its own right, was born. As MacNeil and Hutchings state, "cultural legal studies strays from the hermetically sealed space of . . . the law school's 'laboratory'—that is, the library, with its dull, dusty and dreary tomes—and turns to an array of *fictions*."[15] This turn toward fiction embraces novels and literary works, or law and literature; film, or law and film; and television and music, or law and popular culture.

The study of law and popular culture takes us into a realm where modern socio-legal scholars have, as yet, only ventured in a limited way. Law and popular culture furthers the enquiry about how law and justice really operate. It looks not just at the actions and practices of the justice system but at what factors help to drive the success or failure of laws and legal systems. By taking seriously the culture of law in the form in which it is presented to the public, we generate a richer picture than previously available. Law and popular culture, while not a dominant approach to law, does provide important, new possibilities to complement other legal scholars' work.

LAW AND LITERATURE

Before there was law and popular culture, however, there was law and literature. As long ago as 1913, John Marshall Gest's *The Lawyer in Literature* was the first of a stream of writing about law which showed its link to literature. Building on Wigmore's 1908 list of legal novels,[16] Gest's early collection was very much in the spirit of establishing the lawyer as a fully rounded scholar and was followed by other collections. As Michael Freeman points out, this link to literature was the recognition of something that has fascinated scholars for hundreds of years.[17] Freeman notes that law's engagement with popular culture goes back to the mists of time. Within the Old Testament there are jurisprudential issues aplenty and these expand greatly in ancient Greece. With their roots in Gest's collection, there has been scholarship on the interface between law and literature for the past century.

The law and literature relationship is understood in two principal ways. The less practiced approach is to study the literary forms that judges and lawyers employ in their legal writing; law as literature. We find this approach, for example, in the 1998 *The Literature of the Law*, which contains extracts from some of the more literary judgments of common law judges on topics as diverse as law and the downtrodden, law in wartime, the law and justice, and judicial infirmities.[18] The more common and more read approach to law and literature is to focus on how law is represented within novels and plays; law in literature. Scholars consider what examining works of literature can bring to the understanding of law both within the legal community and outside it. The editors of one collection of essays on law and literature, for instance, suggest that drawing on the insights of literature allows key legal issues to be brought to life in ways which orthodox legal materials simply cannot.[19]

Representations of law in literature are the principal focus of much of the scholarship.[20] Coverage of writers, novelists, and playwrights such as Bertolt Brecht, Angela Carter, Charles Dickens, Susan Glaspell, Thomas Hardy, Henrik Ibsen, Franz Kafka, Harper Lee, Herman Melville, Arthur Miller, Edgar Allan Poe, Sir Walter Scott, and William Shakespeare is therefore very common. Not only are legal themes mined within literary sources but there is also some attention paid to the literary elements within traditional legal sources such as trials. law and literature's dedicated journals are fulsome, the Association for the Study of Law, Culture, and Humanities is vibrant, and there are courses on law and literature in many law schools. The work of law and literature scholars sits alongside that of writers on the products of the twentieth-century, film and television, however, it is quite distinct. As Lincoln Faller puts it

> literary texts are . . . able to escape or smooth over strongly felt contradictions in belief and practice that other kinds of texts have difficulty dealing with. This can make them powerful instruments for "solving" social and political problems . . . or alternatively escaping the insufficiency in the face of such problems of other, supposedly more reality-orientated forms of discourse.[21]

This, then is the promise and insight provided by law and literature. It allows us to contemplate such "contemporary" issues as consent, power, and rape by looking at the relationship between Alex and Tess in *Tess of the D'Urbervilles*,[22] or the broader theme of violence against women.[23] The work of Alice Walker in *The Color Purple* similarly provides an element of distance from viewers' own preconceptions and perspectives to allow debate to be framed in a way such that viewers are likely to be less threatened.[24] By looking through the eyes of characters, the issues are no less real, but they are less personalized, allowing for better reflection.

Unfortunately, however, law and literature is seen as marginal. The texts are not always accessible. The language is frequently murky. The writings examined by scholars tend not to be contemporary. Greek myths feature heavily in the scholarship of law and literature, a strong intellectual pedigree is essential, and engagement with more recent work is rare.[25] For example, the legal novels from the early 1990s written by John Grisham, Scott Turow, and William Bernhardt have been largely ignored in favor of "classics." As a result, law and literature is perceived to be a niche area with a recognized body of scholarship and adherents who still face the suspicion that what they are doing is merely a diversion or amusement for the high-minded. What is needed is engagement outside the narrow group of law and literature scholars with civil society and into law school syllabi. We believe that linking film and TV to create a more robust field of law and popular culture is more promising than attempting to link the literary and the visual worlds.

LAW AND FILM

Since 1996 the interest in law and film as a field of inquiry has grown. We count at least eighteen books, ten edited collections and eight special journal issues in law and film as noted in our bibliography. Law and film asserts that film influences how we see law and justice. As Marshall McLuhan reminds us,

> the business of the writer or the filmmaker is to transfer the reader or viewer from one world, his *own*, to another, the world created by typography and film. That is so obvious, and happens so completely, that those undergoing the experience accept it subliminally and without critical awareness.[26]

The field is dominated by those with legal rather than film studies backgrounds.[27] The accounts from Australian scholars of the emergence of visual cultural legal studies is specific to the Antipodes.[28] The German perspective on law and film, too, demonstrates quite specific elements,[29] as do the accounts from American scholars.[30] Scholars do agree that film has an effect on law, but that it is very difficult to measure. As we do more empirical work, law and film may expand beyond its current adherents in law schools.[31]

Jessica Silbey has pointed out that there has been a split in emphasis between "law" and "film" somewhat akin to the "law in literature/law as literature" division noted earlier. Law "in" film looks at how debates within law are conducted within film. How does law order our world in film? Within the broad field of law in film, Silbey has noted that the scholarship tends to examine how film shapes our expectations of law and justice in the real world. Her suggestion that "film, *no less than law* [our emphasis] changes our perceptions of reality" is foundational to law and film and law and popular culture.[32] Other writers, including Macaulay,[33] Sherwin[34] and Denvir[35] have made similar suggestions. This notion has inspired writers to explore a range of films. The rather less well-trodden path of some scholars in the field is to suggest that "film-as-law" is a study of filmic practices that are as pervasive and effective as legal ones in the ways in which they influence and inspire social order.[36] All law and film scholars, like socio-legal scholars, are interested in the social construction of law and law's socio-political nature.

The concern of early law and film scholarship was to draw attention to how law was mis-portrayed in film as well as to use the medium to capture the attention and interest of law students.[37] The use of film as an illustrative teaching/pedagogic tool continues to be a worthwhile endeavor for lecturers and students alike, and professors have written about the utility of popular culture for law teaching.[38] Much scholarship has been on individual films,[39] or using films' content to illustrate the operation of power and changes in the way social issues are treated.[40] For example, film portrayals have been used to chart the rise of women lawyers. From *I Am the Law* (1939) through *Adam's Rib* (1949) and *Jagged Edge* (1987) to *Legally Blonde* (2000), we can see the changes in the visibility and role of women in the law.[41] Feminist law and film scholarship, like feminist law and literature scholarship, is well represented.[42] However, the fate of ethnic minorities and the LGBTQ2 community under the law has received rather less coverage by law and film scholars.[43]

Law and film material finds its way into doctrinal law classes much more often than law and literature material, mainly due to students' visual literacy. Visual media approaches are also found in courses on feminist legal theory, jurisprudence, and sociology of law, not to mention in bespoke law and film courses. We believe the visual media focus of modern law and film can break out of the ghetto of academic marginalization that has bedeviled law and literature. Law and film approaches, readings, and articles are fresher in some senses and help meet the need for a modern version of the rounded lawyer.

Linking law and film with professional practice makes a great deal of sense due to the story-telling nature of film. In much of Western legal culture, the adversarial nature of the legal process involves narrative techniques and persuasion as much as technical legal knowledge. The ways in which both juries and lawyers understand the process of legal decision-making suggests that legal material is increasingly presented in story-telling and cinematic terms.[44] It is not just that juries expect the cases to resemble what they have seen on screen. Lawyers and judges themselves derive their role models from fictional presentations of law.[45] This interpenetration of reality and popular culture means that the scope of law and popular culture has moved beyond testing the fictional against the "real." The "real" is constructed by lawyers who tactically mold their arguments to fit into their audiences' popular cultural expectations.[46] Lawyers do this both in technological terms and in narrative terms. Juries are assisted by a range of audiovisual aids. In complex trials, the issues are presented in the narrative forms with which the jury is familiar, that of the fictional film or TV trial. This development has important implications for the next generation of lawyers, law schools of the twenty-first century, and scholars who are interested in the representation of the law and its actors within popular culture.

LAW AND TV

While scholarship on law and film has flourished, there has been relatively little published on the small-screen lawyer and legal processes from within the legal academy. This is strange because by the time children in the United States in the 1980s reached secondary school, they had been exposed to 10,000 hours of crime on television and this shaped their outlook on law and order issues.[47] The dearth of scholarship devoted to television as opposed to film in the law and popular culture field is difficult to understand. Television reaches the vast majority of the population. It is more democratic in its processes and distribution mechanisms than film. It provides news, dramas, documentaries, and comedies seven days a week, twenty-four hours a day. Cinema, the pre-eminent source of mass entertainment since the early 1920s, is on the decline. Going to the movies is now a luxury and is reserved for a relatively small population of Western audiences. The rise of television as the dominant source of entertainment and information, in light of the world's growing focus on the rule of law and international relations, demands consideration in law and culture scholarship. Robust studies of law and television will complement law school courses on law and literature, law and film, and law and popular culture more broadly.

Outside of the legal academy, the notion that television is an arena where hegemonic ideas on such issues as gender and sexuality are reproduced, challenged, and negotiated is well established.[48] In addition, there is work indicating how TV can influence how social conditions are made sense of and responded too.[49] At the micro-level, there is work on such issues as media representations of sexual violence[50] and male-on-male rape.[51] When we look to contributions from legal scholars, we find scholarship from Britain, the United States and Canada that analyzes the nature of the television product, the production process, and its reception.[52] There is work from American and Canadian scholars on the depiction of women lawyers on TV, as distinct from women lawyers in film,[53] as well as television's take on particular legal processes, such as mediation.[54] In Spain, where cultural images of law have been examined in extensive detail in a forty-nine volume series titled *Cine y Derecho*,[55] the broader *cultura popular y derecho* is still neglected. Television representations scarcely feature at all,[56] only *The West Wing* is discussed.[57] The same holds true for French and Italian scholarship. In Germany, by contrast, there has been extensive debate and scholarship about law and television,[58] and the United States has produced some work.[59]

Most North American, British, and European television about law focuses on the police and not on legal processes or lawyering.[60] The separateness of the trial process from detention and imprisonment is a consistent feature of a considerable body of programs in Britain and the United States. The split between the apprehension and the adjudicatory phases is stark with the former dominating television coverage across the world.[61] In our study of fourteen countries in 2014, almost 95 percent of the law and justice programming on television was about the police and crime detection.[62]

It is important to link the work on law and television with socio-legal studies and empirical questions of effect. Popular culture may be devised to pacify the masses and accommodate them to the needs of capital,[63] or it could be made by the people for themselves, as a form of resistance.[64] While it is true that most popular culture supports the interests of dominant groups, more recently, "popular culture itself has become a prime site for contestations of value"[65] and scholars ruminate on the impact of TV on people's beliefs about law. Rather than simply assume that television has an impact on behavior and that is why governments have always tried to censor what the people watch, scholars are trying to illustrate how this occurs. This was first attempted in 1973 by Vincenzo Tomeo in *Il Giudice Sullo Schermo*,[66] and over forty years later we still do not have definitive answers.[67]

In the twenty-first century, there have been a number of attempts to address the question of what effect law films and television have on viewers. For example, one team of international scholars conducted a study across six disparate jurisdictions on the ways in which law students derive their notions about justice and its relation to law. Their study revealed that the media, including films and TV, did indeed play a major role in the formation of ideas about justice and the legal system.[68] By contrast, Kimberlianne Podlas[69] as well as Victoria Salzmann and Philip Dunwoody[70] have examined the impact of television and found its impact to be rather less than had been assumed. Further attempts to assess the impact of television on audiences have been chronicled by Machura[71] as well as Machura, Love, and Dwight.[72] We too have conducted empirical research.[73]

Our first book together was the first transnational study of law on TV.[74] We, together with our contributing authors, empirically examined all the legally themed television broadcast in fourteen different countries in November 2014, and our results were published in 2016. One of the goals of our transnational study was to clarify the different ways television services are run in different jurisdictions, highlighting the different role of the state, advertising and politics in the production process. We also sought to identify the focus of the principal kinds of programming, noting trends and developments over the years. Our studies revealed that the assumed dominance of American TV is actually variable. It dominates in Canada for example but is only slightly present in Britain, and not at all in Israel. The extent of local TV series was a major discovery. However, given the existence of the multichannel televisual universe, the pervasiveness of reality channels, and the continued presence of old shows on rerun channels, we were not sure which of the shows in each jurisdiction were watched in significant numbers. What we were certain of is the fact that across all jurisdictions, the majority of law and justice-themed television is focused on policing, not lawyering.

THIS COLLECTION

In this volume we seek to go beyond our previous work together. Here we determine which legally themed shows are the most watched in each jurisdiction, and then we go deeper to examine ethnicity, gender, and diversity in each of them. We analyze legally themed TV series shown in November 2017 in eight different countries: Brazil, Britain, Canada, Germany, Greece, Poland, Switzerland, and the United States of America. We concentrate on the shows with the greatest impact in terms of ratings and viewership and thus each chapter in this volume presents the three most watched legally themed TV series in each country.

Television watching is markedly changed in 2018 from the early days of law and popular culture analysis. In this book, we proceed from the basis that television and other series that viewers watch on their TVs, computers, phones, tablets, and other devices, has an influence on law. Indeed, that is why the cover image of this book includes both a television and a tablet, to demonstrate the modern realities of television viewing. All of our authors found that viewers in their countries watch a combination of "regular" TV as well as specialty channels and subscription video-on-demand (SVOD) services, such as Netflix, so this book attempts to include all of them. All of us had similar issues in seeking to assess the significance of highly watched programs as well as assessing SVOD shows for which viewership numbers are not provided. We all recognize the particularity of different national and cultural contexts, and yet employ clear, common methodology, simple language, and an unambiguous focus: diversity. Our contributing authors examine areas of law and justice on television which are both specific to their individual jurisdictions, but which, we suggest, illustrate broader themes of relevance outside these jurisdictions. In this collection, we believe we have the beginnings of a valuable link between law and TV and what is going on in "real life."

Our contributing authors have paid particular attention to diversity—gender, age, ability, ethnicity, race, class, sexual orientation, nationality, and religion in law and justice TV series. These are socio-culturally constructed representations, categories, markers, and identities, and what TV "says" about them is important. Specific representations of gender, ethnicity, sexuality, and class are generated every day on television, and the most popular shows are seen by millions of people. These representations are circulated as norms and thus they must be examined by law and popular culture scholars.

Thus, for our book cover, we wanted a photo that demonstrated the multifaceted ways TV is watched in 2018, and we also wanted to feature a woman, as this book is explicitly concerned with gender. We succeeded on those fronts. However, our book is also explicitly concerned with ethnicity and diversity, and we were not successful there. We were required to choose a cover image from stock photos, and unfortunately, the stock photo that was available was of a Caucasian woman—telling in and of itself—and mirroring our findings that while women are now better represented on legally-themed TV, ethnicity and diversity often are not.

Popular culture is a source from which people can acquire values and behaviors. The stereotypes, both positive and negative, embedded in cultural products like television shows, are relevant in people's acquisition of values.[75] Therefore, we must be cognizant of the types of depictions we see of women, people of color, ethnic minorities, gay and lesbian characters, and other marginalized people on television. As Julie D'Acci notes: "TV is a technology and a social, economic, cultural and ideological institution, it exists as such within a whole range of different relationships to the countries in which it is produced and/or consumed, and to the economic, religious, and ideological frameworks of those countries."[76] In these pages, readers will find the first transnational empirical look at ethnicity, gender, and diversity on legally themed television shows.

From Pedro Fortes and Germano Schwartz we learn that in Brazil, while the production of legal TV series is rare, the highest watched Brazilian TV shows involve televisual justice. Telenovelas such as *The Other Side of Paradise* are extremely popular, where the authors argue symbolic affirmative action can be seen. Brazilians are also very interested in real news coverage of the *Car Wash Operation.* This real police operation has attracted more attention from viewers than any fictional series. Viewers are fascinated by the political corruption and money laundering in this TV narrative of justice, as well as in its offshoot, a Netflix series called *The Mechanism,* a fictional story inspired by the *Car Wash Operation.* In Brazil, telenovelas, news coverage, and TV series focus on corruption and social injustice.

In Britain, Peter Robson finds that the images on TV in terms of roles and focus are located within the broader politics of British identity. He provides a history of television in Britain and notes that the three most watched shows are the British gangster series *Peaky Blinders*, wherein law is a minor irritant; the American *NCIS: New Orleans* that focuses on forensic justice, and a two-part British documentary on life in prison, *Lifers Behind Bars* and *Violent Men: Behind Bars.* Robson notes that while often the law is not adverted to in these popular shows, the changing role of women and useful illustrations of some of the issues around ethnicity and diversity are.

Jennifer L. Schulz finds that in Canada, two American shows, *NCIS* and *Bull*, and one Canadian show, *The Indian Detective*, were the most popular law shows in November 2017. All three of these shows focus on criminal law and all three feature male, heterosexual, able-bodied, middle- to upper-middle-class leads in their forties and fifties. In the American shows, those leads are white. In the Canadian show, the lead is, as he puts it, brown. All three shows feature at least one strong female character, but none of the shows have LGBTQ2, disabled, or poor characters. Overall, the top three shows have good gender and ethnic diversity in their casts, but they are not representative of the actual diversity that exists in Canada.

Franziska Stürmer determines that the three most popular crime series in Germany are the American shows, *NCIS* and *Criminal Minds*, and *Tatort*, the longest-running German crime series. She found that the US productions are more sensitive toward diversity issues such as gender, age, and race than the regional German production. While *Tatort* has good gender diversity, racism, refugees, class, and disability are discussed but not reflected in the casting. Non-native German characters appear mostly as objects of discussion or as corpses, not as subjects in their own right. Since *Tatort* claims social relevance and insights into German life, Stürmer says it still has a long way to go in terms of diversity.

Nickos Myrtou, Stamatis Poulakidakos, and Olga Derzioti studied law shows in Greece and found that *NCIS*, *Criminal Minds*, and *Hannibal*, three American productions, were the most watched. Their research method is textual analysis, which permits academic assumptions about the cultural directions of the shows, and they ask six research questions about female and non-white characters. They find a predominance of white male characters in the shows. Men and women of color are underrepresented. The one more "active" black male character has a stereotypical troubled past. The white female characters, while dynamic, are mostly under the supervision or protection of male characters. The Greek authors conclude that popular culture is a fruitful domain for critical feminist and race analysis.

In Poland, Zofia Zawadzka focused on attitudes toward refugees and homosexual relationships as evidenced in the three most popular shows, which were all Polish: *Ojciec Mateusz*, *Belfer*, and *Wataha*. Gender is not directly brought up in any of these legally themed TV series, but it is most noticeable in *Ojciec Mateusz*. *Belfer* positively portrays a high school lesbian relationship, and *Wataha* perfectly depicts a social climate of fear of refugees. The top Polish legally themed shows address age, ethnicity, class, religion, migrants, and xenophobia. Zawadzka notes that the series, especially those on public channels, tend to avoid tackling the highly controversial, social and ethical Polish problems of the present.

Lucas Musumeci and Fabian Odermatt focus on the extremely popular German-language Swiss crime show, *Wilder*, in multilingual Switzerland. They apply seduction theory to *Wilder* to demonstrate how the representation of diversity-related conflicts creates ambivalence in viewers. The diversity-related conflicts in *Wilder* include a juxtaposition of the patriarchal village community with two strong female characters; a divide between rich and poor; a crucial upcoming Arab investment in the homogenous community that increases the financial divide; and avoidance of gay stereotypes despite the presence of a homosexual policeman in the conservative town. All of these conflicts contribute to seducing viewers, thereby influencing their perceptions of law.

Finally, in the United States, Christine A. Corcos finds that the three legally themed shows with the highest ratings in November 2017 were *Bull*, *How to Get Away with Murder*, and *Law & Order: SVU*. Corcos argues that these American legal dramas present tension between minority lawyers (female, disabled, LGBTQ2, and lawyers of any ethnicity) and the norm (white male heterosexual middle- or upper-middle-class lawyers) in ways that demonstrate that the lawyers who fall outside the norm must fight for acceptance and against discrimination. Corcos predicts that as American audiences fragment further, networks will offer shows that recall traditional TV formats, while taking some opportunities to offer characters and situations that reflect changes in US society.

It is our view that we can work to negotiate, resist, change, and develop depictions of marginalized characters on television and that this will enrich the legal academy, student experience, the practice of law, and society generally. We began by noting that many wish to uncover how it is that the legal system, which promises equal treatment, so consistently does not deliver equality. By making more overt attempts to engage with gender, age, disability, ethnic, racial, class, sexual orientation, national and religious discrimination, as Law and Popular Culture can, a transformation on the legal and social fields might begin.

NOTES

1. Asimow et al. (2005).
2. Robson (1979, 2012); Abel Smith and Stevens (1965).
3. Huffman (1998); Maharg (2007) chapter 3; Gordon (2008).
4. Laguette (1987); Lonbay, Brown, Platt, and Tridimas (1990).
5. *Jex-Blake v Senatus of Edinburgh University* 1873 11 M 784.
6. Snidjers (1998); Bund (1998); Sharp and Leiboff (2016).
7. Robson (1979).
8. Guy Mannering (1815) chapter 37.
9. MacNeil and Hutchings (2001).
10. Coombe (1998) at 21.
11. Ibid.
12. Chase (1986).
13. Ibid. at 528–29.
14. Ibid. at 566.
15. MacNeil and Hutchings (2001) emphasis in original.
16. Wigmore (1922–1923).
17. Freeman (2005) at 1.
18. Harris (1998).
19. Morison and Bell (1996) at 1.
20. See, for example, Freeman and Lewis (1999).
21. Faller (1993), xv (cited in Morison and Bell at 1).
22. Freeman and Lewis (1999) per Melanie Williams at 167.
23. Graycar (1996).
24. Walker (1982).
25. Meyer (2001); Robson (1996, 2014).
26. McLuhan (1965) at 285.
27. See Picart, Jacobsen, and Greek (2016) who link their work to film studies.

28. Sharp and Leiboff (2016).
29. Machura (2016).
30. Sarat (2000).
31. Per James Elkins (2004) at 824.
32. Silbey (2007) at 567.
33. Macaulay (1987).
34. Sherwin (2000).
35. Denvir (2004).
36. Silbey (2007) at 557 fn 29.
37. Bergman and Asimow (1996, 2006).
38. Corcos (2019); Schulz (2019, 2009a).
39. See, for example, Puaux (2002); Nieto and Fernandez (2004); and Strickland, Foster, and Banks (2006).
40. Greenfield, Osborn, and Robson (2001, 2010).
41. Kamir (2005) and Lucia (2005).
42. See, for example, Caplow (1999); Schulz and Youn (2016); Schulz (2009b, 2009c), Corcos (1998); Graham and Maschio (1995–1996); Kamir (2000a, 2000b); Lucia (1997); Russell (1997); Shapiro (1995, 1998); Tushnet (1996).
43. Moran (1998).
44. Silbey (2001).
45. Meyer (2001).
46. Sherwin (2000).
47. Stark (1987).
48. Maratea and Monahan (2015).
49. Kitzinger (1999) and Henderson (2007).
50. Schwark (2017).
51. Akrivos (2018).
52. Robson and Silbey (2012).
53. Klein (1998) and Schulz (2009c).
54. Schulz (2011).
55. Published by Valencia publishers Tirant Lo Blanch—discussed in Robson (2009) at 117.
56. www.tirant.com (last consulted June 2, 2018).
57. *Law Política Como Promesa* from October 2016.
58. Machura (2012).
59. Jarvis and Joseph (1998); Rapping (2003); Asimow (2009); and Villez (2005, 2010).
60. Rafter (2000, 2006); Lenz (2003).
61. Robson and Schulz (2016).
62. Robson and Schulz (2016).
63. Edensor (2002) at 13.
64. Fiske (1989).
65. Edensor (2002) at 16.
66. Tomeo (1973)—no English translation is available at present but the matter is in hand with the editors.
67. Robson and Schulz (2016) *passim.*

68. Asimow et al. (2005).
69. Podlas (2009, 2012).
70. Salzmann and Dunwoody (2005).
71. Machura (2011).
72. Machura, Love, and Dwight (2014).
73. Robson and Schulz (2016).
74. Robson and Schulz (2016).
75. Gálvez, Tiffenberg, and Altszyler (2018) at 1.
76. D'Acci (2004), 373–88 at 374.

BIBLIOGRAPHY

Abel-Smith, Brian and Stevens, Robert (1967) *Lawyers and the Courts* (London: Heinneman).

Akrivos, Dimitris (2018) *Crime and Popular Culture* (London: Palgrave).

Allen, Robert C., and Hill, Annette, eds. (2004) *The Television Studies Reader* (London: Routledge).

A Symposium on Film and the Law Oklahoma City University Law Review (1997) 22 (1).

Aristodemou, Mària (2000) *Law and Literature* (Oxford: Oxford University Press).

Asimow, Michael, ed. (2009) *Lawyers in Your Living Room: Law on Television* (ABA, Washington).

Asimow, Michael, Brown, Kathryn and Papke, David, eds. (2014) *Law and Popular Culture: International Perspectives* (Cambridge: Cambridge Scholars Press).

Asimow, M., Greenfield, S., Guillermo, J., Machura, S., Osborn, G., Robson, P., Sharp, C., and Sockloskie, R. (2005) "Perceptions of Lawyers: A Transnational Study of Student Views on The Image of Law and Lawyers," *International Journal of the Legal Profession* 12: 407.

Asimow, Michael and Mader, Shannon (2004) *Law and Popular Culture* (New York: Peter Lang).

Bergman, Paul (2009) *Rumpole and the Bowl of Comfort Food* (in *Lawyers in Your Living Room: Law on Television*, Asimow [ed.] [ABA, Washington: ABA]).

Bergman, Paul and Asimow, Michael (1996) *Reel Justice—The Courtroom Goes to the Movies* (Kansas City: Andrews and McMeel).

Bergman, Paul and Asimow, Michael (2006) *Reel Justice—The Courtroom Goes to the Movies* (2nd ed.) (Kansas City: Andrews and McMeel).

Black, David (1999) *Law in Film: Resonance and Representation* (Urbana and Chicago: University of Illinois Press).

Bund, Elmar (1998) *The Study of Law and the First National Law Examination in the Federal Republic of Germany* (in Grant, Jagtenberg and Nijkerk 1998).

Caplow (1999) "Still in the Dark: Disappointing Images of Women Lawyers in the Movies," *Women's Rights Law Reporter* 20: 55.

Chase, Anthony (1986) "Toward a Legal Theory of Popular Culture," *Wisconsin Law Review* 527.

Chase, Anthony (2002) *Movies on Trial: The Legal System on the Silver Screen* (New York: The New Press).

Coombe, R. J. (1998) *Contingent Articulations: A Critical Cultural Studies of Law* (in Sarat and Kearns 1998).

Corcos, Christine A. (1998) "Portia and Her Partners in Popular Culture: A Bibliography," *Legal Studies Forum* 22: 269.

Corcos, Christine A., ed. (2019) *Teaching Law with Popular Culture* (Durham, NC: Carolina Academic Press).

D'Acci, Julie (2004) *Television, Representation and Gender* (in Allen and Hill).

Denvir, John, ed. (1996) *Legal Reelism: Movies as Legal Texts* (Urbana and Chicago: University of Illinois Press).

Denvir, John (2004) "The Slotting Function: How Movies Influence Political Decisions," *Vermont Law Review* 28: 799.

Edensor, T. (2002) *National Identity, Popular Culture and Everyday Life* (Oxford: Berg).

Elkins, James (2004) "Reading/Teaching Lawyer Films," *Vermont Law Review* 28: 797.

Faller, Lincoln (1993) *Crime and Defoe: A New Kind of Writing* (Cambridge: Cambridge University Press).

Fineman M. A. and McCluskey, M. T., eds. (1997) *Feminism, Media & Law* (New York: Oxford University Press).

Fiske, J. (1989) *Reading the Popular* (Boston: Unwin Hyman).

Freeman, Michael and Lewis, Andrew, eds. (1999) *Law and Literature* (Oxford: Oxford University Press).

Freeman, Michael, ed. (2005) *Law and Popular Culture* (Oxford: Oxford University Press).

Gálvez, Ramiro, Tiffenberg, Valeria, and Altszyler Edgar (2018) *Half a Century of Stereotyping Associations between Gender and Intellectual Ability in Films* (https://ssrn.com/abstract=3110865 or http://dx.doi.org/10.2139/ssrn.3110865, last consulted August 15, 2018).

Gardiner, Gerald and Martin, Andrew, eds. (1963) *Legal Reform Now* (London: Gollancz).

Gest, John (1913) *The Lawyer in Literature* (Sweet & Maxwell, London) (reprinted 1999).

Getty, J. Arch (1991) "State and Society under Stalin: Constitutions and Elections in the 1930s," *Slavic Review* 50 (1): 19.

Goodrich, Peter (1996) *Law in the Courts of Love: Literature and Other Minor Jurisprudences* (London: Routledge).

Gordon, Robert (2008) *The American Legal Profession 1870–2000* (Cambridge: Cambridge University Press).

Graham, L. and Maschio, G. (1995–6) "A False Public Sentiment: Narrative and Visual Images of Women Lawyers in Film," *Kentucky Law Journal* 84: 1027.

Grant John, Jagtenberg R. and Nijkerk, K. J., eds. (1998) *Legal Education: 2000* (Aldershot: Avebury).

Graycar, Regina (1996) *Telling Tales: Legal Stories about Violence against Women* 8 (2), Boalt Hall: Law and Literature Symposium. Part 1 (Autumn–Winter), 297–315.

Greenfield, Steve and Osborn, Guy (2005) *The Double Meaning of Law: Does it Matter if Film Lawyers are Unethical* (in *Law and Popular Culture*, Freeman M [ed.]) 638.

Greenfield, Steve and Osborn, Guy, eds. (2006) *Readings in Law and Popular Culture* (Abingdon: Routledge).

Greenfield, Steve, Osborn, Guy, and Robson, Peter (2007) *Genre, Iconography and British Legal Film* 36, *Baltimore Law Review Law and Cinema Special Issue* 371.

Greenfield, Steve, Osborn, Guy, and Robson, Peter (2001) *Film and the Law* (London: Cavendish).

Greenfield, Steve, Osborn, Guy, and Robson, Peter (2010) *Film and the Law: The Cinema of Justice* (Oxford: Hart).

Guéry, Christian (2007) *Justices à l'écran* (Institut des Hautes Etudes sur la Justice, Paris).

Gunn, David, ed. (1993) *The Lawyer and Popular Culture: Proceedings of a Conference* (Fred B Rothman, Littleton).

Harding, Roberta (2005) *Reel Violence: Popular Culture and Concerns about Capital Punishment in Contemporary American Society* (in *Law and Popular Culture* Freeman M [ed.]), 358.

Harris, Thomas (1987) *Courtroom's Finest Hour in American Cinema* (Metuchen, NJ and London: The Scarecrow Press, Inc.).

Harris. Brian, ed. (1998) *The Literature of the Law* (London: Blackstone Press).

Henderson, Lesley (2007) *Social Issues in Television Fiction* (Edinburgh: Edinburgh University Press).

Huffman, J. (1998) *Legal Science is Alive and Well in American Law Schools* (in Grant, Jagtenberg, and Nijkerk 1998).

Hutchings, Peter (2001) *Beyond the New Wave: Realism in British Cinema 1959–1963* (in *The British Cinema Book*, Murphy [ed.] [London: BFI]).

Jarvis, Robert and Joseph, Paul (1998) *Prime Time Law: Fictional Television as Legal Narrative* (Durham, NC: Carolina Academic Press).

Kamir, Orit (2000a) "X–Raying Adam's Rib: Multiple Readings of a (Feminist?) Law-Film," *Studies in Law, Politics, and Society* 22: 103.

Kamir, Orit (2000b) "Feminist Law and Film: Imagining Judges and Justice," *Chicago-Kent Law Review* 75: 899.

Kamir, Orit (2005) *Framed: Women in Law and Film* (Durham, NC: Duke University Press).

Kitzinger Celia (1999) "Researching Subjectivity and Diversity" *Psychology of Women Quarterly* 23: 267–76.

Klein, D. (1998) "Ally McBeal and her Sisters: A Quantitative and Qualitative Analysis of Representations of Women Lawyers on Prime-Time Television 18," *Loyola of Los Angeles Entertainment Law Journal* 259.

Kornstein, Daniel (1994) *Kill All the Lawyers? Shakespeare's Legal Appeal* (Princeton: Princeton University Press).

Korzec, Rebecca (2007) "Viewing North Country: Sexual Harassment Goes to the Movies," *Baltimore Law Review Law and Cinema Special Issue* 36: 303.

Laguette, Serge-Pierre (1987) *Lawyers in the European Community* (Brussels, Commission of the European Communities).

Law and Cinema Special Edition Baltimore Law Review (2007) vol. 36.

Law and Film Journal of Law and Society (2001) vol. 29.

Law and Popular Culture (1998) *Legal Studies Forum* vol. 22, 3.

Law in Film/Film in Law Vermont Law Review (2004) vol. 28, 797.

Lenz, Timothy (2003) *Changing Images of Law in Film and Television Crime Stories* (New York: Peter Lang).

Levi, Ross (2005) *The Celluloid Courtroom: A History of Legal Cinema* (Westport, CT: Praeger).

Linera, Miguel, Presno, Angel, and Rivaya, Benjamin, eds. (2006) *Una introducción cinematográfica al derecho* (*A Cinematic Introduction to Law*).

Lonbay, Julian, Brown, L. Neville, Platt, Margaret, and Tridimas, Takis (1990) *Training Lawyers in the European Community* (London: The Law Society).

Lucia, Cynthia (1997) *Women on Trial: The Female Lawyer in the Hollywood Courtroom* (in Fineman and McCluskey 1997).

Lucia, Cynthia (2005) *Framing Female Lawyers: Women on Trial in Film* (Austin: University of Texas Press).

Macaulay, Stewart (1987) "Images of Law in Everyday Life: The Lessons of School, Entertainment and Spectator Sports," *Law and Society Rev*iew 21: 185.

Machura, Stefan (2011) *Media Influence on the Perception of the Legal System* (in *Understanding Law in Society*, Papendorf, K., Machura, S., and Andenæs, K. [eds.] [Zurich and Bwerlin: Lit Verlag]).

Machura, Stefan (2012) "The German Sociology of Law: A Case of Path Dependency," *International Journal of Law in Context* 8: 506–23.

Machura, Stefan, Love, Thomas, and Dwight, Adam (2014) "Law Students' Trust in the Courts and the Police," *International Journal of Law, Crime and Justice* 42: 287–305.

Machura, Stefan (2016) *Law and Cinema Movement* (in Picart, Jacobsen, and Greek [2016]).

Machura, Stefan and Robson, Peter, eds. (2001) *Law and Film* (Oxford: Blackwell).

MacNeil W. and Hutchings, P. (2001) "Law's Cultural Mediations: An Introduction by Way of Introduction," *Griffith Law Review* 10:1, Special Issue: *Law's Cultural Mediations*.

McLuhan, Marshall (1965) *Understanding Media: The Extensions of Man* (Cambridge, MA: MIT Press).

Maratea, R. and Monahan, Brian (2015) *Social Problems in Popular Culture* (Chicago and Bristol: University of Chicago Press).

Masson, Antoine and O'Connor, Kevin, eds. (2007) *Representations of Justice* (Bruxelles: Peter Lang).

Meyer, Phil (2001) "Why a Jury Trial is more Like a Movie than a Novel," *Journal of Law and Society* 28 (1): 133.

Moran, Leslie (1998) "Heroes and Brothers in Love: The Male Homosexual as Lawyer in Popular Culture," *Studies in Law, Politics & Society* 18.

Moran, Leslie, Sandon, Emma, Loizidou, Elena, and Christie, Ian, eds. (2004) *Law's Moving Image* (London: Glasshouse Press).

Morison, John and Bell, Christine, eds. (1996) *Tall Stories? Reading Law and Literature* (Aldershot: Dartmouth).

Nieto, Francisco Soto and Fernández, Francisco J. (2004) *Imágenes y Justicia: el derecho a través del cine* (*Images and Justice; law through cinema*) (Madrid: Lay Ley).

Ogletree, Charles and Sarat Austin (2015) *Punishment in Popular Culture* (New York: New York University Press).

Osborn, Guy (2001) *Borders and Boundaries: Locating the Law in Film* (in *Law and Film*, Machura and Robson [eds.]).

Picart, Caroline, Jacobsen, Michael, and Greek, Cecil, eds. (2016) *Framing Law and Crime: An Interdisciplinary Anthology* (Madison, Teaneck: Farleigh Dickinson University Press).

Podlas, Kimberlianne (2009) "Impact of Television on Cross-Examination and Juror 'Truth,'" *Widener Law Review* 14: 483.

Podlas, Kimberlianne (2012) "Testing Television: Studying and Understanding the Impact of Television's Depictions of Law and Justice" (in *Law and Justice on the Small Screen*, Robson, P. and Silbey, J. [eds.] [Oxford: Hart]).

Posner, Richard (1988) *Law and Literature* (Cambridge, MA: Harvard University Press).

Puaux, Francoise, ed. (2002) *La justice à l'écran 105 CinémaAction* (Corlet-Telerama, Conde-sur-Noireau). "Race, Law and Film" (1998) *Asian Law Journal* 1.

Rafter, Nicole (2000) *Shots in the Mirror* (Oxford: Oxford University Press).

Rafter, Nicole (2006, 2nd ed.) *Shots in the Mirror* (Oxford: Oxford University Press).

Rapping, Elayne (2003) *Law and Justice As Seen on TV* (New York: New York University Press).

Robertson, Michael (2005) "Seeing Blind Spots: Corporate Misconduct in Film and Law" (in *Law and Popular Culture*, Freeman M. [ed.]) 385.

Robertson, Michael (2008) "Property and Privatisation in RoboCop," *International Journal of Law in Context* 4 (3): 117.

Robson, Peter (1979) *Housing and the Judiciary* (Glasgow: University of Strathclyde).

Robson, Peter (1996) *Images of Law in the Fiction of John Grisham* (in *Tall Stories? Reading Law and Literature*, Morison, J., and Bell, C. [eds.] [Aldershot: Dartmouth]).

Robson, Peter (2001) *Adapting the Modern Law Novel: Filming John Grisham* (in *Law and Film*, Machura and Robson [eds.]).

Robson, Peter (2002) "Fade to Grey: Portraying the Ethnic Minority Experience in British Film," *International Journal of the Sociology of Law* 3: 235.

Robson, Peter (2005) *Law and Film Studies; Autonomy and Theory* (in Freeman [2005]).

Robson, Peter (2006) *The Justice Films of Sidney Lumet* (in *Readings in Law and Popular Culture*, Greenfield and Osborn [eds.] [London and New York: Routledge]).

Robson, Peter (2007a) "Lawyers and the Legal System on TV: The British experience," *International Journal of Law in Context* 2 (4): 333–62.

Robson, Peter (2007b) *Developments in Law and Popular Culture: The Case of the TV Lawyer* (in *Representations of Justice*, Masson and O'Connor [eds.] [Bruxelles: Peter Lang]), 75–93.

Robson, Peter (2009) "Law, Hollywood and the European Experience," *Studies in Law, Politics and Society: Symposium on Film*, 117.

Robson, Peter (2014a) "The Law through the Eye of Courtroom Comedy: The Light Legal Procedural in Context" (in *Law and Popular: International Perspectives* Asimow, Brown and Papke [eds.] [Cambridge: Cambridge Scholars Press]).

Robson, Peter (2014b) "Women Lawyers on TV—the British Experience," *Nordic Journal of Law and Social Research* 5: 101–16.

Robson, Peter (2016a) *Beyond the Courtroom: Vigilantism, Revenge and Rape-Revenge Films in the Cinema of Justice* (in Picart, Jacobsen, and Greek [eds.] [Madison, Teaneck: Farleigh Dickinson University Press]).

Robson, Peter (2016b) "Vengeance in Popular Culture," *Oxford Research Encyclopaedia Criminology and Criminal Justice* (www.criminology.oxfordre.com, last consulted June 2, 2018).

Robson, Peter and Schulz, Jennifer L., eds. (2016) *A Transnational Study of Law and Justice on TV* (Oxford: Hart).

Robson, Peter and Silbey, Jessica L., eds. (2012) *Law and Justice on the Small Screen* (Oxford: Hart).

Russell, M. M. (1997) *Law and Racial Reelism: Black Women as Celluloid 'Legal' Heroines* (in Fineman and McCluskey [1997]).

Salzmann, V., and Dunwoody, P. (2005) "Do Portrayals of Lawyers Influence How People Think About the Legal Profession," *Southern Methodist University Law Review* 58: 411.

Sanderson, Peter and Somerlad, Hilary (2006) *Gender, Power and Law in Screwball Comedy: Re-Viewing Talk of the Town and Adam's Rib* (in Greenfield and Osborn [eds.]).

Sarat, Austin (2000) "Imagining the Law of the Father: Loss, Dread and Mourning in the Sweet Hereafter," *Law and Society Review* 34: 5.

Sarat, A. and Kearns, T., eds. (1998) *Law in the Domains of Culture* (Ann Arbor: The University of Michigan Press).

Sarat, Austin, Douglas, Lawrence, and Umphrey, Martha, eds. (2005) *Law on the Screen* (Stanford: Stanford University Press).

Schulz, Jennifer L. (2009a) "Using Film in the Classroom: Comment on Dinner for Two," *Canadian Journal of Women and the Law* 21: 207.

Schulz, Jennifer L. (2009b) "The Cook, the Mediator, the Feminist, and the Hero," *Canadian Journal of Women and the Law* 21: 177–95.

Schulz, Jennifer L. (2009c) *Girls club Does Not Exist* (in Asimow [2009]).

Schulz, Jennifer L. (2011) "Settlement and Mediation in Canadian Legal Television," *Journal of Arbitration and Mediation* 1: 77–104.

Schulz, Jennifer L., and Youn, JiHyun (2016) "Monsters & Madwomen? Neurosis, Ambition and Mothering in Women Lawyers in Film," *Journal of Law, Culture and the Humanities*: 1–21.

Schulz, Jennifer L. (2019) "Enlarging the Pie or Slicing the Bug? ADR Education via Animated Short," *Journal of Legal Education* 67 (3).

Schwark, Sandra (2017) "Visual Representations of Sexual Violence in Online News Outlets," *Frontiers in Psychology* 8: 774.

Shapiro, C. (1995) "Women Lawyers in Celluloid: Why Hollywood Skirts the Truth," *University of Toledo Law Review* 25: 955.

Shapiro, C. (1998) "Women Lawyers in Celluloid, Rewrapped," *Vermont Law Review* 23: 303.

Sharp, Cassandra, and Leiboff, Marett, eds. (2016) *Cultural Legal Studies: Law's Popular Cultures and the Metamorphosis of Law* (Abingdon and New York: Routledge).

Sherwin, Richard (1996) "Cape Fear: Law's Inversion and Cathartic Justice" *University of San Francisco Law Review* 30: 1023.

Sherwin, Richard (2000) *When Law Goes Pop: The Vanishing Line Between Law and Popular Culture* (Chicago: University of Chicago Press).

Silbey, Jessica (2001) *Patterns of Courtroom Justice* (in Machura and Robson [eds.]).

Silbey, Jessica (2007) "Truth Tales and Trial Films" *Loyola of Los Angeles Law Review* 40: 551 at 557 fn 29.

Silbey, Jessica (2009) *A Witness to Justice* (in *Studies in Law Politics and Society*, Sarat [ed.]), 61–91.

Snidjers, H. J. (1998) *Entry to the Legal Profession in the Netherlands* (in Grant, Jagtenberg, and Nijkerk [1998]).

Stark, Steven (1987) "Perry Mason meets Sonny Crockett: The History of Lawyers and the Police as Television Heroes," *University of Miami Law Review* 42: 229.

Strickland, Rennard, Foster, Teree, and Banks, Taunya, eds. (2006) *Legal Reelism: The Hollywood Film as Legal Text* (Littleton, CO: Fred B. Rothman).

"Symposium on Law and Film" (1991) *Legal Studies Forum* 15: 199.

"Symposium: Picturing Justice: Images of Law and Lawyers in the Visual Media" (1996) *University of San Francisco Law Review* 30: 891.

Thornton, Margaret, ed. (2002) *Romancing the Tomes* (London: Cavendish).

Tomeo, Vincenzo (1973) *Il Giudice Sullo Schermo* (Bari: Laterza).

Tushnet, Mark (1996) *Class Action: One View of Gender and Law in Popular Culture* (in Denvir [1996]).

Valverde, Mariana (2006) *Law and Order: Images, Meanings and Myths* (London: Routledge and Cavendish) at 42 ff.

Villez, Barbara (2005) *Séries Télé: visions de la justice* (Paris: Presses Universitaires de France) (available in English [2010] *Television and the Legal System* [London: Routledge]).

Wagner, Anne and Sherwin, Richard (2014) *Law, Culture and Visual Studies* (New York and London: Dordrecht, Heidelberg).

Walker, Alice (1982) *The Color Purple* (New York: Harcourt Brace Jovanovich).

Ward, Ian (1995) *Law and Literature* (Cambridge: Cambridge University Press).

Ward, Ian (1999) *Shakespeare and the Legal Imagination* (London: Butterworths).

Wigmore, J. (1922–1923) *List of One Hundred Legal Novels* 17 Ill L.R. 26.

Chapter 2

Brazil

Dramas of Televisual Justice

Pedro Fortes and Germano Schwartz

The purpose of this chapter is to examine the most popular television programs on law in Brazil, focusing specifically on their depiction of the justice system and representations of ethnicity, gender, and diversity. Importantly, the development of Brazilian television is essential for the understanding of characteristics of its networks, genres, and programs. In contrast to countries like the United Kingdom, Germany, and Japan, for instance, television is not financed through the payment of a specific tax or public fee charged by the state. Even if the diffusion of telecommunication services is a public concession granted by the state, the economic resources are provided by private advertisement—in the case of open television—or by a combination of private fees and advertisement—in the case of cable television.

Importantly, there is one dominant network, which has been the leading corporation for over forty years: TV Globo. This company controls the market with quasi-monopolistic powers and is only very rarely challenged by the other networks. For instance, its industry of telenovelas has dominated prime time for decades with audiences of some 50 to 60 percent since the 1980s.[1] Additionally, the most viewed news report is their program, titled "National News," which is watched regularly by 35 to 45 percent of all television viewers.[2] Moreover, TV Globo also provides the official broadcasting of the FIFA World Cup, Olympic Games, the Brazilian national and regional football tournaments, F1 races, and other major sports events. In summary, a typical prime time evening on weekdays at TV Globo consists of a combination of telenovelas, the news report, and eventually a football match.

Brazilian telenovelas and documentaries are extremely well produced and exported to over one hundred countries across the globe. A collateral effect of their success, however, is the relatively low number and relevance of television series in the Brazilian networks. In quantitative terms, TV Globo launched around 100 series over the last fifty years and only very few of these programs were related to law and justice. For instance, *Open City* (1965–1966) and *News Alert* (1979–1981) followed journalists who covered police investigations and somehow got involved in discovering relevant evidence to solve the cases. *Police Station for Women* (1990) described the routine of policewomen trained to investigate and repress criminal offences committed against female victims. *The Punisher* (1997) revealed the activities of an informal secret squad that informally sanctioned criminal suspects that were not punished within the formal justice system. *Carandiru: Other Stories* (2005) provided narratives related to prisoners of a well-known penitentiary in São Paulo. *Task Force* (2009–2011) followed the division of internal affairs of the military police in their investigation of crimes committed by police officers in Rio de Janeiro. *In the Form of the Law* (2010) covered the murder of a law student and the difficult challenges to punish a wealthy and powerful criminal suspect for the homicide through conventional means. *The Web* (2014) told the story of a chief police investigator who solved an important airport robbery. *The Hunter* (2014) showed the efforts of an ex-con police officer to demonstrate his innocence after serving his prison time. *Double Identity* (2014) covered the investigation of a serial killer. Interestingly, most of these series consisted of only one season with a very limited number of episodes—except for *News Alert* and *Task Force*, which each had three seasons. Likewise, most of these programs were not translated into foreign languages or sold in the international market for other countries—except for *Task Force*, which was broadcast in nine countries, including the United States, Poland, and South Korea.

Therefore, series do not occupy a prominent position in the Brazilian television industry. Germans praise the longevity of *Tatort* and its crime scene investigations with more than 1,000 episodes of their different investigative teams in various cities—from the picturesque villages of Münster and Weimar to the metropolis of Berlin and Hamburg.[3] The Dutch cherish the particularities of their own local law and justice system with their specific rules and pragmatic approach to solve people's problems as revealed in the routine cases solved by their itinerary judge or the *Driving Judge*.[4] The United States developed a tradition of televisual justice and their programming contains many televisual judges[5] and courtroom drama shows—from the classics *Perry Mason* and *LA Law*[6] to the more recent *Suits*[7] and *Better Caul Saul*.[8]

Examining the sparse and rare production of legal series in the Brazilian television industry, a foreign observer could perhaps conclude that the audience has very limited interest in criminal investigation and courtroom dramas. Such a conclusion would simply be wrong. Brazilians have a strong interest in their dramas of televisual justice, but they are just broadcast elsewhere. For instance, in the last year, the highest watched Brazilian television involved dramas of televisual justice.[9] For instance, the telenovela *The Other Side of Paradise* captured the attention of around 60 percent of viewers,[10] who watched the episode with the trial of the local police chief and his conviction for sexually abusing his stepdaughter.

Likewise, Brazilian audiences have been fascinated by the news coverage of the *Car Wash Operation.* The country simply stopped to watch every single episode with various search warrants, arrest orders, accusations, and convictions. Starting March 17, 2014, *Car Wash Operation* already had fifty episodes and has not yet finished its investigation of political corruption, money laundering, and illegal campaign financing. Entering into its fifth year, this real police operation has attracted much more attention from the public than any fictional series and has generated a dramatic narrative of televisual justice in the media. Additionally, Netflix has recently launched the series *The Mechanism*, a fictional story inspired by the *Car Wash Operation*, which quickly became a topic for heated debate in Brazil.

In contrast to the popularity of the telenovela *The Other Side of Paradise* and the coverage of *Car Wash Operation*, the television series *The Prohibited City* had only 25 to 33 percent of the audience. The show was about a detective investigating adultery in the 1950s and executives of TV Globo considered it to be unsuccessful. For a quasi-monopolistic corporation used to, at least half of the viewing audience, a market share of one-third or one-fourth is a failure and *The Prohibited City* will not have a second season.

In this chapter, we will examine the three most popular television programs related to law, crime, and justice in Brazilian television: the telenovela *The Other Side of Paradise*; the coverage of *Car Wash Operation*; and the series *The Prohibited City*. Importantly, we used November 2017 as our month of reference to assert popularity, but our analysis covers a longer period to provide the necessary context and information for an international audience. First, we will examine the representations of law and justice in the telenovela *The Other Side of Paradise*. This section will explain the structure of Brazilian telenovelas with their multiple plots, dramatic turns, character arcs, and the appeal of legal dramas within the narratives. Additionally, this section will discuss the representation of gender, ethnicity, and diversity within Brazilian telenovelas and how there is much more inclusion nowadays than in the past.

Second, we will examine *Car Wash Operation*, revealing the various facets of media coverage, including the news reports, the roundtables, the press releases, the ideological disputes in the Internet, and the fictional narratives generated from this police operation. This section will also analyze the publicity and transparency of the Brazilian Supreme Court; its hearings and judgments are generally open to the public and accredited journalists, and are televised live at a cable network organized and sponsored by the judiciary called TV Justice. In contrast to most countries, Brazilian justices are also performers in the sense that they prepare their opinions for public debates, televised argumentation, and the diffusion of their ideas into the public sphere. Third, we will examine the television series *The Prohibited City* and representations of gender, ethnicity, and diversity in it. We will discuss whether progressive ideas of social inclusion are incorporated into the public debates through fictional narratives and if television may cultivate affirmative action in Brazilian society.[11]

In terms of methodology, this chapter is empirical and interpretative. Following the pattern established by the editors of this collection, we mapped the three most popular television programmes on law and justice in contemporary Brazil. Based on our empirical observation, we analyzed the representations of the Brazilian legal and judicial system, interpreting the meaning of these shows and providing a contextualization for our readers. Additionally, we also addressed the symbolic inclusion and exclusion of minorities through the analysis of representations of gender, ethnicity, and diversity in Brazilian television.

THE OTHER SIDE OF PARADISE: REPRESENTATIONS OF CORRUPTED JUSTICE

Historically, the genre of the telenovelas is linked to eighteenth-century French literature and the development of the *Feuilleton* or *folhetim*—a fictional series of stories that were published in episodes in the newspapers.[12] Some of the classics of Brazilian literature by José de Alencar and Machado de Assis, for instance, were originally published in this format, and only later were published as complete books. This format established a tradition of short and sharp episodes, in which the attention of the reader had to be constantly captured through drama, comedy, farce, satire, and continuous entertainment. At the beginning of the twentieth century, this narrative structure reached the radio-novelas, which became very successful among Brazilian audiences. In the 1950s, with the inauguration of TV Tupi, the first telenovelas were developed and they gradually evolved into a typical Brazilian narrative style—different from the soap operas in the United States and the highly melodramatic Mexican telenovelas.[13]

Brazilian stories are expected to last around 150 episodes and to provide a definitive and clear closure to all the characters, which comes in the climax of the final episode, broadcast on a Friday and rebroadcast on a Saturday. Therefore, a regular final episode of a Brazilian telenovela normally contains scenes of a wedding, vengeance, forgiveness, and eventually the solution of a criminal investigation or a similar mystery. However, at the beginning of a telenovela, it is impossible to predict the final outcome, because there are only fifteen episodes written and produced. The writers develop the various plots, arcs of characters, and the narrative according to the responses of the audiences to the stories of a telenovela. Based on their success or rejection by the public, protagonists may prematurely die and supporting characters may become the leading stars of a telenovela.

Therefore, the telenovela is a bricolage of various sorts of genres, developed to keep the audience attracted to its multiple plots and parallel stories. As part of this strategy, since the mid-1980s, telenovelas have become more realistic incorporating contemporary social and political problems into their narratives and serving as a fictional platform for reflection upon controversial legal issues, such as agrarian reform, racism, abortion, homosexuality, and corruption.[14] On the one hand, telenovelas provide representations that are mirrored on the lives of millions of Brazilians. On the other hand, these narratives also provide a public forum with opportunity for reflection and debate on how to transform social reality toward a different future.[15]

In this context, the telenovela *The Other Side of Paradise* contains a plot based on the laws of reciprocity and the belief that sooner or later, justice is applied to everyone. Importantly, the idea of justice is related more to vendetta than to the formal application of judicial decisions. Freely inspired by the movie *Kill Bill*, a young woman, Clara, seeks revenge against her mother-in-law Sophia, because of Clara's forced hospitalization in a psychiatric asylum for ten years. Sophia ruined Clara's life not only by destroying her relationship with her close family but also by taking over her lands for emerald mining. When Clara finally escapes from the psychiatric asylum, her revenge is supported by the collaboration of a lawyer who provides legal advice, investigates criminal wrongdoings, and litigates on her behalf.

Importantly, however, justice never comes from the formal judicial system, but rather through the mysterious ways of the laws of reciprocity. The motto that "everything you do, will be done against you one day" is captured by the opening video in which the audience follows the view from a boomerang and listens to the song *Boomerang Blues*, "And if you do wrong, with the evil later you will have to live." Therefore, punishment comes more from tragedy than from judicial sanctions, revealing a corrupted justice system whose operations are limited and unable to vindicate the wrongdoings suffered by Clara.

The lenience and corruption of the judicial system is addressed by public humiliation, violence, and disease. For instance, in episode two of the telenovela, Gael violently rapes Clara on their wedding night, after drinking too much champagne and ripping off her wedding dress. Therefore, as part of her revenge in episode fifteen, Clara invites Gael to come to her home, where he again gets drunk, rips off her low-cut dress, and hits her in the face. Her lawyer immediately appears and takes Gael to prison. Even if Gael was quickly released from jail, his public humiliation arguably stands in for the lack of judicial sanctions.

Another victim of Clara's vengeance is the physician who medicated her, determined that Clara suffered from mental insanity, and stated she had to be incarcerated at the psychiatric asylum. After confronting this physician, Clara confirmed that he doped her and falsified his medical opinion about her mental state. The physician's punishment also came through humiliation by the public revelation of his homosexuality, made at his hospital by his wife. Clara forced the physician "out of the closet" by providing evidence of his cross-dressing and of a homosexual affair to the physician's wife and his mother.

Likewise, the chief of local police was a target of Clara's revenge due to his participation in the conspiracy against her. Particularly in his case, Clara discovered that the chief of police sexually abused his stepdaughter and then encouraged her to press charges against him. Episode 104 showed the jury trial. It seemed initially that there would not be sufficient evidence for his conviction, because the only evidence of his crime was the victim's testimony. However, Clara's lawyer found another key witness, who used to work as a cleaning lady at their house. In her testimony, this witness confirmed that the chief of police was a pedophile. Describing how she routinely found blood in the child's underwear and bruises on her body, her testimony confirmed the sexual abuse. It was persuasive that the mother of the girl also decided to change sides. The wife of the policeman finally admitted that her daughter was really raped and that her husband was a psychopath and a sexual monster. Finally, the chief of police confessed that he raped his stepdaughter, stating that he never really loved his wife, he only married her to have access to the child. Convicted and incarcerated, he was murdered in prison by the other inmates. Again, punishment did not come from the formal sentence, but through the "boomerang effect" and the laws of reciprocity.

Episode 104 of the *Other Side of Paradise* reached 62 percent of the audience in São Paulo and 67 percent of the audience in Rio de Janeiro. The plot that captured the attention of two-thirds of viewers consisted of televisual representations of corrupted justice. During his testimony, the chief of police admitted that he felt that he could commit these crimes because people feared him. Likewise, he confessed that he accepted bribes (including from Sophia) and corrupted the outcome of many investigations. Moreover, he announced that the criminal judge was also corrupt and sold his sentences. Finally, the chief of police regretted that he did not kill Clara and predicted that her revenge would reach everyone. This narrative reveals a corrupt justice system, in which police officers consider themselves beyond the judicial system and feel that they can commit crimes, receive bribes, and even kill without further consequences. On the other hand, there is also a message that contradicts this idea, because the chief of police is judged, convicted, imprisoned, and killed. The role of the lawyer was essential for televisual justice and perhaps the message for the audience is that the rule of law may overcome a corrupt justice system.

THE EVOLUTION OF INCLUSION IN BRAZILIAN TELENOVELAS: SYMBOLIC AFFIRMATIVE ACTION

Brazilian telenovelas provide a mirror of our social habits, moral values, and personal behaviors, and also a window for observation and discussion of real issues.[16] In general terms, the plot of a telenovela changes constantly, because the reception of the viewers is continuously measured, analyzed, and used in the planning of subplots, character arcs, and narrative development.[17] Therefore, the views of the general public are normally respected and the stories tend to be more conservative, reproducing the status quo and mainstream discourse. However, like in Hollywood movies, there are opportunities for counterintuitive narratives that promote diversity and protect minority rights in Brazilian telenovelas.[18]

In terms of the evolution of inclusion, our analysis starts with the landmark *Anything Goes*. Importantly, this extremely successful telenovela brought a strong social critique to the wide public.[19] It discussed the possibility of getting rich in Brazil without respecting the institutional rules of the game through scams, frauds, and corruption. In the period of Brazilian re-democratization and the enactment of a liberal progressive constitution, this narrative showed Brazil as a country with a weak rule of law, patronage among the rich, discrimination against the poor, and the idea that "anything goes" to get rich.

In terms of inclusion, the leading character is a female entrepreneur who becomes wealthy and successful through hard work and mutual respect with customers and workers. One of the few ethical characters in this telenovela, Raquel set a role model for Brazilian women to succeed in a patriarchal society. Additionally, Laís, and Cecília formed one of the first LGBTQ couples in the history of Brazilian telenovelas. Moreover, the villain Odete Roitman opposed social rights and repeatedly discriminated against minorities based on sexual orientation, ethnicity, and financial conditions—a way of denouncing the worst side of our society.[20] *Anything Goes* pioneered realist narratives with open discussion of corruption and social injustice in Brazilian televisual dramas.

Gender issues are often discussed. In the last thirty years, Brazilian telenovelas have advanced symbolic affirmative action and have functioned as arenas for discussion of social injustice and promotion of diversity. In terms of gender, there are representations of mothers reconciling their jobs with their family life, of strong female leaders being successful in business, and of sexual trophies victimized by the sense of entitlement typical of a patriarchal society and the macho attitude of wealthy white men.

Brazilian telenovelas also portray the economic growth and inclusion of the lower middle classes into the markets. There are representations of residents of favelas and poor suburbs of Rio de Janeiro and São Paulo, which show the emergence of a new middle class, increase of their purchase power, and also their challenges as workers, consumers, and individuals in contemporary Brazil. Critiques of political patronage, politics of friendship, and the absence of meritocracy are constant themes of these stories, especially showing the influence of wealthy characters within social networks and the conflicts of the poor characters to live larger lives.

Sexual orientation and racism are no longer taboo subjects. In the twenty-first century, Brazilian telenovelas have black actors as protagonists and the first gay and lesbian kisses in Brazilian prime time television. The respect for pluralism on the screen includes an understanding of different religions. For example, some stories explained Hinduism and Islam to an audience of Christian viewers. *India: A Love Story* is an Emmy–winning telenovela with multicultural characters, prohibited romance, and representations of religious diversity, the caste system, the untouchables, and arranged marriages. *The Clone* depicted the prohibited romance between Luke—a Christian man from Rio de Janeiro—and Jade—a Muslim woman from Morocco. Both productions required careful anthropological research and constant consultation with religious authorities to prevent mistakes, misrepresentations, and stereotypes.[21]

This overview leads us to the analysis of *The Other Side of Paradise*. This telenovela advances minority rights such as gender, LGBTQ, and class. First, the leading character is a strong female character, whose narrative reveals a struggle against rape, parental alienation, and forced incarceration. All these issues are representative of the feminist political agenda and became real for large audiences of this telenovela. Second, the subplot of the physician's gay relationship advances LGBTQ rights, because it featured an episode of public humiliation followed by the normalization of the same-sex partnership after the character came out of the closet. Third, the conflict between the main characters resembles a class struggle, because the poor heroine fights against the wealthy family that controls the economy and politics in a small city. Therefore, this telenovela follows the tradition of representing minorities seeking emancipation in Brazilian society. The next section will examine the second most popular television program: *Car Wash Operation*.

THE *CAR WASH OPERATION*: REPRESENTATIONS OF CORRUPTION JUDGED

The *Car Wash Operation* is a criminal investigation of money laundering, corruption, and illegal campaign financing that already had fifty episodes of staged police actions in the last five years. It started in 2014 with the evidence that a criminal suspect had bought a Land Rover automobile for a former director of Petrobrás.[22] The investigation revealed a corrupt scheme within the state-owned Brazilian oil company that caused the misappropriation of billions of dollars. The money was laundered through financial operations with political parties, and bribes were remitted to off-shore accounts and Swiss banks. Each episode of the *Car Wash Operation* captured the attention of its audience, which followed the imprisonment of directors of Petrobrás, owners of major construction companies, and several important politicians, like the former governor of Rio de Janeiro, the former president of the House of Representatives, and the former president of the Republic.

The news coverage of this operation became one of the most popular television programs in recent years, dominating prime time television, cable news networks, and the Internet. For instance, the *National News* revealed the accusations of corruption against the current Brazilian president and of obstruction of justice against the former Brazilian president, capturing the attention of around 50 percent of television viewers.[23] Even though it is not a fictional drama, the coverage of the *Car Wash Operation* is also episodic, dramatic, and provides extremely important representations of political corruption being judged not only by the judicial system but also by the media and the audiences in the arena of public opinion. Moreover, debates polarized the different social groups and discussions over the imprisonment of some key Brazilian politicians resulted in extreme perspectives and heated political debates over social networks in the Internet. The movie *Federal Police: The Law Is Applied to Everyone* and the Netflix series *The Mechanism* offer fictional narratives inspired by the real events related to the *Car Wash Operation.*

Initially, the investigation focused on Alberto Youssef, responsible for money laundering. The title *Car Wash* is related to a gas station used undercover for the fraudulent distribution of money. As a result of a Land Rover automobile given to former director of Petrobrás, Paulo Roberto Costa, the investigators discovered the scheme of misappropriation of resources from the oil company. Based on plea bargain agreements with Youssef and Costa, there was sufficient evidence for twenty-one arrest orders and forty-nine search warrants against executives from the most important Brazilian construction companies. This phase of the investigation was nicknamed "The Final Judgment," an allusion to the biblical trial at the end of time, and it mobilized 300 federal police officers on November 14, 2014.

Between January and March 2015, episodes 8, 9, and 10 resulted in the imprisonment of other directors from Petrobrás, who were responsible for collecting bribes for other political parties involved in the corruption scheme. In April and May 2015, episodes 11, 12, and 13 were labeled "the Origin" and led to the imprisonment of two former federal representatives and the accountant of the labor party. In June 2015, the CEO of the biggest Brazilian construction company, Marcelo Odebrecht, was arrested in episode 14 called "Applied for Everyone." Between July and December, episodes 15–21 expanded the scope of the investigations to corruption in the nuclear energy industry and collected evidence of corruption by other executives of Petrobrás and politicians. In this period, the federal police arrested two close friends of the former president Lula: José Dirceu, the former chief of his cabinet, and José Bumlai, a cattle rancher.

In 2016, the operation finally reached well-known politicians. In March, the target of phase 24 was Lula, the former Brazilian president, who was made to testify at the federal police bureau in São Paulo. In April, former senator Gin Argello was arrested for receiving bribes to obstruct a parliamentary commission of enquiry related to corruption at Petrobrás. In September, former Ministers of Finance Guido Mantega and Antonio Palocci were arrested. In November, the federal police arrested the former governor of Rio de Janeiro, Sérgio Cabral. In 2017, the operation continued, leading to the imprisonment of Aldemar Bendine, a former president of Petrobrás, and Cândido Vaccarezza, a former leader of the Labour government in the Federal House of Representatives. In March 2018, the *Car Wash Operation* completed four years and fifty episodes.

The Federal Judge Sergio Moro, responsible for the judicial decisions based in Curitiba, became a well-known public figure. For some, he is a hero of a crusade against corruption. For others, the judge is a villain whose decisions are more political than juridical. The leader of the task force of federal prosecutors, Deltan Dallagnol, also became a divisive public figure. For some, he emerged as a symbol of ethical transformation. For others, the prosecutor persecutes politicians for personal vanity, without sufficient evidence. The Federal Attorney General, Rodrigo Janot, also became widely known in Brazil, especially for investigating the president of the Senate, the president of the Republic, and the president of the House of Representatives for crimes of corruption. Justice Zavascki, rapporteur of the *Car Wash Operation* in the Supreme Court, was a very discrete judge and suddenly had to deal with enormous publicity. His death in an airplane crash in February 2017 caused a national commotion and was one of several dramatic social events that happened in parallel with the investigative phases of the operation.

The *Car Wash Operation* affected the Brazilian political setting decisively. First, the theme of corruption dominated the political campaign for presidency in 2014. Second, the impeachment of former president Dilma Roussef is related to the operation, especially the investigation of Lula and Roussef's initiative to nominate him as a Ministry of State after his testimony in March 2016. Third, the extremely low popularity of the current president resulted from the broadcasting of a recorded conversation in which he told a businessman to keep paying for the silence of the former president of the House of Representatives.[24] Fourth, the chances of the former leader of the opposition becoming the president of the Republic evaporated, because he was caught asking a businessman for money for payment of his lawyers. Fifth, the conviction and imprisonment of former president Lula eliminated the most popular contender for president of the Republic in 2018. Representations of the investigation and the criminal judgments shaped the public debate and influenced public opinion.

FROM REALITY INTO FICTION: THE MECHANISM OF CORRUPTION

In March 2018, Netflix launched the first season of the television series *The Mechanism*, a story freely inspired by the *Car Wash Operation*. The pilot episode was titled *Car Wash*, exactly like the first phase of the police investigation. Additionally, the last episode of this first season was titled *The Final Judgment*, exactly like the seventh episode of the real *Car Wash Operation*. Moreover, some twenty characters are clearly inspired by real-life public agents, politicians, and businesspeople. Brazilian viewers may also easily identify some fifteen organizations, like construction companies, political parties, and public bureaus.

However, this realism does not correspond entirely to the facts, as there is some myth making, distortion, and political activism in this television series. *The Mechanism*'s leading character is a police officer willing to sacrifice his life for the investigation because of his empathy for the suffering of the Brazilian people. This narrative choice frames the story not simply as a detective story, but rather as a social critique of a corrupt society. In the fictional narrative, police officer Marco Ruffo lives a miserable life because of the unstoppable corruption that misappropriates public funds. This character and his family are not present in the journalistic book that was adapted into the screenplay. The writers and producers wanted to develop more empathy with the audience and to invite a political reflection on such a "mechanism."

There are some significant differences between fiction and reality. For instance, character Marco Ruffo collected shredded paper from the garbage and manually reconstituted the bank receipts of the criminal suspects, but in reality the federal police used information technology to discover the evidence of these crimes. Additionally, the series showed judicial decisions and legal analyses through informal conversations and discussions between characters, perhaps necessary for the televisual narrative, but probably suggesting that some procedural rules were broken. Moreover, the complexity of some characters was not captured, especially the former Minister of Justice, who was not only a well-respected criminal lawyer but also responsible for the modernization of the Brazilian federal police and the technological structure for investigating white-collar crimes. Finally, the former president Lula was described as the political leader who wanted to stop *Car Wash Operation* and a sentence from a senator—"we have to staunch this bleeding"—was attributed to him in the television series.

These distortions led to critiques, protests, and a campaign to boycott Netflix. The series producer and director, José Padilha, wrote an op-ed in which he explained that the mechanism of corruption does not have an ideology. It is embedded in the public administration, serves political parties for campaign financing, and corporations to secure fraudulent contracts with the state.[25] Padilha explained that neither the television series, nor *Car Wash Operation* were partisan, but that a larger number of politicians from the labor party were arrested and convicted because they had operated corruptly for fourteen years.[26] In his conclusion, Padilha expressed frustration at being criticized by both the left and the right. He expected Brazilians would transcend ideological divides to fight together against the corruption instead of indirectly collaborating with corruption by merely criticizing the representation of it on Netflix.[27] This response nicely captures the political division of Brazilian society today. The polarization of debates within social networks is leading the public to extreme views.[28] This phenomenon is observed not only on the Internet[29] and on the streets[30] but also in the media.[31]

The Mechanism focuses on the police investigation and represents the leading federal investigator as a strong female character, whose dedication and seriousness made the difference. Interestingly, another investigator is played by a black male actor in what may be interpreted as a case of symbolic affirmative action. Class struggle is also relevant in the series, as the narrator is played by a former police officer living in relative poverty with economic problems. Therefore, just like in *The Other Side of Paradise*, there is a conflict between a poor and honest character against rich and vile enemies.

JUDGING IN PRIME TIME: BRAZILIAN SUPREME COURT LIVE SHOW

One important aspect of media coverage on law and justice in Brazilian television comes from the live broadcasting of the judgments of the Supreme

Court. Since 2002, all plenary sessions are shown on TV Justice. Normally, lawyers constitute the main audience, because the general public is not interested in watching judicial decisions. However, the court decided several landmark cases in recent years, especially the political scandal known as *Mensalão* ("Monthly Bribe"), which related to the purchase of support for the labor government in the Federal House of Representatives.[32] During the trial of this case in 2012 and 2013, images of debates between justices were reproduced on cable news television and prime time national news. Justice Joaquim Barbosa, rapporteur of the *Mensalão* case in the Supreme Court, prepared strong opinions for conviction and punishment of the accused politicians, developing an image of a champion of the rule of law and an anti-corruption campaigner. In the media and popular culture, Justice Barbosa was represented as a hero who fought against corruption. After retiring from the Supreme Court in 2014, Joaquim Barbosa benefitted from his popularity as a former justice and even considered becoming a candidate for the presidency of the Republic in the general elections of 2018.

Importantly, the Brazilian Supreme Court is unique, because elsewhere judges have the opportunity to discuss legal arguments and their opinions in a secret room or private chambers. In contrast, Brazilian justices have their discussions in public through transparent and open plenary sessions, in which their opinions are broadcast live. Therefore, every Justice is prepared for a performance, that is, for an oral presentation of arguments that is expected to capture the viewer. Because they are always on stage and have to defend their arguments in front of the cameras, there is less opportunity for genuine deliberation with exchange of ideas, suggestions, and feedback. Negotiations of meaning more often emphasize differences rather than build consensus within the court. In the end, the Supreme Court live show demonstrates that the eleven Justices compete for prestige, which fragments the body politic of the court into eleven supreme courts.[33]

Sometimes the Supreme Court's discussions sound more like a telenovela than a judgment. On March 21, 2018, for example, after being offended by a colleague, Justice Barroso counter-attacked: "leave me out of your bad feelings. You are a horrible person. . . . You are a combination of evil and backwardness with drops of psychopathy. . . . You are a shame and an embarrassment for this tribunal." These discussions between the Justices are reproduced in all media outlets and there are currently several journalists, academics, and professional lawyers commenting on the Brazilian Supreme Court. In a pioneering initiative, Fundação Getúlio Vargas law school offered the support of a permanent situation room to inform journalists with questions on the trial of the "Monthly Bribe" in 2012 and 2013.[34] Later, a team of law professors started to provide weekly commentaries on the Supreme Court at *Supra*.[35] Legal academics have been constantly invited to comment on the decisions on television, and cable news has dedicated several programs and roundtables to speculating on the future of the *Car Wash Operation.*

The plenary session or trial of former president Lula for corruption on April 4, 2018, was covered by eleven hours of television debates and decisions related to his potential imprisonment. A majority of sixty-five justices decided to reject the habeas corpus and Lula was arrested on April 7, 2018. Before the trial, journalists predicted the outcome, analysts discussed the technical legal issues, and reporters interviewed people on the streets, collecting opinions from supporters and opponents of the labor party. During the trial, cable television broadcasted the opinions of justices, which were summarized and explained in more colloquial language in prime time news coverage.

After the trial and the issue of the judicial order for his imprisonment, Lula went to the Union of Metallurgical Workers and organized a final public act before going to prison. Surrounded by supporters from his party, the union, and social movements, Lula obtained permission from the Federal Police for a final one hour speech, wherein he thanked the people, reaffirmed his innocence, suggested that his imprisonment resulted from his resilience in protecting the poor, and told the audience that he could no longer be arrested, because he represented not just an individual, but the ideal of social justice. Commentators suggested that the labor party wanted to produce a counter-narrative in contrast to the narrative produced by the *Car Wash Operation*. According to a German newspaper, the Brazilian ex-president was producing his own telenovela.[36] *Car Wash Operation* reveals the importance of TV Justice for the representation of law in contemporary Brazilian television.

The media coverage of *Car Wash Operation* and the *Mensalão* Supreme Court case also generates discussion about gender, ethnicity, and diversity. In the news programs, there is a growing presence of female and black journalists. However, they still play secondary roles and the leading position is played by predominantly white male journalists. In courts, there is also growing diversity. The prominent rapporteur of the *Mensalão* case was the first black justice. Likewise, there are more women represented at the court. On the other hand, the impeachment of the first female president in the midst of the corruption scandal generated debate on sexism and misogyny behind the political process.[37] Finally, Lula's supporters also suggested that Lula's prosecution and imprisonment was motivated by his leadership of the working class and that Brazilian elites were behind his conviction.[38] Therefore, minority issues are an essential part of the representation of these corruption scandals—both in fiction and in media coverage. The next section will examine the third television program: *The Prohibited City.*

THE DISCONTINUATION OF TV SERIES: *THE PROHIBITED CITY*

The television series *The Prohibited City* introduced the private detective, a former police officer, Zózimo Barbosa, to prime time audiences. Inspired by a Brazilian graphic novel, Zózimo Barbosa investigated cases of female adultery in 1950s Rio de Janeiro. However, instead of adopting a professional distance from his cases, Zózimo often fell in love for the women that he followed. Each of the twelve episodes of the first season was named after an investigated woman. His circle of friends is composed of Paranhos—a black police investigator who does not comply with the orthodox rules of investigation, Handsome—a gigolo whose lifestyle is paid for by his lovers, and Marly—a prostitute who constantly tries to seduce Zózimo and hopes to become his girlfriend.

There are some progressive messages in the show's narrative. For instance, Paranhos holds a position of power as the chief deputy of the police station in Rio de Janeiro in the 1950s, when a black individual would not be expected to become a prominent state official. Brazil only abolished slavery in 1888 and Brazilian society still struggles with racial discrimination today.[39] Another progressive message comes from the rage that Paranhos feels toward men who beat women. According to the narrative, Paranhos suffered from domestic violence during his childhood, because his father often got drunk and then hit Paranhos's mother. In the series, Paranhos always intervenes and protects women from abusive men. On the other hand, the characters of *Prohibited City* belong to a macho universe typical of Rio de Janeiro in the 1950s. Even if the actress Regiane Alves considered her character Marly to be a woman ahead of her time, a prostitute is unlikely to be a role model for contemporary female viewers. Likewise, characters Zózimo and Handsome developed sexist relationships with women. Even though a contemporary production, the series offered an old-fashioned narrative that did not please prime time audiences.

The executives of TV Globo had guaranteed that *Prohibited City* would have a second season before the exhibition of the first season. However, with the cold response from viewers and audiences (between 25 percent and 33 percent),[40] they decided to discontinue the show. Only a third or fourth of viewers seemed a failure for an expensive production featuring some of the finest telenovela stars in its cast. The quasi-monopoly of TV Globo is currently threatened by competition with other channels, cable television, and the emergence of new medias.[41] Therefore, it seems it is really difficult to capture the hearts and minds of the majority of viewers, while promoting diversity and the protection of minorities.

THE CHALLENGE OF SOCIAL INCLUSION: GENDER, ETHNICITY, AND DIVERSITY

Brazilian society still faces several challenges related to social inclusion. Female, black, and LGBTQ individuals normally have fewer opportunities for success in the legal profession.[42] On the Brazilian screen, both in fiction and in reality, straight white men normally dominate positions of power and are successful lawyers. However, there is a growing presence of minorities in both the judiciary and televisual representations of law and justice. For instance, the current chief justice and the current federal attorney general are both women. The potential presidential contender Joaquim Barbosa was the first black Justice in the Brazilian Supreme Court. Nonetheless, the representation of minorities in powerful positions is still very limited on television.

It also seems that there are fewer possibilities for symbolic affirmative action through counter-hegemonic narratives in prime time television than in cinema[43] or in rock and roll,[44] because the necessity to please large televisual audiences may induce authors to be less activist than film-makers or musicians who produce art for particular niches of fans and may therefore experiment more easily with symbolic affirmative action. To be sure, gender issues are seriously considered on TV, because of the large number of female viewers. Many protagonists of telenovelas are strong women and one of the most prominent telenovela writers centered all of his shows around a leading actress who performed the role of "Helena," though his "Helenas" were feminine, not feminists. Additionally, there is never a plot or a subplot that challenges the conventional Catholic morality, nor advances the protection of reproductive rights for Brazilian women. On the other hand, *The Other Side of Paradise* provides an interesting case study of a telenovela with strong female characters and a progressive view of domestic violence and sexual abuse.

In terms of race, there are very few examples of black protagonists in the telenovelas. Worse still, Brazilian audiences rejected the first black actress as the leading star of a telenovela, when Thaís Araújo played the role of Helena in 2009s *To Live the Life*.[45] As a result of low viewership and the lack of empathy of viewers with the black top model, Thaís Araújo's role was downgraded into a supporting role. More recently, Lázaro Ramos played the male protagonist of telenovela *Irrational Heart* and managed to entertain audiences, but his character was a womaniser. Likewise, the first gay character to receive a leading role was the very evil Felix in *The Love for Life*. In this telenovela, he finally gave the first gay kiss on Brazilian prime time television in 2014. In 2005, another TV writer wrote a final scene with a gay kiss for *America*, which was even recorded, but vetoed by executives of TV Globo for fear of the reaction of conservative audiences. The first lesbian kiss was broadcast in 2015 in *Babylon* and the telenovela lost a significant number of viewers after that scene.[46] In summary, there are some possibilities for symbolic affirmative action in television, but these are limited by the obligation to meet the expectations of large, often conservative, audiences.

CONCLUSION

The dramas of Brazilian televisual justice go beyond detective and courtroom stories. They invite the audiences to undertake an existential reflection on the kind of people and society that Brazilians hope to develop. Behind the romance, the suffering, and the revenge of fictional narratives, there are social critiques of a corrupt and unequal society. Telenovelas, news coverage, and TV series engage with viewers through representations of corruption and social injustice. The polarization of perspectives in social networks often reproduces telenovela narratives, being reduced to a debate on whether the government should prioritize fighting against poverty or corruption—as if the political agenda could not accommodate both issues. In the past decades, representations of gender, ethnicity, sexual orientation, and class have increased in prime time television, even if sometimes minorities faces opposition and rejection from the majority. The analysis of symbolic affirmative action reveals the growing presence of women, black, LGBTQ, and poor characters in leading roles on Brazilian television.

Brazilian televisual justice follows the pattern of the telenovela with multiple genres, subplots, and dramatic turns of narrative. In April 2018, a lawyer referred metaphorically to his case as a telenovela with various different episodes before the end. He is involved in another case at the Supreme Court that may restore liberty to Lula. This reference to a telenovela as a metaphor for Brazilian justice may well be justified by the complexity, instability, and variety of decisions in Brazilian courts with numerous appeals. Slicing complex decisions into a series of episodes is also a strategic decision to better communicate to the public, as Justice Joaquim Barbosa did in the *Mensalão* ("Monthly Bribe") case—breaking the decision into a series of debates about each act, the trial mobilized the audience like a telenovela.[47] In the end, Brazilian audiences pick their heroes and villains in the benches of the Supreme Court and follow the episodes of *Car Wash Operation* as a story about themselves. Lost between the fictional reality of infotainment and the realist fiction of telenovelas, Brazilian viewers discuss their future over representations of corruption and social injustice in telenovelas, news reports, and series.

NOTES

1. Ricco, Flávio and José Armando Vannucci (2017), *Biografia da televisão brasileira*, volume 2. São Paulo: Matrix, 168.

2. https://www.terra.com.br/diversao/tv/blog-sala-de-tv/bom-de-ibope-jn-se-aproxima-dos-30-pontos-de-media-no-ano,b40044f0fe3a0f13adb74a0cc7ca918e2qqn6w6c.html (checked on 07.13.2018).

3. Machura, Stefan and Michael Böhnke, Germany (2016), in Peter Robson and Jeniffer Schulz (editors), *A Transnational Study of Law and Justice on TV*. Oxford: Hart.

4. Gaakeer, Jeanne (2014), 'It's My Culture, Stupid!': A Reflection on Law, Popular Culture, and Interdisciplinarity, in Michael Asimow, Kathryn Brown, and David Papke (editors), *Law and Popular Culture: International Perspectives*. Newcastle: Cambridge Scholars Publishing; Heynders, Odile and Philip Paiement (2014), A Mobile Judge: An Analysis of a Dutch Television Hit, in Michael Asimow, Kathryn Brown, and David Papke (editors), *Law and Popular Culture: International Perspectives*. Newcastle: Cambridge Scholars Publishing.

5. Friedman, Lawrence (2012), Judge Judy's Justice, *Berkeley Journal of Entertainment and Sports Law*, 1: 125; Marder, Nancy (2009), Judging Judge Judy, in Michael Asimow (editor), *Lawyers on Your Living Room: Lawyers on Television*. Chicago: American Bar Association.

6. Friedman, Lawrence (1989), Law, Lawyers, and Popular Culture, *The Yale Law Journal* 98(8): 1579–1606.

7. Robson, Peter (2017), The Portrayal of the Corporate Lawyer on TV: the US and British Models from LA Law to Trust and Suits, in Pedro Fortes and Michael Asimow (editors), *Law, Popular Culture, and Classical Culture: Representations of the Underworld in Arts and Media*, Special Issue of the *Journal of the Oxford Centre for Socio-Legal Studies*: 46–58.

8. Gómez, Manuel (2017), Outside But Within: The Normative Dimension of the Underworld in the television series *Breaking Bad* and *Better Call Saul*, in Pedro Fortes and Michael Asimow (editors), *Law, Popular Culture, and Classical Culture: Representations of the Underworld in Arts and Media*, Special Issue of the *Journal of the Oxford Centre for Socio-Legal Studies*: 32–44.

9. https://www.otvfoco.com.br/o-outro-lado-do-paraiso-bate-recorde-de-ibope-no-penultimo-capitulo-confira-os-consolidados-de-quinta-feira-10-05-18/ (checked on 07.13.2018).

10. https://www.otvfoco.com.br/o-outro-lado-do-paraiso-bate-recorde-de-audiencia-em-sp-e-rio-confira-os-consolidados-de-segunda-feira-07-05-18 (checked on 07.13.2018).

11. Fortes, Pedro (2017). Lights, Camera, Affirmative Action: Does Hollywood Protect Minorities? in Pedro Fortes and Michael Asimow (editors), *Law, Popular Culture, and Classical Culture: Representations of the Underworld in Arts and Media*, Special Issue of the *Journal of the Oxford Centre for Socio-Legal Studies*: 60–75; Fortes, Pedro (2014), Affirmative Cinema: When Filmmakers Defend Minorities, in Michael Asimow, Kathryn Brown, and David Papke (editors), *Law and Popular Culture: International Perspectives*. Newcastle: Cambridge Scholars Publishing.

12. Rêgo, Cacilda (2003), Novelas, Novelinhas, Novelões: The Evolution of the (Tele)novela in Brazil, *Global Media Journal* 2(2): 5.

13. Rêgo (2003); See also Morais, Fernando (1994), *Chatô: O Rei do Brasil*. São Paulo: Companhia das Letras.

14. Rêgo (2003).

15. Rêgo, Cacilda (2014), Centering the Margins: The Modern Favela in the Brazilian Telenovela, in Naomi Pueo Wood (editor), *Brazil in the Twenty-first Century Popular Media: Culture, Politics, and Nationalism on the World Stage*. Lanham, MD: Lexington Books.

16. Rico, Flávio and José Armando Vannucci (2017), *Biografia da Televisão Brasileira*. volume 2. São Paulo: Matrix.

17. Idem.

18. Pedro (2017, 2014).

19. Rico and Vannucci (2017).

20. Rico and Vannucci (2017).

21. Rico and Vannucci (2017).

22. Netto, Vladimir (2016), *Lava Jato: O Juiz Sérgio Moro e os Bastidores da Operacão que abalou o Brasil*. Rio de Janeiro: Primeira Pessoa.

23. https://portal.comunique-se.com.br/duplicar-globo-jornal-nacional-hora-duracao (checked on 07.19.18).

24. https://br.reuters.com/article/topNews/idBRKBN1AC2L0-OBRTP (checked on 07.19.2018).

25. Padilha, José (2018), O Mecanismo Agradece. Folha de São Paulo, 01 de abril de 2018.

26. Ibid.

27. Ibid.

28. Sunstein, Cass (2009), *Going to Extremes: How Like Minds Unite and Divide*. Oxford: Oxford University Press.

29. https://infograficos.oglobo.globo.com/brasil/fgv-pronunciamento-dilma.html (checked on 07.19.2018).

30. https://brasil.elpais.com/brasil/2016/03/08/politica/1457471624_673376.html (checked on 07.19.2018).

31. https://cultura.estadao.com.br/blogs/estado-da-arte/basta-de-silencio-a-insuportavel-polarizacao-politica-no-brasil (checked on 07.19.2018).

32. Falcão, Joaquim (2013), *Mensalão: Diário de um Julgamento*. Rio de Janeiro: Campus-Elsevier.

33. Falcão, Joaquim, Diego Werneck Arguelhes and Felipe Recondo (2017), *Onze Supremos: O Supremo em 2016*. Belo Horizonte: Letramento.

34. Falcão, Joaquim (2014), The Activist Law School, paper presented at the II Graduate Conference on Law and Policy in Latin America at the St. Antony's College, University of Oxford.

35. https://www.jota.info/tudo-sobre/supra (checked on 07.19.2018).

36. Hermann, Boris (2018), Brasiliens Ex-Präsident inszeniert eine Telenovela, Süddeutsche Zeitung, April 8, 2018.

37. https://www.bbc.com/portuguese/brasil/2016/05/160513_temer_imprensa_internacional_repercute_fd (checked on 07.19.2018).

38. http://www.pt.org.br/imprensa-internacional-acompanha-perseguicao-a-lula (checked on 07.19.2018).

39. Moreira, Adilson (2017), *O que é discriminação?* Belo Horizonte: Letramento; Moreira, Adilson (2016), Miscigenando o círculo do poder: ações afirmativas, diversidade racial e sociedade democrática, *Revista da Faculdade de Direito da UFPR* 61(2): 117–48.

40. https://observatoriodatelevisao.bol.uol.com.br/noticia-da-tv/2017/10/cidade-proibida-derruba-ibope-e-perde-quase-3-em-cada-10-telespectadores-na-globo (checked on 07.19.2018).

41. Hoineff, Nelson (1996), *A Nova Televisão: Desmassificação e o impasse das grandes redes*. Rio de Janeiro: Relume Dumará.

42. Bonelli, Maria and Pedro Fortes (2018). The Transformation of the Brazilian Legal Profession: Fragmentary Development, Democratisation and Globalisation, in Richard Abel, Ulrike Schulz, Hillary Sommerlad, and Ole Hammerslev (editors), *Lawyers in 21st Century Society*. Oxford: Hart, forthcoming.

43. Pedro (2017, 2014).

44. Schwartz, Germano (2015), Direito e Rock: When Two Worlds Collide or Break on Through . . . To The Other Side, in Pedro Fortes (editor), *Direito, Cultura Pop e Cultura Clássica.* Rio de Janeiro: FGV; Schwartz, Germano (2014), *Direito e Rock: O BRock e as expectativas normativas da constituição de 1988 e do maio de 2003*. Porto Alegre: Livraria do Advogado.

45. https://extra.globo.com/tv-e-lazer/publico-critica-atuacao-de-tais-araujo-na-novela-das-oito-391130.html (checked on 07.19.2018).

46. https://noticiasdatv.uol.com.br/noticia/televisao/para-autor-de-babilonia-boicote-a-beijo-gay-tem-motivacao-ditatorial-7049 (checked on 07.19.2018).

47. This point was made recently by Joaquim Falcão in a interview with Pedro Bial. See https://globoplay.globo.com/v/6808485 (checked on 07.19.2018).

BIBLIOGRAPHY

Bonelli, Maria and Pedro Fortes (2018), The Transformation of the Brazilian Legal Profession: Fragmentary Development, democratisation and globalisation, in Richard Abel, Ulrike Schulz, Hillary Sommerlad, and Ole Hammerslev (editors), *Lawyers in 21st Century Society*. Oxford: Hart, forthcoming.

Falcão, Joaquim (2013), *Mensalão: Diário de um Julgamento*. Rio de Janeiro: Campus-Elsevier.

———. (2014), *The Activist Law School, paper presented at the II Graduate Conference on Law and Policy in Latin America at the St. Antony's College*, University of Oxford.

Falcão, Joaquim, Diego Werneck Arguelhes and Felipe Recondo (2017), *Onze Supremos: O Supremo em 2016*. Belo Horizonte: Letramento.

Fortes, Pedro (2014), Affirmative Cinema: When Filmmakers Defend Minorities, in Michael Asimow, Kathryn Brown, and David Papke (editors), *Law and Popular Culture: International Perspectives*. Newcastle: Cambridge Scholars Publishing.

———. (2017), Lights, Camera, Affirmative Action: Does Hollywood Protect Minorities? in Pedro Fortes and Michael Asimow (editors), *Law, Popular Culture, and Classical Culture: Representations of the Underworld in Arts and Media*, Special Issue of the *Journal of the Oxford Centre for Socio-Legal Studies*: 60–75.

Friedman, Lawrence (1989), Law, Lawyers, and Popular Culture, *The Yale Law Journal* 98(8): 1579–606.

———. (2012), Judge Judy's Justice, *Berkeley Journal of Entertainment and Sports Law* 1: 125.

Gaakeer, Jeanne (2014), "It's My Culture, Stupid!": a reflection on Law, Popular Culture, and Interdisciplinarity, in Michael Asimow, Kathryn Brown, and David Papke (editors), *Law and Popular Culture: International Perspectives*. Newcastle: Cambridge Scholars Publishing.

Gómez, Manuel (2017), Outside But Within: The Normative Dimension of the Underworld in the Television Series "Breaking Bad" and "Better Call Saul," in Pedro Fortes and Michael Asimow (editors), *Law, Popular Culture, and Classical Culture: Representations of the Underworld in Arts and Media*, Special Issue of the *Journal of the Oxford Centre for Socio-Legal Studies*: 32–44.

Herrmann, Boris (2018), Brasiliens Ex-Präsident inszeniert eine Telenovela, Süddeutsche Zeitung, April 8, 2018.

Heynders, Odile and Philip Paiement (2014), A Mobile Judge: An Analysis of a Dutch Television Hit, in Michael Asimow, Kathryn Brown, and David Papke (editors), *Law and Popular Culture: International Perspectives*. Newcastle: Cambridge Scholars Publishing.

Hoineff, Nelson (1996), *A Nova Televisão: Desmassificação e o impasse das grandes redes*. Rio de Janeiro: Relume Dumará.

Machura, Stefan and Michael Böhnke, Germany (2016), in Peter Robson and Jeniffer Schulz (editors), *A Transnational Study of Law and Justice on TV*. Oxford: Hart.

Marder, Nancy (2009), Judging Judge Judy, in Michael Asimow (editor), *Lawyers on Your Living Room: Lawyers on Television*. Chicago: American Bar Association.

Morais, Fernando (1994), *Chatô: O Rei do Brasil*. São Paulo: Companhia das Letras.

Moreira, Adilson (2016), Miscigenando o círculo do poder: ações afirmativas, diversidade racial e sociedade democrática, *Revista da Faculdade de Direito da UFPR* 61(2): 117–48.

———. (2017), *O que é discriminação?* Belo Horizonte: Letramento.

Netto, Vladimir (2016), *Lava Jato: O Juiz Sérgio Moro e os Bastidores da Operacão que abalou o Brasil*. Rio de Janeiro: Primeira Pessoa.

Padilha, José (2018), O Mecanismo Agradece. Folha de São Paulo, 01 de abril de 2018.

Rêgo, Cacilda (2014), Centering the Margins: The Modern Favela in the Brazilian Telenovela, in Naomi Pueo Wood (editor), *Brazil in the Twenty-first Century Popular Media: Culture, Politics, and Nationalism on the World Stage*. Lanham, MD: Lexington Books.

Rêgo, Cacilda (2003), Novelas, Novelinhas, Novelões: The Evolution of the (Tele) Novela in Brazil, *Global Media Journal* 2(2): 5.

Rico, Flávio and José Armando Vannucci (2017). *Biografia da Televisão Brasileira*, volume 2. São Paulo: Matrix.

Robson, Peter (2017), The Portrayal of the Corporate Lawyer on TV: The US and British Models from *LA Law* to *Trust and Suits*, in Pedro Fortes and Michael Asimow (editors), *Law, Popular Culture, and Classical Culture: Representations of the Underworld in Arts and Media*, special issue of the *Journal of the Oxford Centre for Socio-Legal Studies*: 46–58.

Schwartz, Germano (2014), *Direito e Rock: O BRock e as expectativas normativas da constituição de 1988 e do maio de 2003*. Porto Alegre: Livraria do Advogado.

———. (2015), Direito e Rock: When Two Worlds Collide or Break on Through . . . To The Other Side, in Pedro Fortes (editor), *Direito, Cultura Pop e Cultura Clássica*. Rio de Janeiro: FGV.

Sunstein, Cass (2009), *Going to Extremes: How Like Minds Unite and Divide*. Oxford: Oxford University Press.

Chapter 3

Britain

The Justice System on TV

Peter Robson

This chapter examines the background to the study of law and justice on British television. It notes how the reach of television has continued in the second decade of the twenty-first century. Two major trends can be identified—sources and modes of consumption. On the one hand, there has been an expansion of the sources of programing. This has involved an explosion of niche channels free to view through either Freesat or Freeview. The number of channels free to view has proliferated into the hundreds. This has largely involved the emergence of specialist channels showing a highly restricted service such as, for instance, *Talking Pictures*. Talking Pictures offers a diet of mainly black and white British films from the 1950s and 1960s with no other material—no news, documentaries, or other entertainment/educational material. Complementing these niche-free channels has been the emergence of low-cost subscription services such as Netflix or Amazon that offer films and TV series "on demand" rather than any kind of news or current affairs.[1]

In addition, the mode of consumption has changed. Programing has altered from a single "family" TV set in the living area to a proliferation of both television sets and other devices on which to consume the material such as computers, tablets, and mobile phones. The preference of young people, for instance, for viewing their favorite programs on such devices has led the government to address the loss of revenue through such devices not requiring a TV licence and impacting on the revenue source of the BBC.[2] This did not, however, impact on people watching other free on-demand content provided by channels such as ITV, Channel 4, or Channel 5, nor on demand subscription services.

These developments are of major importance to what drove our original project goal, namely the assessment of the impact of the medium of television on the representation of the justice system. That message has become highly diffused. Whilst print newspapers and other media continue to review and assess programs when they are aired on major TV channels, this increasingly does not reflect audience viewing behavior.[3]

The "great debate" in the world of TV policy continues to center on the role and nature of the major British cultural icon, the BBC. Due, in part at least to the distraction of the narrow vote to leave the European Union in June 2016, the review of the BBC Charter has left the licence fee funding intact.[4] The issues of inclusivity and diversity have, however, become rather more prominent in the new arrangements.

The images we find on British TV in terms of roles and focus are located within the broader politics of identity. The ineffectiveness of policies to address inequalities of access and outcomes for women and a range of minorities continue to be a major feature of British political life. These range from the slow progress of women to recognition in the boardroom to the more mundane continued gender pay gap discussed next.[5] The commitment to addressing such issues as the policing of minority ethnic Britons and their representation as protagonists of the justice system continue thirty-five years after the McPherson Report.[6] These issues have also been at the heart of discussions about the BBC from its description in 2001 as a "hideously white" institution by its then director general Greg Dyke[7] to its embarrassment in 2018 at finding its own pay policy favored male presenters significantly over the female counterparts.[8]

This chapter notes how there has been a gathering momentum in relation to the issue of gender in the world of TV policing. Although, as was noted in our 2016 study, *A Transnational Study of Law and Justice on TV*, women were not absent from the world of law and justice, their role was limited. A new tranche of programs in the second decade of the twenty-first century has seen over half of the new dramas headed by women and featuring storylines that address such chronic social issues as violence against women.

What we noted in the survey of programing in November 2014 was the dominance of the apprehension phase of the justice process. Although of interest to specialists in the area and extensive over a period of time, lawyer-focused programs on British TV were dominated by the courtroom histrionics of Judge Judy. By the same token there was limited coverage of prison series. In broad terms, these observations remain true today despite the rise to prominence of Robert Rinder as a home-grown judicial star on British TV[9] and the critical success of *Orange Is the New Black*.[10] Given, however, the overall lack of new material on law and justice on British TV, it is noteworthy that prison life is a focus of the most popular documentaries screened in November 2017.[11]

Our observations on the difficulty of judging the impact of programs from a simple examination of their frequency of appearance in a multi-channel, on-demand TV world led us to focus on programing of significance in this follow-up collection. Here we concentrate on the shows with the greatest impact in terms of ratings and viewership.

There is no doubt that the crime drama *Peaky Blinders* fits into this category with its portrayal of a world in which the forces of law and order and the justice system provide, for the most part, a minor irritant. The series is in its fifth season in 2018 with twenty-four one-hour episodes in the first four series. On its return in November 2017, it drew audiences of over 4 million on BBC 2.[12] Although not "home-grown," the selection of *NCIS: New Orleans* reflects another theme which permeated our first collection across all jurisdictions, namely the impact of American TV products. This program is the tip of the forensic justice iceberg of the last decade with the successful showing of the full range of CIS products on British mainstream TV. Finally, we look at a short documentary series on prison, *Behind Bars*, which reflects what was one of the recurring elements in the world of non-fictional TV justice—the prison experience.[13]

The study of the world of TV justice in Britain toward the year 2020 shows a high degree of continuity. In broad terms, the same kind of programs is being offered. What has changed is who is starring in the programs and who is producing, writing, and directing them. The impact of women is not wholly surprising given the fact that it is ninety years since women achieved formal equality to vote in Britain.[14] What is much less clear is what changes have been effected in other areas such as ethnicity and sexuality. Some areas like disability continue to be noticeable by their almost complete absence from the screen.

CONTEXT—BRITISH TV CHANNELS AND THEIR GOVERNANCE

The world of television reception continues to alter at a rapid pace. There have been two quite distinct major developments worth noting. There continues to be an expansion in the number of channels available to licence holder viewers free of charge on modern television channels. There are some seventy TV channels available to modern TV sets in Britain, which have Freeview automatically available via antennae.[15] There are more than 200 channels available to those who have the alternative satellite reception through the BBC/ITV service Freesat.[16]

In addition, the ways of watching the programing has altered. The availability of watching programing via the Internet using "catch up" and box sets has altered patterns of media consumption. It now seems likely that the viewing habits of younger viewers, with their preference for streamed online content over linear viewing, is likely to change the way television is produced in the future just as the same pattern has affected CD sales with the rise of music streaming.[17] Viewing of broadcast TV by children (four to fifteen years old) and sixteen- to twenty-four-year-olds fell 33 percent between 2010 and 2017, and about 9 percent compared with 2015, according to Ofcom's annual Communications Market Report published in August 2017.[18]

Finally, what counts as law and justice material requires clarification. Our focus on apprehension, adjudication, and disposition did mean that some tangential material was excluded[19] such as government agents[20] and private individuals[21] as being outside the justice system scope. As far as the programs available in connection with the operation of the justice system, in addition to traditional new police shows,[22] innovative material has come on stream.[23] There are also shows that are closely related to the traditional apprehension model, centered on the direct work of the police, such as forensic science shows,[24] internal police investigations,[25] and specialist work.[26]

The mixture of license-funded public service television alongside the private advertising model continues to operate in Britain. The politicians of the right who have dominated Parliament since 2010 continue to be against the long-term future of funding the BBC from a flat rate licence fee.[27] In the chapter on Britain in the 2016 volume, it was noted that one of the issues which was awaiting decision was the future of the BBC. This is a process which takes place every ten years or so. One of the principal issues in the most recent process centered around how the BBC should be funded. Due to the impasse in British politics at the time of writing between the right and left, the licence fee was left in place when the December 2016 Royal Charter and Framework Agreement was published.[28] This runs for a further decade until December 31, 2027,[29] and replaces the 2006 Charter.

GENDER, ETHNICITY, AND DIVERSITY IN BRITAIN

Recent British social movements for change have centered around emancipation from restricted rights looking at three major areas—gender, ethnicity, and sexuality.[30] Prior to these issues being foregrounded, the principal area of political struggle was focused on universal male suffrage and the exclusion of the working classes from voting. Until 1832, the vote was limited to male property owners. The initial focus in the nineteenth century was for universal male suffrage. Progress on this issue was made in the 1880s with the extension of the vote to men owning or occupying property above the value of £10.[31] It was not, however, until 1918 that the remaining 38 percent of the male population achieved the right to vote with the removal of the limit on the value of property occupied. The progress for women was even slower. Agitation and support for women's suffrage was a feature of nineteenth-century politics.

The vote was initially restricted in 1918 to married women over the age of 30 who satisfied the property qualification.[32] These restrictions were removed in 1928 when women voted in the same terms as men.[33] The principle of "one person, one vote" was not achieved in Britain until 1948.[34] Removal of formal restrictions on access to education and into employment was found in the Sex Discrimination (Removal) Act 1919. The rationale for the different treatment of women was centered on their different abilities and contribution to society. Ranging from lesser cerebral power to greater sensitivity, these arguments were encapsulated in decisions of the courts around the access of women to higher education.[35]

Implementation of formal equality into actuality proved rather more problematic. Companies and institutions continued to operate, for instance, a marriage bar until the 1950s whereby any single woman who married was required to forfeit her post as teacher, civil servant, or bank employee. Men dominated the positions of power in politics, industry, and the professions. Not only did they occupy the senior positions but they also received higher remuneration for doing the same work by dint simply of their gender.

These issues were finally addressed in the Equal Pay Act 1970 and the Sex Discrimination Act 1975. The subsequent half century has seen a slow change in practice and attitudes in relation to women's equality in British society. At the time of writing electoral representation has now reached 208 out of 650 Members of Parliament—32 percent.[36] Women's average rate of pay still lags some 14 percent behind that of their male colleagues[37] and there are only 26 percent of Boards of FTSE 100 companies with women directors.[38]

Within the areas of the justice system the changes have also been slow to arrive. In the highest court in Britain, the Supreme Court, there are two female judges out of a complement of twelve.[39] Women comprise 30 percent of the judiciary in the higher ranks and 40 percent in the lower ranks.[40] The leading courtroom lawyers, QCs, are 65 percent male.[41] Although women are now entering the legal profession at a higher rate than men, they have not achieved parity in the higher echelons as partners in law firms.[42] In the police force, the role of women has altered significantly. Women were first recruited to work in standard roles in the police in 1918.[43] Until 1973 there was a distinction between the two arms of the service. Women's role here was, in practice, limited to certain specific "female-orientated" tasks such as child protection.[44] They now make up some 28 percent of the total personnel and their role is not "gender specific."[45]

It was in this context that women first started to appear on the television screen in Britain. They were seen occasionally in the supporting roles which they played in actual life. In the first television drama centered on the career of a woman barrister, for instance, one of the principal themes, which inform the drama, is the fact that the protagonist, Harriet Peterson, is one of the very few women working as a lawyer in the courts.[46] At the time, some 7 percent of practicing barristers were women.[47]

Britain's history consists of a series of inward movements of population from elsewhere since Roman times. The last hostile movement was the Norman invasion of 1066. Subsequent immigration generally involved those fleeing from persecution or destitution in a variety of different countries from the Protestant Huguenots in the seventeenth century to Jews fleeing the pogroms in Russia in the nineteenth century and the oppression of the Nazis in the 1930s to Asians being expelled from Kenya and Uganda in 1968 and 1972 respectively.[48] In addition, there have been major movements of population within the British Isles. The pacification of Ireland involved the transplanting of Scots into Ulster in the eighteenth century to consolidate British rule over Ireland and the potato famine of the 1840s produced major waves of emigration from Ireland. Many of those who survived and were able to leave remained in Britain.[49] More recently, in the postwar era, there has been immigration from former British colonies. The major difference between the postwar immigration and earlier movements was skin color. Whilst Irish, Italian, and Polish immigrants may have suffered discrimination and ill-treatment on their arrival, they were able to merge into the "host" population without excessive difficulty.[50] People of color may have been subject to informal "color bars" but were never formally excluded from employment or civil rights such as education or voting. The voter registration practices which occurred in the United States were never a feature of life in Britain.[51]

In terms of numbers it is estimated that in 1945 the population of Britain was 96 percent white.[52] There had always been small numbers of non-white Britons in various seaports serving the slave trade like Cardiff, Bristol, and Liverpool. The presence of increased numbers of people of color following the First World War and limited work opportunities led to early instances of blaming with riots in Cardiff in 1919. Later racial tensions following the end of Britain as a colonial power drew on white supremacist racism and xenophobia.[53] These developments were complemented by legislation to outlaw discrimination on the grounds of race and ethnicity from the limited Race Relations Acts of 1965 and 1968 to the more comprehensive Race Relations Act 1976.

Unlike women and people of color, there was never any doubt that relations between same-sex males were a criminal matter. Statutes had criminalized sodomy as far back as the sixteenth century[54] and subsequently the Offences Against the Person Act 1861 criminalized "the abominable Crime of Buggery, committed either with Mankind or with any Animal."[55] The offence of "gross indecency" in terms of the Criminal Law Amendment Act 1885 was more usually used against men in public places.

Moves to decriminalize the expression of same-sex love did not gain traction until the 1950s. The Report of the Departmental Committee on Homosexual Offences and Prostitution (better known as the *Wolfenden report*, after Lord Wolfenden, the chairman of the committee) was published in Britain on September 4, 1957. It recommended that private moral decisions for activities in private be a matter for individual choice. It did not result in a change of the law for a decade when the 1967 Sexual Offences Act for England and Wales removed the taint of criminality from activities between men of 21 or older in private.[56]

Disability was late to receive standard legislative protection from discrimination in Britain through the Disability Discrimination Act 1995.[57] Other issues were even later. The chronology of coverage is itself an interesting guide to the social pressures being exerted from race to gender to disability. The whole question of equal treatment is now found in Britain bin the Equality Act 2010 and its "protected characteristics" of discrimination, which extends the issues covered considerably.[58] It is in this context of a white patriarchal homophobic society that the justice system operates and is in the post–World War II period represented on television.

TV SERIES POST-2010

New TV programs in the second decade of the twenty-first century exhibit the same kind of general focus as was found in the survey of the postwar television age in the 2016 volume.[59] The apprehension and law enforcement aspects of the justice system continue to attract program makers. No less than fifteen new series have started in this decade and all of them have appeared for more than one season. In addition, there has been a number of miniseries on law enforcement. Most have followed the traditional male detective-centered format. One Victorian-set series has three male main protagonists,[60] but another show has a team which includes a supporting female in the "Dr. Watson/Lewis" role.[61]

A number of striking things occur when assessing the new series of this decade. In the first place, the changing role of women is marked both directly and indirectly. Four of the new series are headed up by a woman or women.

Two contain women with important secondary roles. The remaining two series are set over fifty years ago and provide a fascinating perspective on the emerging role of women in the justice system. I will look at these in a little more detail.

Vera (2011–),[62] like many other British police dramas, is based on a long-running fictional character.[63] Set largely in England's rural northeast area of Northumberland, the TV series follow the books of Ann Cleeves quite closely. They have a traditional structure with each of the two-hour episodes solving a single murder. The team is led by Detective Chief Inspector Vera Stanhope, a middle-aged woman who drives around in an old Land Rover Defender clad in a long green weatherproof coat and the kind of hat worn by fishermen against the elements. Vera eschews glamor in her appearance and lifestyle. She treats her colleagues with respect but is a hard "taskmaster." In 2017 the program returned for a seventh season. The TV adaptations were written by a variety of men and women.

Rather more novel and innovative are two police procedurals *Scott and Bailey* (2011–)[64] and *WPC 56* (2013–2015).[65] The former is written by Sally Wainwright, a writer with an impressive track record of TV writing.[66] *Scott and Bailey* is centered on a murder squad in Manchester and on the work of the Major Incident Team of the Manchester Metropolitan Police Service, and in particular on the eponymous Janet Scott and Rachel Bailey. Over five seasons we observe their professional development and their personal lives and how these interact. They are conscientious and hardworking and kept on their toes by a Stakhanovite boss, Detective Chief Inspector Gill Murray. Their work is centered on murder, rape, and other serious matters. The rather shorter-lived *WPC 56* focused on the struggles of a young woman police constable in the Midlands in 1950s Britain.[67] The series ran for three seasons of five episodes and was shown in the afternoons at 2:15 p.m. on BBC 1. Each season centered on an individual case and the restricted role of women in the macho male world in which WPC Gina Dawson worked. Apart from the belittling of her potential, she is also sexually harassed by one of her superiors.[68]

Two of the other programs from this decade are also set in the past. *Grantchester* (2014)[69] features a crime-solving clergyman from Cambridge, Sidney Chambers, who is friendly with a police detective from the northeast of England, Chief Inspector Geordie Keating. Together they investigate and solve a range of crimes in 1950s Cambridge. The series is based on the books of the son of a former Archbishop of Canterbury, Robert Runcie, James Runcie.[70] Both of the principal protagonists served in the Second World War and the series shows them both readjusting to the constraints of immediate postwar Britain. The change in the attitudes to sex outside of marriage as well as the taboo of same-sex relationships provide the background to the murders and other crimes with which the pair grapple. The only female presence is the stern but warm-hearted housekeeper, Mrs. Maguire.

By contrast, the prequel to the long-running detective series *Morse* (1987–1993), *Endeavour* (2012)[71] is set in the 1960s. We see the young Endeavour Morse a raw Detective Constable working in the male world of Oxford policing. The maleness of this world comes into focus in the five seasons of the series[72] with the appearance of WPC Shirley Trewlove. Her brightness and enthusiasm are in sharp contrast to the rather more plodding approach of her male colleagues. Recognition of her ability by the hierarchy is not, however, evident.

There is a shift away from the murder focus of these rather more glamorous shows in the day-to-day grind of small town policing in *Happy Valley* (2014–). This show also comes from the pen of Sally Wainwright and covers the daily work of a police sergeant, Catherine Cawood, with a mildly problematic family.[73] A rather different tone is found in *No Offence* (2015–).[74] Set in the northern powerhouse city of Manchester, this is written by esteemed gritty writer Paul Abbott. Abbott's previous highly successful series have covered the lives of both ordinary working people[75] and those of the "underclass."[76] The main protagonist Detective Inspector Viv Deering is a driven leader of her diverse force. This deals with serious issues as with the other writings and productions associated with Paul Abbott, but the fun of life and gallows humor predominate as Deering's motley crew are faced with the grisly end of policing.[77]

This change from male lead role dominance looks set to continue. In 2016 Anna Friel played London Detective Sergeant Marcella Backland in the ITV drama *Marcella* (2016–),[78] returning to work to investigate an unsolved murder in Season 1 and investigating a serial killer in Season 2. In addition, although it appeared after the period of collecting the empirical data on the kinds of law and justice programs being broadcast in Britain, *Collateral* (2018–)[79] is worth noting for maintaining the higher profile of woman as protagonists in law and justice programing. It has an unconventional woman in the leading role as a detective in charge of examining a convoluted murder with security and political implications. Its writer, David Hare's earlier theatrical work includes highly critical examinations of the Establishment ranging from the legal world[80] to the political[81] to as well as looking at the impact on society of gender inequality.[82]

Along with flagging the changing role of women in the second decade of the twenty-first century, there have been a few signs in the law and justice fictional series of the more diverse population now found in Britain. Two series have a non-white male protagonist. In *Luther* (2010–), Detective Chief Inspector John Luther is dedicated, ruthless, and obsessive. This makes his personal and professional life far from straightforward. The role confirmed the black actor Idris Elba as someone in great demand for major big screen roles in Hollywood,[83] in addition to his role in the sixth season of the TV series. The impact of Luther's own ethnicity and his cross-cultural marriage is not a major element in the series.[84] In *New Blood*, a two-man team of children of immigrants feature.[85] Two junior investigators find themselves working together in modern cosmopolitan London. Stefan Kowolski is from a Polish background and is able to use his Polish language skills to communicate with exploited Polish workers. His Asian-British colleague, Arrash Sayyad, is Muslim.[86]

It is rather in the historical series that we find racism and intolerance centered on skin tone. In 1955 *Grantchester*, the background to one investigation into the death of a visiting cricketer is the racism which is displayed against a Pakistani cricketer. Ten years later in the 1960s, the series *Endeavour* also recognizes the presence of other ethnicities in the romance which the eponymous hero has with one of the other occupants of his Oxford base. The rarity of black faces and of mixed race relationships is highlighted in the relationship between Endeavour and Jamaican Nurse Monica Hicks. After nursing him in Season 2 in 1966 following his being shot on duty, they start a relationship. By the end of Season 2 the relationship has petered out as he tries to protect her from the kind of characters with whom his police work means he must come in to contact. When we advance a year into 1967 in Season 3, Endeavour moves to a different house and we see Monica no more.[87] Another take on diversity can be seen in the Welsh language series *Y Gwyll* (The Dusk) (2013–2016).[88] Initially broadcast on S4C, the Welsh language channel, it migrated to an English language version, *Hinterland*, in 2014 on BBC4. The series follows the work of DCI Tom Mathias as he tracks down murderers in the unlikely setting of rural Wales assisted by DI Mared Rhys. It was part of the commitment to showing more Welsh language life and culture on mainstream TV.

Grantchester, with its setting in the criminalized world of the pre-liberation 1950s, highlights the need for gay men to suppress their sexuality to conform to the moral and legal standards of the day. The curate at Sidney Chambers' church, Leonard Finch, agonizes over his sexuality and faith throughout Season 2, finding himself attracted to a gay photographer. In Season 3, he is pressured by a new archdeacon into retreating into the closet and eventually marrying a woman. The relationship is far from successful and Leonard attempts suicide.[89] He does, however, come out in the final episode of Season 3 where both he and Sidney (who has been in breach of the Church of England's perspective on extra-marital relationships) put their hearts and feelings before strict adherence to the "old morality."

There does not appear to be very extensive coverage of issues of disability either in TV storylines or in characters. The exception to disability invisibility is in *Vera*. One of the backroom staff with an expertise in computers is a wheelchair user. The actor, Lisa Hammond, has a restricted growth condition and is 4″1′ (1.24 meteres). She played the part of Intelligence Officer Helen Milton from April 2015 through Seasons 5 and 6, and left the series at the end of Season 7 in 2017.[90] She was often a key figure in the narrative providing links to the suspects.

SIGNIFICANT PROGRAMS IN NOVEMBER 2017

For this collection, as for *A Transnational Study of Law and Justice on TV*, we undertook an overview of the programing on law and justice during our chosen month—November 2017. The programing in November 2014, the month of analysis in the previous collection, and November 2017 was remarkably similar. There has not been a dramatic shift in terms of the hours devoted to lawyer, police, and prison material. The same dominance of police and a focus on the apprehension phase of justice continues. The only major change in British TV has been the amount of hours devoted to law and justice on the small screen. This has increased by dint of the proliferation of free-to-air channels noted earlier.

As indicated, we are here concerned to evaluate more closely the nature of the programs with the greatest impact in terms of audience. We have chosen to examine in detail the three most popular series looking at law and justice shown during this period. Our particular concern is to pick up the threads of the findings of our 2016 study in relation to ethnicity, gender, and diversity. I have determined this by looking at the audience reach of the programs based on the British Audience Research Bureau statistics.[91]

As I have noted, the second decade of the twenty-first century has seen a number of clear trends in British television—the continued popularity of British series on crime, an affection for slick forensic American imports, and a steady stream of documentaries. To these it would be fair to add a new breed of low key dramas capitalizing on the popularity of dour Scandinavian crime fiction. In November 2017, however, there was no "Scandi noir" available on free-to-air TV.[92]

The three most watched series shown in November 2017 which seem to represent important threads running through the representation of law and justice are the successful long-running gangster series *Peaky Blinders*, the imported American forensic science series *NCIS New Orleans*, and a two-part documentary on life in prison, *Lifers Behind Bars* and *Violent Men: Behind Bars.*[93]

Peaky Blinders has been a commercial and critical success since it debuted on BBC2 in Britain in 2013. Four seasons had been shown by the end of 2017 and a fifth has been commissioned for transmission in 2019. It is set in the 1920s in the second largest city in England, Birmingham. Although centered on a criminal gang and its interactions, the justice system is a crucial element in the set-up. Its sporadic appearance in a series about the struggles of a major criminal gang internally and with other denizens of crime demonstrate the limited role of law and legality in this world as well as its potential to disrupt. This British television action crime drama follows the activities of the Shelby crime family. The major roles are taken by actors with track records in film and TV. Cillian Murphy plays Thomas (Tommy) Shelby, the gang's leader, and Sam Neill as Chester Campbell is a commissioned detective whose task is to suppress the gang. Helen McCrory plays the unusual matriarchal figure of Aunt Polly Gray. The title derives from the name of a nineteenth-century urban youth gang who were active in the city until the 1890s. They sewed razor blades into their caps in order to have handy but easily portable hidden weapons available at all times in an era of permanent headgear use.

The series has political resonances along with racial elements and gender politics made quite explicit throughout the series. The gang of Tommy Shelby established in its opening season their control of the major manufacturing center in England.[94] Their activities center on gambling and gun running from Ireland. There are also various internecine clashes with rivals. The police seek to infiltrate the organization as part of the broader struggle against the IRA. The Irish War of Independence between 1919 and 1921 is the initial backdrop. Two years on and the cat and mouse game with the police, with the background of the authorities' struggle against the IRA, continues in Season 2 as the Shelby gang seek to expand their activities to London and the greater opportunities in the gambling world there. The symbiotic relationship with the police and the role of the IRA is complicated by a mutual love interest between the principal gangster protagonist, Tommy Shelby, and the leading police officer Inspector Campbell. By the third season we have reached 1924 and the gang attempts to expand internationally, providing weapons for the Russian civil war. The series appears to be in danger of "jumping the shark" with a train bombing and a tunnel into the Russian embassy.[95] There is an emerging battle with the Sicilian Mafia too. At the end of the third season, four of the family are arrested and convicted and find themselves facing the death penalty by hanging. The fourth series opens in 1925 with the reprieve of the Shelby family members as Tommy Shelby has damaging information which allows him to force the Home Secretary into granting a reprieve. There is continuing bloody conflict with the Sicilian Mafia and problems emerge with the gang's legitimate front, their factory manufacturing motor vehicles, the Lanchester Motor Company, and various other companies. This is a violent and dangerous world dominated by violent and dangerous men.

What is also of major interest is the role of women in the post–World War I era. Although the gang is led by Tommy Shelby, the roles played by the women in the family are central throughout the series. They change, however, depending on the challenges facing the gang. In series 3 we saw the women characters walking out and joining a strike of women workers. This is an issue which we find in the second episode of Season 4 in November 2017 with the confrontation between Tommy Shelby and Jessie Eden.[96] Although the Great War has allowed Jessie to become a leader in the powerful Trade Union movement, her role is seen by some as temporary. She is urged not to worry that she is still Miss Eden. Her status in the workforce is transient. "Be patient. A good man will come," Tommy Shelby's assistant tells her.

In the episodes shown in November 2017, though, we also see the role of the matriarch, Aunt Polly, in decline in the fourth series with her reliance on drink and painkillers, revive to validate her son's demise by maintaining her major role in the day-to-day strategy and running of the "business."

Racial issues are covered discreetly for the most part. There are non-white faces from the war years and the implied acceptance of those who have fought. The Shelbys' own background is a Romany heritage. There is major focus on the conflict between the Shelby gang and the Jewish gang of Alfie Solomons and the Sicilian gang of Luca Changretta deriving not from any notions of inferiority or racial hierarchy but simply from business rivalry.[97] Non-white figures within the gang are treated no differently from anyone else, likely due to their shared background of fighting against injustice for little reward in post–Great War Britain.

This light on issues of diversity is something which Stephen Knight, the creator and writer of the series, was keen to emphasize. At times the modern resonances are a little questionable. When confronting Tommy Shelby about the wages of the women workers in his factories the discussions adopt the language of the tests developed in the litigation around the Equal Pay Act 1970. One way in which the equal pay legislation was avoided was by ensuring men's work and women's work was quite distinct, avoiding any need for equality. There were thus no comparators. So, in the 1980s the alternative test of "equal pay for work of equal value" was established. We find Jessie Eden addressing this issue some fifty years before it emerged as an issue in a negotiation with Tommy Shelby, noting the absence of comparators in the tasks undertaken by the woman. A prescient if improbable light on an ongoing issue in the continuing fight for equal recognition of women's work today.

NCIS: New Orleans is set in contemporary America with a very different tone. It is one of the two offshoots of the original *NCIS* series. The fictional Naval Criminal Investigative Service investigates crimes involving the U.S. Navy and Marine Corps. The concept and characters were initially introduced in the CBS series *JAG* and came to air in the United States on September 23, 2003, on CBS. The first spin-off was *NCIS: Los Angeles*.

The third season of *NCIS: New Orleans* received its UK premiere on Channel 5 on Saturday November 4, 2017, at 10 p.m. with a double-bill.[98] The show is set in the NCIS New Orleans field office, which handles cases from Pensacola through Mississippi and Louisiana to the Texas panhandle. The drama is produced by CBS Television Studios and its stars have established track records in previous American TV series.[99] During the month of our study the issue which was dealt with was principally murder[100] but the team also dealt with kidnapping[101] and a plane crash.[102] This focus was found across the remaining sixteen episodes of the series shown over the period of December 2017 and January 2018.[103]

The diversity issues we are focusing on emerge on this series obliquely. The workforce is an interesting mix of ethnic backgrounds and equal prominence is given to all six major characters across the series. There is the white middle-aged male boss, Dwayne Pride alongside senior black female Coroner, Dr. Loretta Wade. They are assisted by a young "will they or won't they" couple Sonja Percy and Christopher LaSalle. He is a deep South white country boy, she a hip urban African American. The other two men are both technical rather than operational. One is a socially awkward white geek with scientific expertise, Sebastien Lund, and the other a wheelchair using African American computer wizard, Patton Plame. The cosmopolitan nature of New Orleans means the cast of the show is varied. The perpetrators also reflect a society which is mixed with the principally male lawbreakers seeming to come from all sectors of society. Victims too were random. What we do not find in this series initially is any attention paid to the crimes of the powerful. This is addressed by the arrival on secondment to the team of an ex FBI agent, Tammy Gregorio. Her big "secret," other than her bisexuality, is that she was married to the man who embezzled $80 million from the relief funds for Hurricane Katrina. With most diversity bases covered, each episode neatly concludes with the team overcoming the various threats to life and security in New Orleans. It is refreshingly simplistic and old style in its narrative arcs along with the novel background of a constant threat from local politicians and the FBI in the affairs of the local NCIS.

A far different world of white males is encountered in the documentary series which drew the next highest audience, *Lifers Behind Bars* and *Violent Men: Behind Bars*.[104] These programs comprised a two-part documentary series, shown at prime time on Channel 4 that went behind the bars of prisons in the United Kingdom to interview men serving long sentences for violent crimes.[105] The style adopted is a mixture of fly-on-the-wall filming, interviews with prisoners, relatives and staff, plus some background information from the narrator. Some of the inmates had spent more than half of their lives in prison and talked about their struggles with drugs and other inmates who commit violent crimes inside since they have nothing to lose. The prison in the film is HMP Shotts, a modern facility located between Edinburgh and Glasgow. This is a world of men. The inmates we see are white and working class. The focus on this world gives us no information about the size of the prison population in Scotland and what proportion of it these men represent. Although filmed in Shotts Prison, we gain little insight into context. For example, it is mentioned that many of the prisoners have mental health issues but this is not quantified. Without wishing to require documentaries to be the equivalent of lectures on criminology or penology, they do leave the viewer in the dark. What the difference between the Shotts Prison and its population and that of Low Moss High Security Prison in Glasgow is never clear. (Low Moss featured in a rather less sensational documentary in July 2017 dealing with the visiting hour allowed to prisoners.)[106] In Low Moss, we saw a mixture of prisoners with convictions ranging from murder and drug trafficking to anti-social behavior amounting to breach of the peace. There is in these programs a slightly wider range of social class encountered.

CONCLUSION

What this 2017 research and our 2016 publication have sought to do is provide a much clearer benchmark as to what is happening in the portrayal of law and justice on the small screen. Both studies revealed a high level of focus on the policing function. The coverage is principally focused on entertainment in both the fictional and documentary spheres. Even when we look in greater depth at the most popular programs which feature law and justice issues, we struggle to find any context or background to the crimes. It may be that writers like Macaulay[107] and Sherwin[108] are still right in their suggestion that television is where we go for our information on law and justice, but it continues to be the case that the information available is extremely limited. It would be naïve to imagine that program makers are engaged in providing courses in civil society, but our studies confirm that what is available is highly random. There is a major difference between the kinds of crimes which occupy the majority of police and court time in real life and that shown on television.

The programs which proved most popular covering the realm of law and justice provide an interesting window into the issues of ethnicity, gender, and diversity. They show the changes which have occurred in the formal and informal treatment in British society of women and the way their role has altered over the years. The law itself is hardly adverted to but the changing role of women and their dependent status can be seen in the three most watched programs. In *Peaky Blinders*, this contrast is enabled by the historical context. Set at the culmination of the "first wave" of feminism with its focus on voting rights, we see the limited nature of change in the world of work and within the family. The changes to come are hinted at with the patronizing language of Tommy Shelby in his encounters with a self-confident woman. *Peaky Blinders* is the 1920s seen from the vantage point of the present day. The same can be said of ethnic conflicts. The language and the interactions in the TV show bear little relation to the terms used in the fiction of the time, nor to the day-to-day racial exclusion and anti-Semitism in social life.[109]

Although *NCIS: New Orleans* is clearly involved in a very different culture in respect of ethnicity and the aftermath of extensive use of slavery, there are interesting parallels in the portrayal of a developing multi-ethnic populace as well as in the law and justice workforce. The increasingly equal role of women is foregrounded in both *NCIS: New Orleans* and *Peaky Blinders*. What both *Peaky Blinders* and *Behind Bars* also emphasize is the contrast between women in the world of work in the twenty-first century and the cultural forces inhibiting this and the largely male world of crime. If we are to look to the television for a vision of how the world works then these programs provide, perhaps, a surprisingly useful illustration of many of the issues around ethnicity, gender, and diversity. Which is not to say that those looking for such elements as sexuality and transgender issues will find much here. These matters are covered in twenty-first-century television but they are not encountered in the most watched law and justice shows in Britain. The availability though of a myriad of channels does mean that there is now some space for diversity.

NOTES

1. These are in contrast to the kind of subscription service through the various "bundles" offered in Britain by Sky where in addition to the basic package offering news, soaps, and documentaries there are add-ons for those who want to watch Sport, film, history, or "vintage" television.

2. The Communications (Television Licensing)(Amendment) Regulation 2016/704 which amended the Communications (Television Licensing) Regulations 2004 and the Communication Act 2003 to include in the definition of using a television receiver, "receiving all or any part of a programme included in an on-demand programme service which is provided by the BBC." This came into force from September 1, 2016.

3. The contrast with the viewing figures for a successful program mean that, for instance, the audience for the top rated show in the 1970s, *The Generation Game*, was 25 million (https://www.thesun.co.uk/tvandshowbiz/4285131/bruce-forsyth-generation-game). Its modern "successor," the soap *Coronation Street* is able to be

top the ratings with 8.8 million viewers (http://www.barb.co.uk, week ending April 8, 2018).

4. Subject to shifting the cost of the free licence for viewers aged seventy five and over from the government to the BBC in 2016 until 2020 (https://www.independent.co.uk/news/uk/politics/the-bbc-is-worryingly-close-to-becoming-an-arm-of-the-government-says-its-own-former-chair-10368284.html).

5. See below (https://www.fawcettsociety.org.uk/close-gender-pay-gap, accessed April 5, 2018).

6. Report of the Stephen Lawrence Inquiry Cm 4262 (February 1999) (https://www.gov.uk/government/uploads/system/uploads/attachment_data/file/277111/4262.pdf).

7. "I think the BBC is hideously white. I think the BBC is a predominantly white organization. The figures we have at the moment suggest that quite a lot of people from different ethnic backgrounds that we do attract to the BBC, leave. Maybe they don't feel at home, maybe they don't feel welcome" on BBC Radio Scotland's *The Mix,* January 7, 2001 (https://www.theguardian.com/media/2001/jan/07/uknews.theobserver1). He resigned three years over the unrelated matter of the BBC's coverage of the David Kelly scandal over the Iraq War.

8. http://www.bbc.co.uk/news/entertainment-arts-42872377.

9. The first long-term success of a British reality show leading to the judge's appearance as a contestant on *Strictly Come Dancing* (*Dancing with the Stars* in United States) in 2016 and a series on real-life crime stories—*Judge Rinder's Crime Stories* as well as the daily afternoon show, *Judge Rinder.*

10. Shown in Britain through the subscription outlet Netflix.

11. *Lifers: Behind Bars* (Channel 4) and *Violent Men: Behind Bars* (Channel 4)—discussed in n. 13 below.

12. See http://www.barb.co.uk/viewing-data/weekly-top-30/ for November 2017—BBC2 figures.

13. *Lifers: Behind Bars* (Channel 4) 1.69 million and *Violent Men: Behind Bars* (Channel 4) 88 million (http://www.barb.co.uk/viewing-data/weekly-top-30); For November 2017 (Channel 4) 1.65 million.

14. Initially, the right to vote was accorded to women aged thirty and over who satisfied a property qualification in the Representation of the People Act 1918. This was extended to women on the same terms as men in the Representation of the People (Equal Franchise) Act 1928.

15. Freeview—https://www.freeview.co.uk/#KXCrcbzFeqqYOCaB.97.

16. Freesat—https://www.freesat.co.uk.

17. *The Guardian.* April 25, 2018, "How Streaming Saved the Music Industry," G2, 8 (https://www.theguardian.com/music/2018/apr/24/weve-got-more-money-swirling-around-how-streaming-saved-the-music-industry).

18. https://www.ofcom.org.uk/research-and-data/multi-sector-research/cmr/cmr-2017.

19. By omission rather than design (e.g., *Taggart* [1983–2010]).

20. *The Professionals* (1977–1983); *The Fixer* (2008–2009).

21. *Lovejoy* (1986–1994); *Hustle* (2004—2012).

22. *DCI Banks* (2010–2016); *Death in Paradise* (2011–); *Ripper Street* (2012–2016); *Law and Order UK* (2009–2014—police/lawyer hybrid); *The Tunnel* (2013, 2016, 2017).

23. See section titled "Significant Programs in November 2017" of this chapter.

24. *Cracker* (1993–2006); *Silent Witness* (1996–).

25. *Between the Lines* (1992–1994); *Line of Duty* (2012–).

26. *The Knock* (1994–2000); *Special Branch* (1969–1974); *Dempsey and Makepeace* (1985–1986).

27. The Committee on Culture Media and Sport concluded that there was no "long term future for the licence fee in its current form"—cited in *A Transnational Study of Law and Justice on TV*, chapter 4 at footnote 29.

28. *BROADCASTING: Copy of Royal Charter for the Continuance of the British Broadcasting Corporation* December 2016 Cm 9365 and *BROADCASTING: An Agreement Between Her Majesty's Secretary of State for Culture, Media and Sport and the British Broadcasting Corporation* December 2016 Cm 9366; see also Philip Ward's Briefing Paper *BBC Charter Renewal* from December 2016 for how these documents went through the process of amendment and discussion—http://researchbriefings.files.parliament.uk/documents/SN03416/SN03416.pdf.

29. Charter, op. cit. at para 2 (3).

30. Disability could also be included but the nature of the political pressure groups were rather different—Helen Bolderson *Social Security, Disability and Rehabilitation: Conflicts in the Development of Social Policy* (1991) London, Jessica Kingsley.

31. Representation of the People Act 1884 ss 2–6.

32. They also require to be householders, the wives of householders, occupiers of property with an annual rent of £5, or graduates of British universities.

33. Representation of the People (Equal Franchise) Act 1928.

34. Until the Representation of the People Act 1948 there were individuals who had more than one vote. In addition to being able to vote where they lived, there was the business vote and twelve University seats.

35. *Jex-Blake and Others v. Senatus Academicus of the University of Edinburgh*, [1873] SLR 10_549 (June 27, 1873).

36. Until 1997 the highest number of women in the chamber was 60—since then the number has increased slowly—1997, 120; 2001, 118; 2005, 128; 2010, 143; 2015, 191. See also http://researchbriefings.files.parliament.uk/documents/SN06652/SN06652.pdf and http://researchbriefings.parliament.uk/ResearchBriefing/Summary/SN01250.

37. https://www.fawcettsociety.org.uk/close-gender-pay-gap (accessed April 5, 2018).

38. https://www.cranfield.ac.uk/press/news-2016/women-on-boards-ftse-100-company-has-full-gender-balance-for-first-time.

39. https://www.supremecourt.uk/about/biographies-of-the-justices.html.

40. http://www.bbc.co.uk/news/uk-37575212.

41. https://www.barstandardsboard.org.uk/media-centre/research-and-statistics/statistics/queen's-counsel-statistics.

42. file:///C:/Users/Peter%20Robson/AppData/Local/Packages/Microsoft.MicrosoftEdge_8wekyb3d8bbwe/TempState/Downloads/ASR-2016-executive-summary.pdf.

43. http://library.college.police.uk/docs/theses/CARTRON-Women-in-the-police-forces-in-Britain-1880-1931.pdf.

44. See the film *Street Corner* (1953), which exemplifies this distinction looking at the role of three different women in the early postwar police force. The film was directed by pioneering director Muriel Box.

45. https://www.gov.uk/government/speeches/women-in-policing.

46. Peter Robson (2014) "Women Lawyers on TV—the British Experience" *Nordic Journal of Law and Social Research* 1(5) (2014), Special Issue on Law and Art.

47. https://www.counselmagazine.co.uk/articles/women-the-bar-historical-perspective.

48. David Olusoga, (2016). *Black and British: A Forgotten History*. London: Pan Macmillan.

49. MacRaild, Donald M., (2010). *The Irish Diaspora in Britain, 1750–1939* London: Palgrave Macmillan. Liverpool and the west of Scotland have sizeable populations with Irish Catholic backgrounds with ethnic tensions reflected in the existence of Orange marches and football rivalry in Glasgow to the current day.

50. James Handley, (2001 [1945]). *The Irish in Scotland*. Cork, Ireland: Cork University Press.

51. Complex racially discriminatory tests were required, which had to be addressed in the Voting Rights Act 1965.

52. David Olusoga, *Black and British: A Forgotten History* (op. cit.)—in 2001 it was 92 percent and by 2011 it was 87 percent—2001 and 2011 Censuses.

53. Camilla Schofield, (2014). *Enoch Powell, and the Making of Postcolonial Britain*. Cambridge: Cambridge University Press.

54. Buggery Act 1533.

55. Section 61—until 1980 sex between men was illegal in Scotland. The Criminal Justice (Scotland) Act 1980 decriminalized homosexual acts between men over twenty one and in private, in Scotland. Whilst sexual acts between women have never been specifically outlawed in the United Kingdom, some prosecutions for indecency were made in the past.

56. This change of attitude did not affect policing of "cottaging" (sexual activity in a public lavatory), which continued to be pursued under the Sexual Offences Act 2003. It was not until 1980 that sex between men was made illegal in Scotland. The Criminal Justice (Scotland) Act 1980 decriminalized homosexual acts between men over twenty-one and in private, north of the border. Whilst sexual acts between women have never been specifically outlawed in the United Kingdom, some prosecutions for indecency were made in the past.

57. Although it is should be noted that the Disabled Persons (Employment) Act 1944 provided an early version of positive action with its requirement on larger employers to employ 3 percent or more of their workforce from a register of those with disabilities. This was not a success in practice embodying *inter alia* the demeaning process of signing on the register. For an overview see Patricia Thornton and Neil

Lunt, *Employment for Disabled People Social Obligation or Individual Responsibility?* (1994) (https://www.york.ac.uk/inst/spru/research/pdf/obligation.pdf).

58. The "protected characteristics" are age, disability, gender reassignment, marriage and civil partnership, pregnancy and maternity, race, religion or belief, sex, sexual orientation. Race incorporates color, nationality, and racial or ethnic origins.

59. Robson in *Robson and Schulz* (2016) at 42–46.

60. *Ripper Street* (2012–2016)—DI Edmund Reid, DI Bennet Drake and Police Surgeon Captain Homer Jackson. The female roles are the brothel owner "Long" Susan Hart and prostitute Rose Erskine.

61. *DCI Banks* (2010–2016) DCI Alan Banks and DS Annie Cabot/DI Helen Morton; *Death in Paradise* (2011–) DI Richard Poole and Camille Bordey; DI Humphrey Goodman and Camille Bordey; DI Jack Mooney and Florence Cassel; *Shetland* (2013–) Inspector Jimmy Perez and Detective Sergeant Alison "Tosh" Macintosh.

62. http://www.tv.com/shows/vera/episodes.

63. *The Crow Trap* (1999); *Telling Tales* (2005); *Hidden Depths* (2007); *Silent Voices* (2010); *The Glass Room* (2012); *Harbour Street* (2014); *The Moth Catcher* (2015); *The Seagull* (2017).

64. http://www.imdb.com/title/tt1843678.

65. https://www.imdb.com/title/tt2678thirty-five4.

66. Including *Unforgiven* (2009) and *Last Tango in Halifax* (2012–2016).

67. https://www.bbc.co.uk-wpc, 56.

68. The daughter of a seasoned police officer, WPC Annie Taylor replaces Dawson in series 3.

69. http://www.imdb.com/title/tt3747572.

70. *Sidney Chambers and the Shadow of Death* (2012); *Sidney Chambers and the Perils of the Night* (2013); *Sidney Chambers and the Problem of Evil* (2014); *Sidney Chambers and the Forgiveness of Sins* (2015); *Sidney Chambers and the Dangers of Temptation* (2016); *Sidney Chambers and the Persistence of Love* (2017).

71. http://www.imdb.com/title/tt2701582.

72. A sixth series has been commissioned for filming in 2019 set in 1969 (http://www.whatsontv.co.uk/news/endeavour-return-sixth-series-itv-522089) with viewing figures of almost 7 million viewers for series 5, this seem likely.

73. http://www.imdb.com/title/tt3428912.

74. http://www.imdb.com/title/tt3428912.

75. *Clocking Off* (2000–2003)—4 seasons.

76. *Shameless* (2004–2013)—11 seasons—a US version of the same title was set in south side Chicago from 2011 for 8 seasons and running at the time of writing in 2018.

77. For completeness a single season of eight episodes of a police procedural set in a southern seaside town titled *Cuffs* ran on BBC 1 in 2015 with a diverse cast (https://www.bbc.co.uk-cuffs) and in 2018 a four-part miniseries *Kiri* featured a female social worker dealing with abduction and murder of a young black girl due to be adopted by a white foster family (https://www.imdb.com.kiri).

78. https://www.imdb.com.marcella.

79. http://www.imdb.com/title/tt6729080.

80. *Murmuring Judges* (1991).

81. *The Absence of War* (1993).

82. *Plenty* (1978)—which was adapted for the screen in 1985 starring Meryl Streep and Sir John Gielgud.

83. Including playing Nelson Mandela in *Mandela: Long Walk to Freedom* (2013) and *inter alia* roles in *Prometheus* (2012), *Pacific Rim* (2013), *No Good Deed* (2014), *Avengers: Age of Ultron,* (2015), *The Dark Tower* (2017), and *Molly's Game* (2017).

84. In contrast to the portrayal of the issues over forty years ago in *Black Silk* (1985) with Rudolph Walker as Larry Scott and Kika Markham as his partner Julie Smythe.

85. https://www.bbc.co-new blood.

86. The series is written by the creator of the wartime set detective series, *Foyle's War* and the boss of Stefan is a woman.

87. Writer Russell Davies had originally intended their affair to unravel more slowly but decided that the story had been told and other matters were more press ing—http://dmbarcroft.com/tag/nurse-monica-hicks.

88. https://www.imdb.com.hinterland.

89. Season 3 Episode 4 (shown May 2017).

90. She also had a role in the top-rated daily soap *EastEnders* playing feisty market trader Donna Yates. She occupied this role from 2014 to 2018.

91. There are alternative ways of gauging the significance or popularity of programmes. There are, for instance, popularity polls run on the Internet. Apart from the question of how these are compiled they do tend to be quite specific. One of these in the area of law and justice which confirms our finding that television programmes in the twenty-first century almost never die, limits itself to the best British detective series. It operates as a guide for American viewers keen to know how British people rate their own products. It ranges across private as well as police detectives over the years but its focus is narrower than the whole law and justice field (https://www.ranker.com/list/best-british-detective-series/ranker-tv) aimed at the American viewers and featuring "all-time top British mystery series," the most highly rated British show is the modern afternoon "filler" *Father Brown* (2013–).

92. November did see the start of a Scandinavian drama, *Acquitted.* Only one episode of this, however, was shown on standard TV and the rest of the season was available on All4, a streaming service offered by Channel 4 for their back catalogue.

93. *Lifers: Behind Bars* (Channel 4) 1.69 million and *Violent Men: Behind Bars* (Channel 4) 88 million (http://www.barb.co.uk/viewing-data/weekly-top-30); For November 2017 (Channel 4) 1.65 million.

94. And at the time, 1919, in terms of population the "second city of the Empire."

95. That moment when good TV goes bad—derived from the incident in *Happy Days* when the Fonz did just that. Although it does not appear to have registered with *The Guardian*'s weekly assessment https://www.theguardian.com/tv-and-radio/series/jump-the-shark?page=4.

96. The character was based on an activist of the time, Jessie Eden who played a major role in the General Strike of 1926 and a major strike in 1931 and the show's

creator and writer Stephen Knight was keen to foreground extraordinary women—https://www.telegraph.co.uk/tv/2016/05/26/peaky-blinders-tommy-shelby-is-at-deaths-door-plus-8-other-thing/ and https://www.theguardian.com/tv-and-radio/2017/oct/29/peaky-blinders-jessie-eden-communist-activist-general-strike.

97. There is an exception to this inter-ethnic acceptance in Season 2 Episode 4 when a friend of a gang member gets involved in a fight due to the color of his skin.

98. Thereafter times varied—it was shown on November 11 in a double 2-hour primetime slot with episodes at 7:50 p.m. and 8:45 p.m. and on November 18 and 25 at 10:25 p.m. and 11:20 p.m. Repeats were on weekday afternoons on Mondays and Tuesdays.

99. Scott Bakula (*Star Trek: Enterprise*), CCH Pounder (*Warehouse 13*), Lucas Black (*Fast & Furious*), Vanessa Ferlito (*CSI: NY*), Rob Kerkovich (*Chasing Life*), Daryl Mitchell (*Galaxy Quest*) and Shalita Grant (*Mercy Street*).

100. Episode 1, "Aftershocks" (shown November 4)—a sniper targeting special events; Episode 2, "Suspicious Minds" (shown November 4); Episode 3, "Man on Fire" (shown November 11); Episode 4, "Escape Plan" (shown November 11); Episode 6, "One Good Man" (shown November 18); Episode 7, "Outlaws" (shown November 25); Episode 8, "Music to my Ears" (shown November 25).

101. Episode 4, "Escape Plan" (shown November 11).

102. Episode 5, "Course Correction" (shown November 18).

103. The third season aired some six months earlier in the United States.

104. Thursday November 15 and 22, 2017, Channel 4.

105. The documentary *Raped* was also shown in the month of the study but as noted above it achieved lower ratings than *Behind Bars* (http://www.barb.co.uk/viewing-data/weekly-top-30/, for November 2017—Channel 5).

106. http://www.channel4.com/programmes/life-behind-bars-visiting-hour

107. Macaulay, Stewart, (1987). *Images of Law in Everyday Life: The Lessons of School, Entertainment and Spectator Sports 21 Law and Society Rev*, 185.

108. Richard, Sherwin, 2000. *When Law Goes Pop: The Vanishing Line Between Law and Popular Culture* (Chicago: University of Chicago Press).

109. Olusoga (2016) op. cit. G. C. Lebzelter, 1978. *Political Anti-Semitism in England 1918–1939* by Gisela C. Lebzelter. London: Macmillan.

Chapter 4

Canada

Women, People of Color, and Diversity on Top Law Shows

Jennifer L. Schulz*

DATA COLLECTION

The last time I wrote a chapter about the law featured on prime-time Canadian television, I noted that it is overwhelmingly American, focused on criminal law, and dominated by police shows rather than lawyer shows.[1] I concluded that chapter by indicating that I am interested in women, people of color, and other marginalized legal processes and actors.[2] I am pleased to have the opportunity to focus on them in this chapter. This is important because popular television programs show viewers how the people in the legal world look. The Canadian world should look multicultural and be equal because Canada has explicitly embraced multiculturalism and equality of all people. These principles are enshrined in the *Canadian Charter of Rights and Freedoms*, which has been part of the Canadian Constitution since 1982.[3] The *Charter* sets out the rights and freedoms that Canadians believe are necessary in a free and democratic society, including freedom of expression, Aboriginal peoples' rights, the right to equality, including the equality of men and women, and the protection of Canada's multicultural heritage. Section 15 of the *Canadian Charter of Rights and Freedoms* stipulates that "Every individual is equal before and under the law and has the right to the equal protection and equal benefit of the law without discrimination and, in particular, without discrimination based on race, national or ethnic origin, colour, religion, sex, age or mental or physical disability." The Supreme Court of Canada has held that Section 15 also protects equality on the basis of other characteristics that are not specifically set out in it, such as sexual orientation.[4] While Canada has

* S. J. D., Associate Professor, Robson Hall Faculty of Law, University of Manitoba, Winnipeg, Canada.

enumerated admirable freedoms and guaranteed equality to all, an examination of television's portrayal of women, people of color, and other aspects of diversity reveals we still have a way to go.

In order to identify the top three legally themed shows in Canada in November 2017 and examine their representations of gender, ethnicity, and diversity, I conducted an empirical study. I surveyed the television available to English Canadian viewers in Manitoba, Canada, including regular, free television, and pay-per-view shows such as those found on Netflix.[5] I obtained my data from Numeris, a Canadian audience measurement company. Numeris was established on May 11, 1944 as a division of the Canadian Association of Broadcasters. It is Canada's leading provider of viewership numbers for television broadcasters. Numeris posts its data online and thus I effortlessly obtained the top thirty TV programs for all national networks and Canadian English specialty networks for each week of November 2017.

Numeris gave me the broadcast television data I needed. However, according to a recent survey of Canadians who participate in Nielsen's HomeScan panel,[6] more than one-third of Canadian viewers (37 percent) accessed TV content using subscription video-on-demand (SVOD) services, such as Netflix in 2015.[7] Netflix and other SVOD services—for example, Shomi, Crave TV, Amazon, and Hulu—have changed the way viewers engage with their screens. Canadians watch when, where, and how we want, at whatever pace we prefer. This has even given rise to a new kind of viewer called the binge racer. Binge racers are defined as Netflix customers who complete a season of a show within 24 hours of its release on Netflix. According to Netflix Media Center, Canada is the country with the highest percentage of 24-hour finishers.[8] Canadians' favorite show to binge race in 2017 was a Canadian show, *Trailer Park Boys*,[9] which ranked seventh out of the top twenty binge-raced shows. Number nine out of twenty was the American program *Orange Is the New Black*.[10] Both of these shows fit into our study's definition of a legally themed show because both are about prison and law-breaking.

Given the fact that Canadians are watching subscription video-on-demand shows such as those produced by Netflix, I needed data about Canadians' Netflix-viewing habits. It is, however, very difficult to determine ratings and viewership because Netflix keeps their viewing figures secret; they are not published anywhere. This means I could not obtain accurate data regarding which legally themed Netflix shows are most popular in Canada. A metric service technology firm called Symphony Advanced Media provided some assistance. Symphony Advanced Media compiled independent data on the twenty-five most-watched Netflix shows of 2016 in their first thirty-five days of availability in the United States. Symphony Advanced Media found that Season 4 of *Orange Is the New Black*, a women's prison drama, was the most popular Netflix show of 2016. Tufayel Ahmed listed the top twenty-five original Netflix shows of 2016, based on the first thirty-five days of release, as follows:

Some of these twenty-five shows are certainly legally themed shows, such as: *Orange Is the New Black*, *Marvel's Luke Cage*, *Marvel's Daredevil*, and *Narcos*. However, Ahmed's numbers are from 2016, not November 2017, the month of analysis in this book. Also, these numbers are American; it is not clear whether these shows are being watched by Canadians, nor how regularly.

Table 4.1 Top 25 Original Netflix Shows of 2016

Rank	*Show*	*Viewers* (by Millions)
1	*Orange Is the New Black* (Season 4)	23
2	*Stranger Things*	21.7
3	*Fuller House*	21.5
4	*Marvel's Luke Cage*	12.1
5	*Marvel's Daredevil* (Season 2)	11.6
6	*House of Cards* (Season 4)	8.8
7	*Unbreakable Kimmy Schmidt* (Season 2)	8.4
8	*The Ranch*	5.8
9	*11.22.63*	5.3
10	*Amanda Knox*	4.96
11	*The Get Down*	4.91
12	*Gracie and Frankie* (Season 2)	4.5
13	*Love*	4
14	*Narcos* (Season 2)	3.8
15	*Black Mirror* (Season 3)	3.7
16	*The Crown*	3.5
17	*Bloodline* (Season 2)	3.3
18	*Longmire* (Season 5)	3.2
19	*Chelsea Does*	2.7
20	*The Path*	2.06
21	*Flaked*	2.04
22	*Bojack Horseman* (Season 3)	2
23	*Marco Polo* (Season 2)	1.9
24	*Goliath*	1.8
25	*Bosch* (Season 2)	1.6 [1]

[1]Tufayel Ahmed, "Netflix Ratings Revealed? These are the Top 25 Original Streaming Shows of 2016" (November 2, 2017) *Newsweek*, U S edition.

John Lynch, writing for *Business Insider*, turned to the online reviews aggregator *Rotten Tomatoes* to rank fifty-four original Netflix shows by their composite critical reception.[11] He did not include children's shows, talk shows, or series from other networks. Where there was a tie, he used audience scores rather than critic scores to break the tie. Of the fifty-four original Netflix shows, seven had legal or police themes. I cannot be certain these are highly watched programs in Canada, but they are highly ranked, and based on press coverage and sociocultural "buzz" in Canada, I believe they are watched by many. The shows are:

Table 4.2 Original Netflix Shows with Legal or Police Themes 2017

Show	*Rank (out of 54)*	*Score (composite critical reception) (%)*	*Synopsis*
Luke Cage	#9	96	An ex-con with superhero strength fights to clear his name and save his neighborhood.
Mindhunter	#10	95	FBI agents in the late 1970s delve into the psychology of murder and get close to real killers.
Jessica Jones	#16	92	Private investigator/failed superhero Jessica Jones tries to find her tormentor before he can harm anyone else.
Orange Is the New Black	#18	91	A privileged New Yorker ends up in a women's prison.
Narcos	#23	87	The story of Pablo Escobar, violent gangsters, and Colombia's powerful drug cartels.
Daredevil	#25	86	Blinded as a young boy, Matt Murdock fights injustice by day as a lawyer and by night as the superhero, Daredevil.
The Defenders	#37	75	A group of superheroes, Daredevil, Jessica Jones, Luke Cage and Iron Fist, join forces to take on common enemies in New York City.

When I added *TV Guide*'s research about the best original Netflix shows,[12] it included two law-related shows that Lynch omitted from his list: *Making a Murderer*[13] and *13th.*[14] Remembering that Canadians are binge-watching *Trailer Park Boys*, and taking all of this information together, I suspect that Canadians are also watching the justice-themed Netflix shows *Luke Cage*, *Mindhunter*, *Jessica Jones*, *Orange Is the New Black*, *Better Call Saul*, *Breaking Bad*, *Making a Murderer*, and *Suits*,[15] but there is no empirical data to verify my speculation.

I simply cannot be sure that the American results I found translate to Canada, especially since streaming in Canada is at a lower level than in the United States, where penetration of SVOD has increased now to 46 percent.[16] According to Nielsen's HomeScan panel, traditional TV viewing averages about twenty hours a week for Canadians, and less than six hours per week are subscription video-on-demand. Among those with a SVOD service, 75 percent have also retained their TV service, and 83 percent of Canadians stream less than 12 hours of SVOD content per week. However, usage among families with children, those under 35 years of age, and among Canada's South Asian community is much higher.[17] Penetration of streaming services also increases with income, and usage among the English-speaking Canadian population is much higher than among the French-speaking population (44 percent versus 13 percent), presumably due to the fact that the number of French language programs on Netflix is low. So, it is clear that Canadians are watching regular broadcast television as well as subscription video-on-demand. We do not know how much SVOD is actually being consumed, but we do know that television remains very popular. As John Doyle notes:

> What has not changed is the popularity of television itself. Whether the viewer is watching content on a giant flat-screen unit on the wall, or on a tablet, it's still TV content. There is a hunger for it and television is the defining storytelling medium of this century. The lights have been dimmed in the Canadian TV racket, but they haven't been turned off. Yet.[18]

FINDINGS

By turning to Numeris I was able to obtain accurate Canadian data about broadcast television viewing. Numeris notes that for the week of October 30 through November 5, 2017, the top ten programs contained five TV shows with jury consultant[19] or police themes (*NCIS*, *Bull*, *S.W.A.T.*, *Blue Bloods*, and *Hawaii Five-0*). *NCIS* was ranked fourth, *Bull* was sixth, *S.W.A.T.* was seventh, *Blue Bloods* was ninth and *Hawaii Five-0* was tenth. For November 6 through 12, 2017, the top ten programs comprised four shows with jury consultant or police themes: *NCIS* held at fourth, *Bull* moved up to fifth, *Blue Bloods* moved up to seventh, and *Lucifer* came in at tenth. There were three jury consultant or police-themed shows in the top ten between November 13 and 19, 2017: *NCIS* still at fourth, *Bull* back down to sixth, and *Lucifer* held at tenth. November 20 to 26, 2017, was the first time a Canadian program with a legal or justice theme entered the top ten. The CBC production of *The Indian Detective* premiered on November 23, 2017, at fifth place, followed by *Bull*, steady at sixth, and *NCIS*, which moved down to eighth. In the last week of my study, November 27 to December 3, 2017, Numeris data again revealed three justice-themed shows. The Canadian show, *The Indian Detective*, managed to hold its own at fifth, *Blue Bloods* was ranked seventh, and *Hawaii Five-0* came back at eighth.

Numeris' data makes it clear that Canadians are watching *NCIS*, *Bull*, *Blue Bloods*, *Lucifer*, *The Indian Detective*, and *Hawaii Five-0* on their televisions during regular prime-time broadcasting hours.[20] During the daytime they are likely watching various judge shows, for example, *Judge Judy*, as well as reruns of *Law & Order* and its most popular spin-off, *Law & Order: SVU*.[21] The types and styles of these shows are very similar to what I found in Canada in 2014, the month of analysis in our 2016 book. Police and American shows still dominate the airwaves. Three prime-time, law-related shows were however always in the top six: *NCIS* (typically in fourth), *Bull* (most often at sixth), and *The Indian Detective* (in fifth place). Thus, these are Canada's top three prime-time television shows with law themes in November 2017, and these are the shows I will examine in this chapter.

The top three, legally themed, hour-long prime-time shows watched by Canadians in November 2017 have three things in common. First, *NCIS*, *Bull*, and *The Indian Detective* all focus on criminal law. Second, they all have male leads, and finally, all three shows have outlandish, unrealistic plots. Additionally, the two American shows, *NCIS* and *Bull*, are filled with ethical violations too numerous to document that are beyond the scope of this chapter.

NCIS is an American show on the CBS network that is shown in Canada on Global and is rated 14+, which means it is meant for viewers fourteen years of age or older; "viewer discretion is advised." The program airs on Tuesday nights at 7 p.m. CST. *NCIS* has been on the air for fifteen seasons and it is a very popular show. It has spawned two spin-offs, *NCIS: Los Angeles* and *NCIS: New Orleans*, also popular with viewers. The show was ranked fourth in the first three weeks of my study and eighth in the fourth week, which means it never moved out of the top ten TV programs watched by Canadians, and was usually in the top five. NCIS stands for Naval Criminal Investigative Service. The service is headed by Inspector Gibbs, played by Caucasian male actor Mark Harmon. Gibbs is depicted as all-knowing, with an amazing "gut" that can always be trusted. He, together with his team, investigates major criminal offences committed by US Navy or Marine personnel. As such, each episode focuses on serious violent crimes. Dowler, Fleming, and Muzzatti note that: "It is apparent, given the research of the past three decades, that particularly heinous crimes have tremendous appeal for the media, the public, and politicians."[22] This is certainly true of *NCIS*.

Bull is also an American show on the CBS network that is shown in Canada on Global and is rated 14+. The program airs on Tuesday nights at 8 p.m. CST. The Caucasian male actor Michael Weatherly, who stars as Dr. Jason Bull, was on *NCIS* for thirteen years before moving to *Bull*. Since *NCIS* is the lead-in show to *Bull* and Michael Weatherly is familiar to viewers, a consistent, large audience exists for both shows in Canada. *Bull* was ranked sixth during three weeks of my study and fifth for one week; it too remained in the top ten TV law programs watched by Canadians. Dr. Jason Bull is a psychologist and jury consultant loosely based on jury consultant Dr. Phil McGraw, before he became famous as Dr. Phil on *Oprah*. Dr. McGraw is one of the creators of the show *Bull*. Dr. Jason Bull has his own firm, called TAC, which stands for Trial Analysis Corporation. He travels across the United States with his team of experts to consult on behalf of clients, calling himself a trial scientist, assisting lawyers and legal teams as they prepare for trial. Unfortunately, Dr. Bull is arrogant and employs methods to obtain jury information that are unscrupulous, unethical, and sometimes illegal. For example, Dr. Bull routinely flaunts privacy laws, signals to witnesses, prompts them to deliver pre-prepared testimony, and tampers with juries. Richard Gabriel notes that because the public generally does not know about jury consultants, it becomes easier to accept what happens in *Bull* as reflective of real jury consultants' behavior.[23]

The Indian Detective is a Canadian mini-series that aired four Thursdays in a row, beginning November 23, 2017, at 9 p.m. CST on CTV. It was also rated 14+. The premiere episode was ranked fifth by Numeris. The next week, episode two, also ranked fifth. This is likely due to *The Indian Detective*'s excellent Thursday night timeslot immediately following the two most popular shows on television, *The Big Bang Theory* at 8 p.m. and *Young Sheldon* at 8:30 p.m. By its third week, *The Indian Detective* slipped down to twelfth position, where it stayed for its fourth and final week.[24] The show premiered on Netflix worldwide on December 19, 2017, but viewing numbers are not available. *The Indian Detective* is a one-hour dramedy starring male Indo-Canadian Russell Peters, who is a famous stand-up comedian, ranking ninth on Forbes' 2016 list of the highest earning comedians. The show is filmed on location in Cape Town, Mumbai, and Toronto, and stars Peters as a Toronto police officer, Doug D'Mello, who becomes involved solving drug cartel-related crimes while visiting his father in Mumbai. Doug is actually a constable, not a detective, even though his father tells others that he is a detective.

ANALYSIS: GENDER

Conducting an analysis of gender in the police procedural genre of television shows must be done with an awareness that policing, and shows about policing, are gendered male. It is not surprising that the majority of characters are male, given that the majority of police officers in real life are men. Television generates representations of women in the police genre and reinforces the idea that "this human, social construction is really the real thing. . . . The representation, the social construction, has come to stand in for an imaginary original reality."[25] So what are "real" women like, according to Canada's top three legally themed shows? They are strong. All three shows feature strong women characters. However, one needs to be aware of the women's positions in the plots—are any women the protagonists? None of the women characters in *NCIS*, *Bull*, or *The Indian Detective* are leads in their shows.

Julie D'Acci has identified an integrative approach to studying gender representations on television.[26] Her integrated approach recognizes four interrelated spheres involved in constructing representations of gender: television production, reception, programming, and social/historical context. With respect to production, D'Acci notes that gender inequities in the television workplace have structured the sphere of production.[27] This means that because there are so few women producers, more shows are focused on men, because that is who male producers tend to make shows about. All three of the top shows in Canada are produced by men. With respect to reception, D'Acci notes that there are traditional family hierarchies that dictate who watches what and when.[28] While this may be true, especially during prime time in homes with only one TV set, I suspect that presently, younger Canadian viewers watch on different devices and more than one program may be watched in the same home at the same time.

With respect to programming, D'Acci argues: "we see that gender is represented in the unfolding of the narrative, in the genre, and in each of the techniques such as camera work (close ups and soft focus, for example); editing (romantic dissolves, for example); sound (authoritative speech or voice overs, for example); and mise en scène."[29] All three of the top shows in Canada are of the investigative genre, which is a genre that is gendered male and therefore does not typically use soft focus or romantic dissolves. Similarly, all three of the top shows feature authoritative speech from each of their male protagonists, and also some voice overs in the Canadian show. All three of the top shows also depict their male leads as very smart.

Gálvez, Tiffenberg, and Altszyler conducted a study with films to demonstrate the continued existence of the long-standing stereotype that men are smarter than women. They quantified associations between gender and high level cognitive ability in films spanning the 1967–2016 period, and found that the "brilliance = males" stereotype is present and persistent in films for the past fifty years.[30] Although their study examined Western, high-grossing films over fifty years, there is no reason to suspect the "men are smarter than women" stereotype does not also exist on television. Indeed, all of the male protagonists on the top three shows in Canada are understood to be the "smartest" characters on each of their respective shows. Gálvez, Tiffenberg, and Altszyler conclude that "gender inequality is considerably strong in the contents of films. . . . Given that stereotypes have been found to shape intellectual identity and performance, the need to proactively address the presence of the 'brilliance = males' stereotype in films is evident."[31] It is equally necessary to do so in television.

Each of the three shows I examined featured at least one strong female character who demonstrates that brilliance can also = women. *NCIS* features an eccentric white Italian-American female forensic scientist, Abby Sciuto (played by Pauley Perrette) who is part of the investigative team led by Inspector Gibbs (lead actor Mark Harmon). Forensic science is a nontypical field for women, so it is positive to see a strong, smart woman in that role on the show. Just as forensics is a nontypical role, Sciuto is also not typical; she is depicted as having an interesting, "alternative" personality. She has jet black hair, bright red lipstick, and goth-like attire; she wears dog collars, skull chokers and combat boots, and she sports a large spider web tattoo on her neck. In an interesting juxtaposition, Abby also wears her hair in pony tails, believes in God, and keeps ponies. Abby is very smart and very comfortable with complex technology; in episode eight, "Voices," her analysis of the vehicle in question is responsible for solving the case. Abby's character is a more nuanced, interesting woman scientist than is typical on TV, which gives the message that women can be different from the stereotypical norm, have varying attributes, and still be smart, capable, and interesting to listen to and watch.[32] Chris Chambers Goodman notes that one way of reducing inequality between men and women "may be by increasing the frequency of exposure to females who do not meet typical stereotypes."[33]

Popular culture representations of women can constitute truth, so Agent Sciuto's character on *NCIS* is important. She is a new representation of "woman" that is different from typical TV ideals of femininity. Film and TV position us to identify with the camera's or the protagonist's point of view and the way that film traditionally effaces itself as a medium[34] makes us think that the film is accurately depicting reality. "Unless the movie itself calls attention to itself as a medium, people simply tend not to notice all of the ways in which movies of every kind construct the reality they purport to depict through every cinematographic choice that is made, human or technological."[35] Viewers of popular culture media also bring their habitual patterns of perception and judgment to the task. Thus, we think of ourselves as legitimate knowers of reality or the truth portrayed, missing the fact that it is constructed, incomplete, and contradictory, and that we cannot possibly know it all.

Another white woman character on *NCIS* is Special Agent Jack (Jaqueline) Sloane, played by blonde Maria Bello. She is a smart, strong psychiatrist/profiler, who used to be in psychological warfare in the army. In episode nine, "Ready or Not," Sloane calls an international arms dealer a "racist, misogynistic creep." This is interesting because the writing on *NCIS* is not at a high level nor is it complex. The word "misogynistic" is not one all viewers would know, so it is positive to hear it in episode nine's script. Tellingly, however, both Sloane and Sciuto may be more respected by other characters and by viewers because they have taken on "hard" qualities: Sciuto with her goth-like clothing, and Sloane by assuming the male moniker Jack. They both still have a white male boss; they are always under the supervision of Agent Gibbs.

Bull is about its protagonist, Dr. Jason Bull, another white man. In episode 8, "The Devil, the Detail," Dr. Bull comes up against an extremely worthy adversary, and she is a woman, played by British-Indian actress Archie Panjabi. Ms. Panjabi's character, Arti Cander, is a jury consultant for the defendant pharmaceutical company in Bull's bike messenger case. She is formidable and the usually arrogant Bull is intimidated by her. Throughout the episode this strong, smart, woman of color is positively portrayed and shown to be Bull's equal. However, Bull describes her to a colleague as "that girl," when she is obviously a woman, likely with a PhD, just like Bull. We see further prime-time evidence of the need to diminish and demean successful "threatening" women when we meet the defendant pharmaceutical company's CEO. She is a white woman, which is unusual for a CEO and to be commended, but then, as is typical, her clear intellectual and leadership attributes are completely minimized when a blonde female employee of Bull's says that the CEO is "a burning hot pepper disguised as an ice cream sundae." The white male colleague she tells responds with, "wow—can't wait to meet her!" It is very unfortunate that a smart woman CEO is described in purely physical terms, and worse, that the description is provided by another female character. Woman must support each other and not focus only on appearance if they want men to do the same.

The Indian Detective is also gendered male, but its protagonist, Doug D'Mello, played by comedian/actor Russell Peters, is Indo-Canadian, or as he puts it, "brown." Doug teams up with a smart, principled, Indian female lawyer named Priya Sehgal (played by Mishqah Parthiephal) who wears both saris and western clothes. Priya is a legal aid lawyer but in the first two episodes, we do not see her in court nor in her office. Rather, she works with Doug in the field as an investigator of sorts. Priya Sehgal is a pro bono lawyer who has dedicated herself to serving the poor of the Annapuri Slum in Mumbai. She had to "choose between making money for those who already have it, or provide a defence to the defenceless,"[36] and she chose the latter. Sehgal is portrayed as a smart, noble, excellent lawyer, who truly cares about her clients. She is connected to her Indian culture and she is promised to a man in an arranged marriage. Thus, we see both independent and traditional aspects to her personality; Priya is a well-rounded character. Often women lawyers in popular culture need to choose one or the other—success as a traditional, heterosexual woman, or professional, legal success.[37] Sehgal is different. She has it "all together" and is able to be in some ways a traditional Indian woman and also an excellent, well-respected lawyer.

Closely watching episodes of the three most popular legally themed TV shows in Canada in November 2017 with a view to gender portrayals was interesting and at times disheartening. I was pleasantly surprised to find strong, smart, nuanced female characters on each show. Agent Sciuto, trial consultant Cander, and lawyer Sehgal are all good characters because they, like real people, have contrasting sides to their personalities. Sciuto on *NCIS* defies the stereotypical profile of a serious, male forensic scientist, because she is a woman with a fun personality and she believes in God. Equally, however, she does not fit the stereotypical profile of a professional woman, because she dresses in a "hard," punk or goth-like style and wears her hair in ponytails. These contrasts make Abby interesting and remind viewers that women, scientists, and professionals come in many guises and personalities. Arti Cander on *Bull* is strong, tough, and a true force to be reckoned with; she is also a woman of a color. Unfortunately, she is a guest character and not a series regular. Sehgal on *The Indian Detective* is a leading character. On the one hand, she is obedient to her parents and happy to be in an arranged marriage situation, and on the other, she is a great, smart, ethical lawyer. This is not how woman lawyers, and especially women lawyers of color, are typically portrayed in popular culture.[38]

Despite these positive portrayals, watching these three shows was also at times disheartening. *Bull* was rife with sexist comments along the politically incorrect to offensive spectrum, and *The Indian Detective*'s lead says lawyer Priya is "like a hot Mother Theresa, only not Albanian and not a nun." As in all visual media and in life, women characters are assessed and judged more on their appearance than male characters are, and these three shows are no exception. Studies show that people consider physically attractive people to be more intelligent and persuasive[39] and that being unattractive has greater negative consequences for women than for men.[40] As Peggy Li notes, the highest intellectual ability is attributed to unattractive men, while the lowest ability is attributed to unattractive women.[41] Women lawyers can be forgiven for feeling as if they cannot win. "Looking too good is taboo as it might result in men dismissing us, yet not looking good enough means we will not be hired in the first place."[42] Priya "looks good" and is a good lawyer, but she too must be helped and protected on more than one occasion by Officer D'Mello.

There is still much progress to be made in the construction, depiction, and description of female characters on television. It is especially important that progress be made since 85 percent of women lawyers surveyed in the United States perceive gender bias in the legal profession,[43] two-thirds think that their male peers do not accept them as equals,[44] and the combined effect of gender and racial stereotypes make things even harder for women lawyers of color in Canada and the United States. A Canadian study by the Criminal Lawyers' Association identifies a number of problems that contribute to the steady exodus of women from the criminal law profession, including gender bias.[45] 78 percent of the women surveyed as part of the Criminal Lawyers' Association study said that women are treated differently than men in the system.[46]

ANALYSIS: ETHNICITY

Just as the categories of women and men are socially constructed and marked, so are ethnic categories. Ethnicity includes people of color and visible minorities, as well as indigenous peoples, and other forms of ethnicity that may be less visible. Herman Gray demonstrates the influence of black producers and writers on the production of innovative representations of blackness on certain TV programs.[47] Lucas Shaw echoes how important executive producers are for television. In the 2017 US television season, 89 percent of the executive producers of new series on the four American broadcast networks were white and 79 percent were male.[48] These white men have come under attack for failing to hire more diverse casts, and Netflix has also met with criticism that it overlooks non-white audiences. "Hollywood is hardly the only industry struggling to diversify, but the dominance of white men is particularly striking in an industry with so much power to shape the minds of people all over the world."[49] The producers of *NCIS*, *Bull*, and *The Indian Detective* are all white men.

In 2004, a group of scholars did a content analysis of the 2000–2001 seasons of *NYPD Blue* and *Law & Order*, focusing on the race and gender composition of the offenders, victims, and criminal justice personnel on these popular police shows.[50] The authors opined that the realistic nature of *NYPD Blue* and *Law & Order* may shape attitudes about crime in the United States which could in turn indirectly influence public policy about crime.[51] On both shows, the number of violent crimes, especially murder, was greatly exaggerated as compared to real-life statistics from New York City at that time.[52] People of color had a statistically significant higher ratio than whites of being portrayed as offenders.[53] Robert Entman argues that the race of offenders on TV may contribute to "modern racism"[54] and Chiricos and Eschholz opine that the greater numbers of people of color cast as offenders may reinforce the perception that people of color pose a social threat to whites.[55]

So, what do we see on *NCIS*, *Bull*, and *The Indian Detective* in 2017? *NCIS* stars white actor Mark Harmon as Investigator Gibbs, the leader of an investigative team based in Washington, DC, comprised of male and female investigators. The team includes one Hispanic male, Agent Nick Torres, played by Wilmer Valderrama, who is objectified as "the cutie with the accent" in the November 14, 2017, episode. In episode 6, "Trapped," Agent

Nick Torres speaks Spanish to a Latino suspect and their conversation in the interrogation room is shown to viewers in English subtitles. Agent Torres is successful; he gets the suspect to give up a name. Then Torres pretends to be a Mexican gangster and is successful again. Torres obtains the crime boss' telephone number from the Latina woman who is doing the boss' bidding in Washington. Later, in episode 8, "Voices," we again see Latino Agent Nick Torres portrayed in a positive light. Torres had been saving for a year for a dirt bike. However, he decides to forego the bike and gives $5000 as a donation to Inclusion Town instead, a charity that built a fully accessible playground.[56] When Nick sees the playground, and the children with disabilities having a lot of fun playing there, he is visibly moved. Bradford Kelley argues that by portraying minorities well or even as heroic, as *NCIS* does with Agent Torres, film and TV producers advance the protection of those minorities.[57] In this way, popular culture can be "a vehicle for the dissemination of emancipatory ideas . . . and they travel much more easily than judicial precedents."[58]

On *Bull*, Dr. Bull has a racially diverse team comprised of women, men, Caucasians, African Americans, and Asians. His in-house counsel is male, half Puerto Rican and half white, who regrettably calls women "girls."[59] On episode seven, "No Good Deed," which aired November 7, 2017, the judge in the court scene is a biracial man (Asian and white) and in episode nine we meet one of Bull's staffers, a biracial woman whose father was a red head and whose mother was African American. The seventh episode of *Bull* includes themes related to race (and gender) because it centers around a black female school teacher, Lacey Adams, in the Bronx, New York City, accused of altering a standardized test. She changed one answer on one disadvantaged black student's test. She did so because despite his terrible home life, he is a strong student who scored one point below what he needed to go to college. Episode seven of *Bull* depicts a racially diverse cast, though most of the characters with power are white. The judge on Lacey Adams' case is biracial—Caucasian and Asian.

In the past, visible minority actors were most likely to play defendants, as, for example, on *NYPD Blue*. On *Bull* that is not the case. *Bull* is quite good at diversity in terms of skin tone. Black lawyers question white witnesses in court,[60] and one episode features a very loving young black couple and a white gangster, a nice inversion of the usual racial roles depicted on American crime TV.[61] In episode nine, the district attorney is a powerful white woman and defence counsel is a black man. Richard Gabriel wrote about *Bull* as follows: "The purpose of traditional primetime shows is to entertain the masses and sell them cars, beer, and burgers. However, as 12 to 15 million viewers watch the show every week, it is also unfair to simply dismiss it as entertainment with no consequences."[62] The consequences of *Bull* or the other shows in my study have not been measured, and viewers may interpret shows in different ways than they were intended. At minimum, however, the fact that casts are becoming more ethnically diverse is a positive step.

The Indian Detective begins in an unabashedly Canadian fashion—Doug is watching curling and drinking Canadian beer. What immediately stands out is how overtly this show acknowledges ethnic diversity. Doug describes himself to the female police officer he is interested in as "your favourite brown person." Once Doug gets to Mumbai he feels he does not fit in, even though he is Indo-Canadian. In one humorous exchange, a Mumbai police officer says, upon seeing Doug, "the Canadian idiot is back." The show is set in Toronto and Mumbai, so there are many Indian characters in the cast, including members of the dangerous crime family, the Chandekars. This family is headed by twin brothers, Gopal and Amal (both played by Hazma Haq), one operating in Toronto and one in Mumbai. Characters in *The Indian Detective* have conversations about cultural difference. For example, David Marlowe (played by William Shatner), is a white Toronto billionaire real estate developer and the richest man in Canada. He is involved with the Chandekar crime family, but reluctantly because he is visibly uncomfortable about shaking non-white hands.[63] Marlowe is labeled a racist who "never went into a non-white neighborhood without an eviction notice."

The ethnic diversity on *The Indian Detective* is important because Canada's 2016 census shows 7.7 million Canadians belong to a visible minority, representing 22.3 percent of our population. In Canada, South Asians are the largest visible minority group at 25.1 percent of the total. Another 20.5 percent of visible minorities are Chinese, while 15.6 percent are black.[64] Of the top three shows in Canada, only the Canadian show, *The Indian Detective*, had a large number of South Asians in its cast. None of the three shows had 20 percent Chinese actors, but they all did have approximately 15 percent black actors. Statistics Canada predicts that by 2036, visible minorities could comprise one-third of Canada's total population.[65] It will be interesting to see whether by 2036 one-third of television characters will also be visible minorities.

ANALYSIS: SEXUAL ORIENTATION, ABILITY, AND CLASS

Television's production, schedule, and stories all have active roles in shaping the ways viewers think and feel, including how they think and feel about themselves as gendered, racialized, and sexualized human beings. The fourth sphere in Julie D'Acci's integrative approach to studying gender representations on TV is social/historical context. She says we can see how social movements such as the women's movement and gay rights movements have introduced different representations of gender and sexuality into North American society, and these influence TV.[66] The influence of the women's rights movement is apparent in all three shows I studied in terms of the depiction of women. Agent Sciuto on *NCIS*, Archie Panjabi's guest character in *Bull*, and lawyer Sehgal in *The Indian Detective* are all reflective of modern, strong, ethnically diverse, smart women. However, influences of the gay rights movement are not as prevalent on television.

No references are made to sexual orientation in *NCIS* or *Bull* in November 2017, which suggests that all characters are presumed to be heterosexual. *The Indian Detective* is different. In episode one, Doug's retired father calls him from Mumbai, encourages Doug to come visit, and tells him, "if you're gay, it's okay." Doug happens to be heterosexual, but his father's statement demonstrates openness and progressive thinking. This makes sense in the Canadian context because in 2005 Canada legalized same-sex marriage, becoming the fourth country in the world to do so, after the Netherlands in 2000, Belgium in 2003, and Spain, also in 2005. There is a lot of pro-gay commentary in *The Indian Detective*. The executive producer of the show said, "This production was truly representative of Russell's commitment to diversity and the embracing of all cultures and orientations. I have never seen a crew and production team as reflective of those values as I have on *The Indian Detective*."[67] All the characters in all three shows I studied are heterosexual, and homosexuality is only discussed in the Canadian show. Julie D'Acci asks whether there is repressed homoeroticism on TV male police forces?[68] I did not detect it on *NCIS* nor in *The Indian Detective* and *Bull* is not a police force show. However, it is certainly possible that when a series is watched in its entirety, examples do surface. There were simply none on *NCIS* in November 2017.

Similarly, in the month of our study, disability was also hidden from view on all three shows. The only disabled characters on any of the three series were the children in the episode of *NCIS* who were depicted playing in the fully accessible playground, and they had no lines. Regarding any discernible religious diversity, none was depicted in November 2017 in *NCIS* or *Bull.* Since *The Indian Detective* is partially set in India, religious diversity between Christians and Hindus is implied, but not discussed in the show.

In terms of class, there were a few potential markers in *NCIS*, *Bull*, and *The Indian Detective. NCIS* Agent Torres is partnered with Agent Tim McGee in episode 6, "Trapped." As the Latino and white male agents work together, we find out that McGee's father purchased expensive ham radio equipment and taught ham radio to McGee when he was a boy. Torres' father brought him to cock fights. This could demonstrate either an ethno-cultural difference or a class difference; it is not clear. In the November 14, 2017 episode of *Bull*, "The Devil, the Detail," there is a class- and gender-based negative comment. One of the trial science technicians tells the bike messenger to "stop ogling over the help," which demeans fellow office workers and sounds classist. Dr. Bull, while working on the bike messenger's case, demonstrates his wealthy, upper-class status by offering the court clerk $10,000 tickets for a new Broadway musical in order to obtain the jury list. Only a very small percentage of the population can afford to spend $10,000 on two theater tickets. Later, Bull attempts to write off that bribe as an expense. In *The Indian Detective*, Doug's father's position of relative wealth is demonstrated by the fact that he has an in-home manservant in Mumbai, and as already mentioned, Marlowe is depicted as Toronto's wealthiest man and the Chandekars are a wealthy crime family. All the other characters on all three shows are middle class and none of the shows feature any poor or "lower-class" characters. There is also no real diversity with respect to age. The vast majority of all characters on all three shows fit in the thirty-five to fifty-year-old category; the age range television advertisers typically wish to attract.

CONCLUSION

My task in this chapter was to identify the top three legally themed television shows in Canada in November 2017 and analyze their depictions of gender, ethnicity, sexual orientation, ability, and class. Based on data I collected from Canada's leading provider of viewership numbers for television, I was able to determine that the most popular, prime-time, legally themed dramas in English Canada in November 2017 were *NCIS*, *Bull*, and *The Indian Detective.* Two of these shows are American and one is a Canadian mini-series. They all showcase heterosexual, able-bodied men as protagonists and two of the three of them are white. All three shows feature at least one strong female character, though not as the lead character, and in the case of *Bull*, as a guest character, not a series regular. None of the shows have LGBTQ2, disabled, or poor characters, but all of the shows have good gender and ethnic diversity in their casts. This means that millions of Canadians are watching women and people of color in, while not leading roles, important, strong, smart, roles. This indicates progress has been made in terms of gender and ethnic diversity, but the top three legally themed television programs in Canada are still not representative of the actual diversity that exists in Canada, nor do they demonstrate the equality the 1982 drafters of the *Canadian Charter of Rights and Freedoms* would have imagined for 2018.

NOTES

1. Jennifer L. Schulz, "Canada," in Peter Robson and Jennifer L. Schulz, eds., *A Transnational Study of Law and Justice on TV* (Oxford: Hart Publishing, 2016). In November 2014 there were 1,255 law-related programs broadcast per week in Canada. 72 percent of them were American and 81 percent of the shows were about police officers, not lawyers (at 59–61).

2. Ibid at 65.

3. Canadian Charter of Rights and Freedoms, Part I of the Constitution Act, 1982, being Schedule B to the Canada Act 1982 (UK), 1982, c 11.

4. *Egan v. Canada* [1995] 2 SCR 513 and *Vriend v. Alberta* [1998] 1 SCR 493.

5. The author thanks the Legal Research Institute of Manitoba for funding that enabled her to hire a research assistant, Ms. Anna Tourtchaninova, who assisted with data collection for this chapter.

6. Nielsen's HomeScan data came from an online HomeScan survey fielded between October 19, 2015, and November 8, 2015, to the heads of household from Nielsen's HomeScan Household Panel. There were 6,448 Canadian respondents aged 18 and older. Given the patriarchal nature of the term "head of household," one can expect that more men responded than women, which may of course provide skewed results.

7. Online HomeScan survey fielded between October 19, 2015, and November 8, 2015.

8. Netflix Media Center, "Ready, Set, Binge: More Than 8 Million Viewers 'Binge Race' Their Favorite Series," October 17, 2017, https://media.netflix.com/en/press-releases/ready-set-binge-more-than-8-million-viewers-binge-race-their-favorite-series.

9. Ibid.

10. Ibid. Top shows were identified as those with the largest number of Binge Racers globally. Binge Racing ranking has no relation to overall viewership.

11. John Lynch (November 9, 2017) *Business Insider*, http://www.businessinsider.com/best-netflix-original-shows-ranked-2017-11/#54-disjointed-17-1.

12. http://www.tvguide.com/streaming/gallery/best-netflix-originals-ranked.

13. *Making a Murderer* is a docuseries that tells the real story of a man who served almost twenty years in jail for a crime he did not commit, then was released, and arrested again for a different murder.

14. *13th* is a documentary on race in the criminal justice system which argues that slavery has evolved into modern day mass incarceration.

15. *Suits* stars Meghan Markle, who became engaged to Prince Harry in November 2017. Queen Elizabeth II is the titular head of Canada and Canadians are interested in the British royal family. Given the royal engagement, the resulting pop culture interest in Meghan Markle, and the fact that *Suits* is filmed in Canada, it is likely that some Canadians watched *Suits* in November 2017 to see Meghan Markle, as now that she is married to Prince Harry she will no longer act.

16. http://www.nielsen.com/ca/en/insights/news/2016/content-and-convenience-power-canadians-increased-use-of-subscription-video-on-demand-services.html.

17. Ibid, online HomeScan survey fielded between October 19, 2015, and November 8, 2015.

18. John Doyle, "Canadian TV, as We Know It, Is Screwed. For Now" (November 23, 2015) *The Globe and Mail*, https://www.theglobeandmail.com/arts/television/john-doyle-canadian-tv-as-we-know-it-is-screwed-for-now/article27440984.

19. A jury consultant is a person who advises lawyers as to the types of people who would make the most strategically useful jurors. They are typically experts in human behavior and are hired as consultants in criminal and civil trials.

20. Canadians are also consistently watching one Canadian justice-themed show, even though it did not make the top ten in November 2017, and that is *Murdoch Mysteries*, a CBC production. This prime-time drama is in its eleventh season, over 150 episodes have been broadcast, and it is seen in 120 countries around the world. John Doyle notes that *Murdoch Mysteries* is "a big, successful show, except in the US market." John Doyle, "Murdoch Mysteries puzzles American Critics" (January 8, 2016, updated March 25, 2017) *The Globe & Mail,* https://www.theglobeandmail.com/arts/television/john-doyle-murdoch-mysteries-puzzles-american-critics/article28078232). *Murdoch Mysteries* is set in Toronto during the Victorian Era and is based on Maureen Jennings' books. The show features Detective William Murdoch, played by Yannick Bisson, who uses cutting-edge forensic techniques, for that time period, to solve crimes. The coroner, a woman, unusual for that time, struggles for recognition on the show. The week of November 6–12, 2017, *Murdoch Mysteries* was ranked 23rd and in the week of November 13–19, 2017, it ranked 20th (http://en.numeris.ca/media-and-events/tv-weekly-top-30).

21. According to Numeris, in the week of November 6–12, 2017, *Law & Order: SVU* was ranked 19 and in the week of November 27–December 3, 2017, it was ranked #11.

22. K. Dowler, T. Fleming and S. L. Muzzatti, "Constructing Crime: Media, Crime, and Popular Culture" (October 2006) *Canadian Journal of Criminology and Criminal Justice* 837 at 842.

23. Richard Gabriel, "Trial Consultants, TV Law, and a Load of Bull" (Winter 2016), 28 *The Jury Expert: The Art and Science of Litigation Advocacy* 1–3.

24. http://en.numeris.ca/media-and-events/tv-weekly-top-30.

25. Julie D'Acci, "Television, Representation and Gender," in Robert C. Allen and Annette Hill, eds., *The Television Studies Reader* (London: Routledge, 2004), 373–88 at 375.

26. Ibid. at 380.

27. Ibid. at 382.

28. Ibid. at 383.

29. Ibid. at 384.

30. Ramiro H. Gálvez, Valeria Tiffenberg, and Edgar Altszyler, "Half a Century of Stereotyping Associations between Gender and Intellectual Ability in Films" (January 26, 2018) 1 at 6, https://ssrn.com/abstract=3110865 or http://dx.doi.org/10.2139/ssrn.3110865.

31. Ibid. at 8.

32. For a different read of Agent Sciuto, see the Greece chapter in this volume.

33. Chris Chambers Goodman, "Nevertheless She Persisted: From Mrs. Bradwell to Annalise Keating, Gender Bias in the Courtroom" (2017) 24 *William and Mary Journal of Women and the Law* 167 at 194.

34. Neal Feigenson, "The Visual in Law: Some Problems for Legal Theory" (2011) *Law, Culture and the Humanities* 1 at 6, http://ssrn.com/abstract=2145585

35. Ibid.

36. "The Indian Detective," Episode 2.

37. C. A. Corcos, "'We Don't Want Advantages' – The Woman Lawyer Hero and Her Quest for Power in Popular Culture," *Syracuse Law Review* 53 (2003): 1225, 1228; Laura Grosshans, "Accurate or Appalling: Representations of Women Lawyers in Popular Culture," *Cardozo Pub L Pol'y & Ethics J* 4 (2006): 457, 473; and Jennifer L. Schulz and JiHyun Youn, "Monsters and Madwomen? Neurosis, Ambition and Mothering in Women Lawyers in Film" (2016), *Law, Culture and the Humanities*, 1–21.

38. As contrast, see the black woman lawyer and law professor, Annalise Keating (played by Viola Davis) in *How to Get Away with Murder*, ABC, USA, http://abc.go.com/shows/how-to-get-away-with-murder.

39. Kathleen A. Bergin, "Sexualized Advocacy: The Ascendant Backlash Against Female Lawyers," *Yale Journal of Law and Feminism* 18 (2006), 191 at 212, citing several studies in notes 128–31.

40. Chris Chambers Goodman, "Nevertheless She Persisted: From Mrs. Bradwell to Annalise Keating, Gender Bias in the Courtroom," *William and Mary Journal of Women and the Law* 24 (2017), 167 at 186.

41. Peggy Li, "Physical Attractiveness and Femininity: Helpful or Hurtful for Female Attorneys," *Akron Law Review* 47 (2015), 997 at 1002.

42. Jennifer L. Schulz, "*girls club* Does Not Exist," in M. Asimow, ed., *Lawyers in Your Living Room! Law on Television* (Chicago: ABA Press, 2009) at 249–50.

43. Chris Chambers Goodman, "Nevertheless She Persisted: From Mrs. Bradwell to Annalise Keating, Gender Bias in the Courtroom," *William and Mary Journal of Women and the Law* 24 (2017): 167 at 169.

44. From the "Lectric Law Library's Stacks: What Lawyers need to Know About Gender Bias in the Legal Profession," Letric Law Library, http://www.lectlaw.com/files/att06.htm [http://perma.cc/T9SP-4HUV].

45. Natasha S. Madon (Toronto, 2016) Criminal Lawyers' Association, "The Retention of Women in the Private Practice of Criminal Law: Research Report" http://www.criminallawyers.ca/wp-content/uploads/2016/03/CLA-Womens-Study-March-2016.pdf.

46. Breese Davies, "Shining a light on gender bias," June 2, 2016, https://www.thelawyersdaily.ca/articles/2082/shining-a-light-on-gender-bias.

47. Herman Gray, *Watching Race: Television and the Struggle for "Blackness"* (Minneapolis: University of Minnesota Press, 1995).

48. Lucas Shaw, "Oh diversity, where art thou in fall's lineup?" August 26, 2017, *Winnipeg Free Press*, E8.

49. Ibid.

50. S. Eschholz, M. Mallard, and S. Flynn, "Images of Prime Time Justice: A Content Analysis of *NYPD Blue* and *Law & Order*," *Journal of Criminal Justice and Popular Culture* 10 (2004): 161.

51. Ibid. at 162.

52. Ibid. at 171.

53. Ibid. at 168.

54. Robert Entman, "Blacks in the News: Television, Modern Racism and Cultural Change," *Journalism Quarterly* 69(2) (1992): 341–61.

55. T. Chiricos and S. Eschholz, "The Racial Typification of Crime and the Criminal Typification of Race: The Social Construction of Social Threat by Local TV News," *Journal of Research in Crime and Delinquency* 39 (2002): 400–20.

56. Similar positive role modelling occurs in *Bull*, Episode 9, "Thanksgiving." Dr. Bull's black male employee's daughter gets into New York University.

57. Bradford J. Kelley, "The Rainbow Sea Change: The Impact of Popular Culture on Homosexual Rights," *Scholar* 19 (2013–2014): 283.

58. Pedro Rubim Borges Fortes, "Lights, Camera, Affirmative Action: Does Hollywood Protect Minorities?" *Journal of the Oxford Centre for Socio-Legal Studies* (2017), at https://joxcsls.com

59. *Bull*, Episode 9, "Thanksgiving."

60. *Bull*, Episode 8, "The Devil, The Detail."

61. *Bull*, Episode 9, "Thanksgiving."

62. Richard Gabriel, "Trial Consultants, TV Law, and a Load of Bull," *The Jury Expert: The Art and Science of Litigation Advocacy* 28 (Winter 2016): 1–3.

63. *The Indian Detective*, Episode 1.

64. Stats Canada 2016 Long Form Census.

65. Ibid.

66. Julie D'Acci, "Television, Representation and Gender," in Robert C. Allen and Annette Hill, eds., *The Television Studies Reader* (London: Routledge, 2004), 373–88 at 385.

67. Clayton Peters, Executive Producer, CPI Pictures, http://www.bellmedia.ca/pr/press/after-shooting-in-south-africa-and-india-ctvs-new-dramedy-the-indian-detective-starring-russell-peters-wraps-production-in-toronto.

68. Julie D'Acci, "Television, Representation and Gender," in Robert C. Allen and Annette Hill, eds., *The Television Studies Reader* (London: Routledge, 2004), 373–88 at 380.

Chapter 5

Germany

Diversity on Its Way

Franziska Stürmer

BACKGROUND

The chapter focusing on Germany in the book *A Transnational Study of Law and Justice on TV* (2016) provided basic information about the development of television services both in West and East Germany and in the Berlin Republic since 1989. The authors Machura and Böhnke also analyzed the legal system as communicated to the viewer and presented an overview on their data, sorted by percentage, content, genre and country of origin. They highlighted occasional shows to mine the legal message. They also included a brief overview on diversity issues, which will now be the main focus of this essay on televised law in Germany.

DIVERSITY IN GERMANY

In 2015, Germany was rated as the country with the second-highest immigration rate worldwide, following the United States.[1] Therefore, ethnic diversity today is quite an issue in public discussions. Racism, intolerance, xenophobia, and right-wing nationalist politics are major topics in Germany, especially at the time of this study. Elections held shortly before (September 2017) showed a significant increase in votes given to the right-wing party AfD,[2] who in its election campaign drew mainly on fears and worries related to the current European Refugee Crisis. Postwar immigration into Germany started in the 1950s, contributing to the so-called economic miracle ("Wirtschaftswunder") in West Germany. Between 1955 and 1973, about 14 million guest workers from Italy, Turkey, and other Southern and Eastern

European Countries arrived and about 3 million stayed in Germany and settled with their families.[3] German law and politics did not recognize this fact—Germany as an immigration country—for a long time; even today, dual citizenship frequently comes under attack and surveys show that acceptance of immigrants is relatively low.[4] Consequently, this demographic fact—Germany as a country with an ethnically diverse society—has not yet arrived in German media, as will be seen from my analysis of *Tatort*, the only German series included in this chapter. The US series, by contrast, seem to be far more sensitive toward this issue and strive to portray an ethnically diverse population in their series.

Gender equality as a constitutional right is part of the German constitution (Grundgesetz, GG) since its revision after World War II, in 1948–1949.[5] It states that "men and women are equal."[6] However, the practical implementation of constitutional equality took a long time and is still a work in progress. Although women were allowed to vote in 1918 (making Germany the fourth European country with female suffrage),[7] they needed their husbands' permission to go to work until 1958.[8] The working conditions of men and women are still under a lot of criticism—in many cases, women get lower wages and are less represented in leading positions than men. Moreover, it is still mostly a female task to balance family and working life—although men have equal rights with regard to parental leave, and so on, in reality, it is mostly mothers who stay at home and thus have to struggle to maintain their careers despite having children.[9] In the media, recent depictions of men and women appear to be quite sensitive toward gender issues. Stereotypes of what is "male" and "female" often are no longer implemented, but caricatured and played with, as can be seen in *Tatort.* Fictional portrayals also frequently address the problems of mothers who want to combine family life and successful careers.

Homosexual marriages have only been legal in Germany since October 2017. Before that, homosexual couples could register "eingetragene Lebenspartnerschaft" (a civil union), which comprised fewer rights than marriage. There has been quite a political controversy about this step. A definite majority in the Bundestag (German Parliament) supported it, while the conservative Christian party CDU/CSU almost completely voted against it[10]—and right-wing AfD announced it was planning to make a complaint of unconstitutionality. In the media, homosexual life does not play a big part; if so, it is largely in comedy (as is ethnic diversity, by the way—culture clash still is a major stock-in-trade for German comedians from migration backgrounds).[11] Gays are likewise underrepresented in the American series most watched in Germany during the time of our study, so there seems to be a blind spot in popular representations.

LAW ON TV

The objective of this study is to highlight diversity issues in the three law-related TV programs, which are most watched in Germany. Research on this was hampered by the unwillingness of all the big streaming portals to reveal their data, so that it was not possible to determine the most popular series by first-hand information. Amazon Prime, Maxdome, Netflix, and Sky all refused my requests; only public TV, represented by the ARD-Media Group, readily shared its data as soon as it was available for November 2017, our month of research. Therefore, the basis for determining the three most watched law-related series in Germany in November 2017 has to rely on second-hand deductions from existing studies, surveys, and estimations such as those made by quotenmeter.de.[12] However, statistics on media usage in Germany show that less than one quarter of the population (23 percent) regularly (i.e., at least once a week) use video streaming as a means of watching their favorite programme, so perhaps we can still do without precise numbers.[13] To a far greater extent (31 percent), people use YouTube, another 10 percent watch online TV, and 14 percent use the material offered online or on streamed services. In terms of streaming services, the public channels ARD and ZDF are by far the most popular.[14] Those 24 percent are part of the data provided by ARD and ZDF. According to their data,[15] crime series and films filled about 15 percent of the average viewing time during November 2017 (thirteen hours, thirty-eight minutes of eighty-eight hours in total). Das Erste, ZDF, and ZDF Neo account for about 60 percent of the crime shows actually watched. The most popular shows on these channels are *Tatort* and *Polizeiruf 110*. Commercial channels mainly rely on licensed US series, the most popular being the various *CSI* formats, *NCIS*, *Hawaii Five-0*, *Bones*, *Criminal Minds*, *Bad Cop*, and *Crossing Jordan*.

Likewise, surveys and statistics[16] show that the American show *NCIS* is the most popular crime series in Germany, at 12 percent. Tied for second place is the notorious German *Tatort* series (11 percent), and the USA's *Criminal Minds* (11 percent), followed by *Akte X—Die unheimlichen Fälle des FBI* at 10 percent. Another German production *Alarm für Cobra 11* managed to reach 9 percent. Unfortunately, this data is from 2016; it was conducted among more than 1,000 participants aged fourteen to forty-nine who watched television at least once a month online or on TV in July 2016. As far as audience ratings are concerned, *Tatort* takes the lead for 2016, reaching an average of 8.3 million viewers. This does not include those viewers who made use of streaming services or watched *Tatort* online on Channel 1, which is also highly popular with *Tatort* fans.[17]

Research conducted by Splendid Research in September 2017[18] showed a slightly different outcome, which might be due both to the different time of the survey and to the inclusion of participants up to the age of sixty-nine (instead of forty-nine). They, too, conducted their survey among a representational group of more than 1,000 participants (n=1.031). According to their data, both *NCIS* (9.3 percent) and *Criminal Minds* (8.3 percent female only/5.8 percent mixed) still are among the most popular law-related TV shows in Germany. Around 30 percent of all participants claimed to have seen all episodes of these series (*NCIS* 30.7 percent, *Criminal Minds* 28.3 percent), therefore proving themselves to be regular watchers. As Splendid Research's survey focused more heavily on streamed series, *Tatort* does not appear, nor do any other German productions, although their findings prove free TV is still the most commonly watched media (68.7 percent), while streaming is used by 20–30 percent (Amazon Video 26.7 percent, Netflix 21.4 percent, Sky 14.5 percent, and Maxdome 6.3 percent).

Comparing the older statistics and the data provided by *Das Erste* for November, one may safely deduce that although with younger watchers streaming is increasingly popular, free TV still plays the major part in broadcasting in Germany. The two most popular international crime series are *NCIS* and *Criminal Minds*, while *Tatort* is still the most popular German crime series.

TATORT

NCIS is discussed in three other chapters[19] in this book and *Criminal Minds* is discussed in chapter 6 so I will mainly focus on the *Tatort* episodes broadcast in November 2017. Moreover, as the only non-US production, comparisons between this series and the other two might shed interesting light on parallels and differences. *Tatort* is the longest-running and most popular German crime series, having broadcast more than 1,000 episodes since 1970. Strictly speaking, there is no *Tatort* series in its own right, rather, there are many. A main characteristic of the series is that it plays in several different areas, all over Germany. The regional *Tatorts* thus form series within the series, bound together by a permanent setting and investigation team (although, of course, there are changes throughout the years). Each of these individual "*Tatort*-intra-series" is characterized by a relatively high dose of local color, both adding to the attraction for viewers related to the particular city or area, and adding to the representational claims of *Tatort* as specific depictions of German life and society. Due to these claims (and its high and enduring popularity in German popular culture), *Tatort* has repeatedly been the focus of attention for various and recent studies on televised law and crime.

However, it is mostly scrutinized in terms of its general representation of German society or of its role and function as a cultural archive.[20] There are, as far as I know, no studies particularly focusing on diversity issues in *Tatort,* apart from the contribution of Kathrin Ruhl to Marion Gymnich's et al. edited volume *Gendered (re)visions*, which addresses gender within the series.[21]

During November 2017, four *Tatort* episodes were broadcast, each playing in a different city: Hannover, Dresden, Münster, and Hamburg. In every city, different agents are at work. With regard to gender, both are evenly distributed throughout the month—the first episode, *Der Fall Holdt*,[22] starring female agent Lindholm; the second, *Auge um Auge*,[23] starring two females, agents Sieland and Gorniak, and one male, Schnabel; the third episode, *Gott ist auch nur ein Mensch*,[24] starring two male agents, Thiel and Boerne; and the last episode of November, *Böser Boden*,[25] again starring one male and one female agent—Falke and Grosz.

Those episodes containing both male and female agents will be of special interest here, as questions of gender are frequently played out within the episodes. For instance, in the Dresden episode *Auge um Auge*, both female agents are rather young, in their thirties, attractive, and torn between their complicated private lives and their highly professional and efficient work as commissioners. By contrast, their director Schnabel is about twenty years older, described as "old school"—"living in a world where men open doors for women and women prepare coffee for men."[26] In the Hamburg episode *Böser Boden*, both characters are roughly the same age but have contrasting life styles and attitudes: male Commissioner Falke is a passionate street cop, while female Grosz is a thorough federal agent. In the male-only episode *Gott ist auch nur ein Mensch*, both male characters have female assistants. Commissioner Thiel is assisted by young Nadeshda Krusenstern, a coroner and male Prof. Boerne is accompanied by a growth-restricted female assistant he calls Alberich.[27] Female agent Charlotte Lindholm from the first episode is the only agent without a partner or an assistant. Instead, she frequently mocks men who tend to underestimate her.[28]

The first November episode *Der Fall Holdt* was seen by 10.22 million viewers and reached a market share of 28.1 percent.[29] Its overall topic was sexual violence against women. Accordingly, issues of ethnicity, age, or class are not addressed in this episode; all protagonists are, roughly speaking, white, middle-aged, well-to-do upper middle-class citizens. The main plot of the episode—a case of kidnapping—is mirrored and influenced by events in the private life of agent Lindholm and thus depicts intricately the vicious cycle of violence both of men against women and, ultimately, of people against one another. The criminal case of the episode remains unsolved, thus further indicating that there is no simple, black-and-white solution to the issues addressed.

The episode starts out with agent Lindholm partying with her new boyfriend. When Lindholm steps out in the parking lot to quickly relieve herself hidden between two cars, she is discovered by three men who film and mock her. She confronts them and demands the video. However, the men overpower her, throw her to the ground, and kick her repeatedly. Lindholm reports sick and stays in her flat after this event. In the meantime, the criminal case of the episode develops. The wife of a successful banker is kidnapped. Like Lindholm, she tries to stand up to her aggressors but they too overpower her and severely beat her up. Her husband Frank Holdt gets a ransom demand of €300,000 and asks his parents-in-law to help him raise the money. His father-in-law informs the police, against Holdt's explicit request not to do so, and Lindholm, although still on sick leave, is put on the case by her male superior. As investigations continue, Holdt becomes a prime suspect himself: evidence of domestic violence and of his wife having an affair mount against him. Lindholm, shaken by her own experience of male aggression, is severely biased against him and puts him under more and more pressure to confess. Finally, Holdt's wife Julia is found dead; she ultimately died of the wounds she received when her kidnappers beat her up. Shocked and shaken, Frank Holdt hangs himself in his prison cell, and Lindholm, who feels responsible for this tragic outcome, is taken off the case, which remains unsolved.

This plot sheds light on the problematic issue of male aggression (bodily and via the exertion of power and hierarchy). As the plot evolves and suspicions about the husband being the kidnapper are first introduced and then thwarted, the plot demonstrates the dramatic results a reductive view—always seeing the male as aggressor and the female as victim—may have. On the other hand, as Claudia Schwartz in the *Neue Zürcher Zeitung* points out,[30] this episode of *Tatort* indirectly draws attention to the social climate, which enables careless aggression between sexes in the first place: Lindholm's party outfit, high heels and a sexy cocktail dress, shows her both more (stereotypically) female and more vulnerable than her usual, professional clothes. Moreover, she feels ashamed of the attack, a typical reaction for female victims of male aggression (which Schwartz links to the current #MeToo debate). Finally, Lindholm's superior exerts a legitimate but nevertheless carelessly cruel form of aggression against females when he arbitrarily puts Lindholm on the case despite her sick leave and then withdraws her again. When doing so, he casually states she looks like "ein gerupftes Huhn," comparing her to "a plucked hen" and thus further debasing her.[31] Lindholm's inability to keep a professional distance between her private traumatic experience and the facts of the case show how devastating aggressive behavior between sexes is for both sides; Lindholm's bias against Holdt was of course induced by her own victimization, but ultimately turns her into another aggressor causing the death of her "victim."

The next episode *Auge um Auge* takes place in Dresden and is the fourth case of female agents Henni Sieland, Karin Gorniak and their male superior Peter Schnabel. It was seen by 9.32 million viewers and reached a market share of 25.7 percent.[32] Again, all protagonists are white; relations between the agents with regard to gender have been sketched above. One critical issue loosely addressed in this episode may be said to be disability and the role of public and private responsibility. The agents have to solve a murder committed in a fictional insurance company, ALVA, which, as it turns out, puts its employees under massive pressure to reduce insurance payments. Among the suspects in this case are therefore dissatisfied employees as well as aggrieved clients who feel destroyed by the ruthless insurance company. One of them is Harald Böhlert, who is in a wheelchair after an accident at work but never received compensation from ALVA, despite long years of legal proceedings against the company. He tries to raise public awareness about ALVA's mismanagement and profit-only policy by chaining himself in front of the company holding a banner saying: "100 percent employable, says ALVA." He gets support from lawyer Martina Scheuring who is, as it turns out, a former ALVA-employee still bearing a grudge. She committed the murder that is being investigated in the episode. At the last minute, the agents are able to stop her from her planned, high-publicity suicide in the ALVA building. This episode touches on disability and is also about racism. Disability is not a major topic in this classical "Whodunit," but the episode does raise questions about the social and political status and support systems for those who are affected by disabilities during the course of their lives. The episode treats Böhlert's disability with lightness but not frivolity. Critics did not receive this well; Christian Buß in *Spiegel online* calls it a "gesellschaftspolitische[s] Thesenstück,"[33] which means sociopolitical thesis play, and laments its lack of humor. There is more about racism in the episode. In the private side plots of the agents, they are concerned with refugees, whom the older and more conservative director Schnabel eyes with great suspicion—if not racism—while agent Sieland gives shelter to a woman from Syria. By demonstrating contrasting positions on refugees, this *Tatort* episode seeks to mirror everyday German life and its ongoing conflict about how to publicly and politically handle the "Flüchtlingsfrage," the issue of refugees coming into the country and the consequences for society. Significantly, refugees (and therefore, different ethnicities) only appear as objects of discussion, rather than acting subjects in their own right.

This is modified to some degree in the last *Tatort* of November, *Böser Boden*. This episode starred male agent Falke and female agent Grosz. It was seen by 7.99 million viewers and reached a market share of 21.8 percent.[34] By numbers, it was therefore the least successful November 2017 episode of *Tatort*. The criminal case in this episode is the murder of Arash Naderi, an engineer who migrated to Germany from Iran only a few months earlier. Evidence soon suggests this murder to be politically motivated; a racist background is suspected. Falke's and Grosz's investigation reveals it was indeed a political murder, but not primarily due to Naderi's origin, but rather his job. Naderi worked as a truck driver for a huge natural gas company and had to transport highly toxic substances through a village of organic farmers. This introduces the second major topic of the episode: fracking and its consequences for the environment and people living nearby. Indeed, the inhabitants of the local village all appear sickish, pale, with matted hair and rashes. They show extremely aggressive behavior against the fracking industry and migrants working in their community. As Agent Falke puts it, they are "Öko-Nazis" or Eco-Nazis.[35] This turns this *Tatort* episode into a mixture of ecological concerns, criticisms of a multinational industry, and nationalistic, protective, and right-wing ideology. These are in no way necessarily associated, so no clear position on any topic can be determined, and the viewer is left puzzling about what to make of this and its social consequences. As far as issues of diversity are concerned, at least Naderi, the Iranian migrant, plays a major part in this episode, even though, admittedly, he plays it as a corpse and therefore indirectly. Still, racism versus ethnic diversity is more central an issue in this episode than in the marginal squabbles between Schnabel and Sieland in the *Auge um Auge* episode.

The third *Tatort* episode broadcast during November 2017, the one before *Böser Boden*, is set in Münster, stars male agent Thiel and male coroner Boerne, and is called *Gott ist auch nur ein Mensch*. It was seen by 12.89 million viewers and reached a market share of 34 percent.[36] By numbers, it was therefore the most successful *Tatort* during November 2017. In this episode, the latest sculpture of the internationally renowned performance artist G.O.D., set directly in front of the town hall, turns out to be the corpse of a local politician dressed up as a clown. Agent Thiel and his female colleague Nadeshda Krusenstern find out that the dead man was only recently acquitted of the charge of statutory rape. However, coroner Boerne and his female assistant Silke Haller find a flash drive containing evidence of his guilt hidden inside the corpse. Soon afterward, another dead body modeled into a sculpture turns up, and all artists currently staying in Münster for the international sculpture festival are under suspicion. Thiel and Boerne delve into the satirically caricatured art scene. While Thiel remains prejudiced and reluctant, arrogant and high-brow coroner Prof. Boerne feels attracted to the posh and exaggerated world of the artists. Therefore, the diversity issue addressed in this episode is class and social status. Rather than openly examining class, it is mocked and depicted humorously by contrasting agent Thiel and Prof. Boerne. The humorous contrast between the two is the trademark of the Münster *Tatort* episodes and responsible for their high popularity with viewers.

The popularity of *Tatort* with viewers depends on the city and the agents carrying out their investigations. Popularity with critics, however, is less influenced by individual characters and their trademarks. Instead, the press frequently discusses the credibility of the plots, the coherency of genre (for instance, *Böser Boden* alludes to Zombie-movies, while *Gott ist auch nur ein Mensch* parodies "serial killer-as-artist" formats like *Dexter*) and the way in which socially relevant issues are treated. With regard to diversity in *Tatort*, the series clearly tries its best: male and female protagonists were evenly distributed during November and numerous other issues like race/ethnicity, racism and xenophobia, social differences and disability as a public responsibility were addressed.[37] There remain, however, various blind spots. For instance, all agents were white, roughly middle-aged (apart from the older Schnabel) and had an (upper) middle-class background (apart from street cop Falke and upper-class Prof. Boerne). Discussions, especially of race and gender, too often appear stereotypical and constrained, for example, as mentioned, the squabbles between Schnabel and Sieland.[38] Characters with a nonnative German ethnic backgrounds or nationality appear mostly as objects of discussion or as corpses not as subjects in their own right. Therefore, especially since *Tatort* raises a claim both to social relevance and to insights into German everyday life,[39] despite good intentions and efforts made, there still is a long way to go in terms of sensitivity toward issues of diversity in *Tatort*.

CRIMINAL MINDS AND *NCIS*

Criminal Minds is an American series focusing not so much on investigations but, as the title indicates, on the criminal mind itself. The series is broadcast on commercial Channel Sat.1; however, all seasons are available online, so it is not as easy as with *Tatort* to determine which episodes were actually watched in November 2017. Generally speaking, the protagonists of the series show quite a high degree of diversity, featuring female as well as male professionals, including different ethnic backgrounds and various ages as well (from twenty-something to sixty-something). They are, however, all highly specialized and very intelligent, have high-level educations and were, presumably, not of the lower working class. Like in *Tatort*, there is always a murder at the center of the episode, and equally like in *Tatort*, the setting of the crime changes from episode to episode. The protagonists, however, stay the same and, as they are a team of specialists, they visit the various crime scenes in order to support the local police and investigation forces. Usually, the crime is solved at the end of each episode and the criminal is either dead or arrested. This criminal plot is, like in *Tatort*, complemented by details from the protagonists' private lives, mostly centering on love affairs and intimate relationships. This is, indeed, an area where the otherwise quite diverse series gives away potential: virtually all relationships depicted are heterosexual. Just like *Tatort*, there is no sexual diversity apparent throughout the series.[40]

Like *Criminal Minds*, *NCIS* is broadcast online as well as on commercial Channel Sat.1. Older episodes are repeated on Kabel 1 and still receive quite high audience ratings.[41] More like *Tatort*, actual investigations and chasing criminals play a major part in this series. Unlike *Tatort* and *Criminal Minds*, the episodes of *NCIS* are not necessarily closed; there are some criminals who are pursued throughout an entire season or who even reappear in later seasons. Furthermore, crimes other than murder are investigated by the *NCIS* team. Similar to *Criminal Minds*, setting changes from episode to episode, but the investigation team stays the same. Like *Criminal Minds*, *NCIS* appears fairly sensitive to diversity regarding gender, age, and race; less so, like all series investigated here, with regard to sexual orientation and class.

CONCLUSION

To sum up, it would appear that US productions are more sensitive toward diversity issues such as gender, age, and race than German productions. *Tatort* clearly endeavors to evenly distribute male and female investigators and strives to address some diversity issues, such as migration, ethnicity, disability, discrimination, racism, and social injustice. However, on *Tatort*, it is noticeable that these issues are discussed, but not reflected in the cast. It may be surmised that in the United States, diversity of class and race is positioned more centrally in the viewer's awareness and therefore, production companies pay more attention to those issues when selecting the casts of their series. All three of the most watched legally themed series in Germany during November 2017 could do with more diversity with regard to, for instance, sexual orientation, religion (which does not play any part at all, as far as I could see), and disability (including disabled protagonists, for instance). Fortunately, there is no discernible discrimination/stereotyping with regard to roles within the three series: no pattern evolves as to race, class, age, gender, etc., of either victims or perpetrators (at least during the month analyzed here). It seems we may have done away with—put polemically—white males in power and lower-class, immigrant criminals. Still, there remains some way to go both for US productions as viewed in Germany and, especially, for the notorious German *Tatort*. Being one of the most popular and well-known German crime series, *Tatort* should embrace this opportunity to take the lead in representations of diversity and strive to depict today's diverse German society more accurately and sensitively.

NOTES

1. International Migration Report 2015—Highlights; http://www.un.org/en/development/desa/population/migration/publications/migrationreport/docs/MigrationReport2015_Highlights.pdf (April 25, 2018).

2. Alternative für Deutschland/alternative for Germany.

3. http://www.bpb.de/gesellschaft/migration/laenderprofile/256269/historische-entwicklung (April 25, 2018).

4. ALLBUS 1996 (ZA2800), 2006 (ZA4500), 2016 (ZA5250); cf. http://www.bpb.de/gesellschaft/migration/laenderprofile/256269/historische-entwicklung (April 25, 2018).

5. http://www.bundestagswahl-bw.de/frauenwahlrecht.html (April 24, 2018).

6. "Männer und Frauen sind gleichberechtigt." Art. 3 Abs. 2 GG.

7. http://www.bundestagswahl-bw.de/frauenwahlrecht.html (April 24, 2018). Together with Austria, Poland, and Russia.

8. http://www.bpb.de/apuz/31161/50-jahre-geschlechtergerechtigkeit-und-arbeitsmarkt?p=all (April 24, 2018).

9. http://www.bpb.de/apuz/31161/50-jahre-geschlechtergerechtigkeit-und-arbeitsmarkt?p=all (April 25, 2018).

10. http://www.zeit.de/politik/2017-06/bundestag-stimmt-fuer-ehe-fuer-alle (April 20, 2018).

11. Only to name a few famous representatives: Kaya Yanar, Bülent Ceylan, Serdar Somuncu (although Somuncu mostly does political satire and less culture clash); in writing, Osman Engin was one of the pioneers, Hatice Akyün writes comic columns and novels on the topic.

12. quotenmeter.de is an online TV magazine covering German television programmes and providing news, statistics and information on market shares etc.

13. ARD-ZDF-Onlinestudie 2017; http://www.ard-zdf-onlinestudie.de/ardzdf-onlinestudie-2017/onlinevideo (December 12, 2017).

14. Ebd.

15. Including the 19 most popular channels which make up for 76.4 percent of TV usage during November. All numbers given in the following passage are provided by courtesy of Christine Gandré, press department of Das Erste.

16. https://de.statista.com/statistik/daten/studie/581038/umfrage/ranking-der-beliebtesten-fernsehserien-in-deutschland (December 12, 2017).

17. http://www.quotenmeter.de/n/96857/quotencheck-tatort-bei-one (December 12, 2017).

18. https://www.splendid-research.com/studie-serien.html (December 12, 2017).

19. See the chapters on Britain, Canada, and Greece.

20. See, for instance, Brück, Ingrid: *Der deutsche Fernsehkrimi. Eine Programm- und Produktionsgeschichte von den Anfängen bis heute*. Stuttgart 2003; Buhl, Hendrik: *Tatort. Gesellschaftspolitische Themen in der Krimireihe*. Konstanz 2013; Gräf, Dennis: *Tatort. Ein populäres Medium als kultureller Speicher*. Marburg 2010; Hißnauer, Christian/Scherer, Stefan/Stockinger, Claudia (eds.): *Föderalismus in Serie. Die Einheit der ARD-Reihe Tatort im historischen Verlauf*. Paderborn 2014;

Karczmarzyk, Nicole: *Der Fall Tatort: die Entschlüsselung eines Kultkrimis*. Marburg 2010; Otte, Björn: *Das Milieu im Fernsehkrimi. Am Beispiel der Krimi-Reihe "Tatort."* Marburg 2013.

21. Ruhl, Katrin: "The Changing Construction of Women in Crime Series: The Case of *Tatort*," in: Gymnich, Marion/Ruhl, Kathrin/Scheunemann, Klaus: *Gendered (re)visions: constructions of gender in audiovisual media.* Göttingen 2010, S. 137–58.

22. The case Holdt.

23. An eye for an eye.

24. God is only human.

25. Evil ground.

26. Cf. The character descriptions on http://www.daserste.de/unterhaltung/krimi/tatort/kommissare/team-dresden-sieland-gorniak-schnabel100.html (February 14, 2018). Author's translation.

27. Cf. http://www.daserste.de/unterhaltung/krimi/tatort/kommissare/team-muenster-thiel-boerne-100.html (February 14, 2018).

28. Cf. http://www.daserste.de/unterhaltung/krimi/tatort/kommissare/ermittlerin-hannover-lindholm-100.html (February 14, 2018).

29. http://www.quotenmeter.de/n/96901 (February 28, 2018).

30. https://www.nzz.ch/feuilleton/neuer-tatort-untermalt-die-metoo-debatte-ld.1326232 (February 27, 2018).

31. My translation; the German original, "wie ein gerupftes Huhn," is even more significant as it compares her to a hen or chicken, further debasing her.

32. http://www.quotenmeter.de/n/97054 (February 28, 2018).

33. http://www.spiegel.de/kultur/tv/tatort-aus-dresden-auge-um-auge-von-stromberg-schoepfer-ralf-husmann-a-1176209.html (February 27, 2018).

34. http://www.quotenmeter.de/n/97363 (February 28, 2018).

35. "öko" used in this way in German has a pejorative connotation, meaning a fanatic environmentalist or even a sort of eco-terrorist.

36. http://www.quotenmeter.de/n/97212 (February 28, 2018).

37. See Ortner, Christina: "Tatort: Migration. Das Thema Einwanderung in der Krimireihe *Tatort*," in Hans-Bredow-Institut (ed.): *Medien & Kommunikationswissenschaft* 1 (2007), Baden-Baden 2007.

38. This appears to be a particular problem of the Schnabel, Sieland and Gorniak-*Tatorte*, as the review of Christian Buß in *Spiegel online* suggests: in another episode from September, sociocritical light is meant to be shed on homelessness and, again, the situation of refugees, but it results, according to Buß, in a bad case of *Pennerklamauk* ("hobo slapstick"), where "*gleich drei Klischee gewordene Obdachlose durch die Stadt*" "*lümmeln und lallen*" ("three walking clichés of homelessness loll and prattle through the city"). http://www.spiegel.de/kultur/tv/tatort-der-koenig-der-gosse-aus-dresden-das-debakel-von-dresden-a-1114248.html (February 28, 2018).

39. See, for instance, Hendrik Buhl, *Tatort: gesellschaftspolitische Themen in der Krimireihe.* Konstanz 2013; Hißnauer, Christian (ed.): *Zwischen Serie und Werk. Fernseh- und Gesellschaftsgeschichte im "Tatort."* Bielefeld 2014.

40. See the November 2017 report for *Criminal Minds* on mediaversityreviews.com: https://www.mediaversityreviews.com/tv-reviews/2017/11/3/criminal-minds-season-13 (February 28, 2018).

41. https://de.statista.com/statistik/daten/studie/581038/umfrage/ranking-der-beliebtesten-fernsehserien-in-deutschland (December 12, 2017).

Chapter 6

Greece

TV Crime Dramas and Some Reflections on Gender and Race

Nickos Myrtou, Stamatis Poulakidakos, and Olga Derzioti

The current chapter is a "sequel" to the chapter concerning the presence of police, law, and prison/postprison series in Greek television.[1] The first chapter served a twofold aim: first, to present a brief overview of the inauguration and development of the television broadcasting services in Greece embedded in the sociopolitical context of Greece since the mid-twentieth century and, second, to provide a quantitative overview of the content of the Greek television focusing on police, law, and prison/postprison content.

The social, political, and historical approach sought to provide an introduction to the political, ideological, and financial schemes contributing to the development of television in Greece, as well as to demonstrate the ideological aspects of the predominantly US-originated law content in Greek TV, either in terms of the political "belonging" of Greece to the West, or in terms of the prevalence of Western popular culture in the formulation of the television program in Greece, both before and after deregulation.[2]

The quantitative analysis of contemporary police, law, and prison/postprison programs demonstrated specific tendencies in terms of both structural characteristics of contemporary Greek TV law content (content, origin, hours, and channels of broadcast), as well as several content characteristics—mostly in terms of race and gender—of the programs under scrutiny. These intoductory quantitative results demonstrated the predominance of white male characters in the main roles of police, law, and prison/postprison programs. Nonwhite and female characters constitute a minority in the main roles of the series under scrutiny. This tendency was evident in both Greek and non-Greek productions broadcast in the free-to-air TV channels during November 2014, demonstrating a specific rationale behind the structure of the cast and the characters, at least in quantitative terms.

The current chapter seeks to move forward and complement the previous one in qualitative terms by focusing on the content of the most popular,in terms of audienceship, series in Greek television that aired in November 2017.[3] In this way, we will be able to address issues emerging from the content of the series, focusing predominantly on issues of gender and race, which have been in many occasions jointly studied.[4] Thus, the current chapter consists of a theoretical approach on issues of gender and race as they emerge in popular TV, with a specific focus on police, law, and prison/postprison series television content. The theoretical background will be informed through the use of textual analysis. Our research methodology will be implemented on the episodes of the three most popular—according to AGB-Nielsen Greece—police, law, and prison/postprison series, aired in November 2017 in the free-to-view TV stations broadcasting nationwide in Greece.[5] The series under scrutiny are *NCIS* (Season 13) with an average of 12 percent during November 2017, *Criminal Minds* (Season 8), with an average of 20 percent audience share, and *Hannibal*, which averaged 15 percent.[6] Before building our theoretical framework on gender and race/ethnicity, which will guide us in the analysis of the three most popular police, law, and prison/postprison series on Greek TV in November 2017, we will first present a very brief overview of gender and race/ethnicity issues in Greece.

ETHNICITY AND GENDER IN GREEK SOCIETY

In terms of ethnicity, Greek society was a rather homogeneous one until the early 1990s.Since then, Greece has experienced a sharp rise in immigration. The majority of immigrants—coming from Eastern and South-Eastern European countries and Asia[7]—have been to a great extent undocumented and looking for work.[8] Since 2009, Greece has been suffering perhaps the country's worst economic recession in recent history. In tandem with the difficult financial context, Greece has become the gateway to Europe for refugees and migrants from Africa, Asia, and the Middle East, due to the latest embattled contexts in countries like Syria, Iraq, Afghanistan, and Nigeria.[9]

The new situation has been characterized by administrative and political confusion with regard to migration policy,[10] since the Greek state found itself rather unprepared to deal with the dramatic increase in asylum seekers and irregular migrants.[11] The phenomenon of migration to Greece became a topic of heated debate, and was increasingly designated as a "social problem" alongside unemployment, national (in)security, and crime.[12]

To a significant extent, reporting on immigrants—especially during the nineties[13]—has been couched in conspiracy theories, rhetoric and an overall perception of "pollution." The Greek or European cultural, ethnic or even religious "purity" is perceived to be threatened.[14] Another major "threat," at least until mid-nineties, is overemphasizing the criminality "generated" by the immigrants[15] and the inherent criminal nature of the immigrants, due to their trespassing of the Greek border (the term "illegal immigrants" or "lathrometanastes" was actually first used during that period).[16]

Since the mid-nineties, the social dynamics, emergence of the antiracist movement,[17] and specific events in which immigrants were the victims, turned public attention away from financial and social risks, allegedly caused by the immigrants, toward issues of racism and xenophobia, as well as the everyday problems encountered by immigrants.[18] This change, though, did not eliminate the negative perceptions of the immigrants, especially on behalf of the conservative media and political and social groups.[19] The crisis context, since early 2010, and the polarized public dialogue on issues of public interest[20] escalated the division between "migrants and indigenous," using the immigrants as scapegoats for the major social and financial issues of Greek society.[21]

As far as gender issues are concerned, examining the course of historic events in contemporary Greece, a reluctant but nonetheless steady progress in women's social standing is noticeable. During the postwar period women faced a plethora of changes such as earning the right to vote in 1952 and actively participating in the labor market,[22] while still retaining the role of the giving homemaker (noikokira). The year 1983 could be characterized as a hallmark for change in Greek family status, since a newly established family law abolished dowry (proika), decriminalized adultery, provided for gender equality in marriage, and stipulated the right of women to keep their maiden names. Since then, a series of gender equality gains were achieved such as the 1986 law regarding the legalization of abortion. In the 1990s and 2000s, Greek women's employment rose sharply due to their high educational level, thus establishing a much fairer distribution of family roles.[23]

However, in the past eight years, the economic crunch, as well as the measures used to remedy to the financial crisis forced Greek women to take the responsibility to meet state deficiencies. While multiple social benefits are being sacrificed on the altar of economic recovery, Greek women are being forced to address the shortcomings of the welfare state in multiple ways within the family,[24] thus threatening progress made toward gender equality. Drawing on recent studies,[25] it becomes evident that owing to pre-existing gender inequality, women all over Greece faced the brunt of the economic crisis and were deeply affected by the gendered impact of policy measures. Recent years' welfare state reforms such as great cuts in social spending led to understaffing in public child care and the closing down of a number of municipal nurseries. Disproportionally affected by public sector cuts, women are expected to step into caring roles and do the lion's share of work.[26]

Taking into consideration Marxist feminist observations and especially Christine Delphy's and Diana Leonard's[27] analyses of domestic mode production, which refer to the family and domestic work as a system of labor relations of economic exploitation, it becomes clear that the burden of domestic work that women have to bear because of shortages is not taken into account by the applied policy. According to Delphy and Leonard,[28] domestic labor, which is not rewarded within the capitalist economy, becomes invisible and hence absent from the gross domestic product and other measures of political significance, rendering it similarly invisible to policy makers.[29] Relating this theory to the contemporary situation in Greece, the formulation of policies against the economic crisis ensures that women, even if they are not losing their jobs, are forced to take on piled up domestic responsibilities that have been handed down from cuts by the state, such as childcare and eldercare. Furthermore, the time consumed by the growing duties of working women in Greece is not included in the years of contribution for retirement. Overall, the gendered implications of the austerity measures undertaken in recent years encapsulate a reversal of prior gender equality gains and seem to have altered Greek women's social standing by reinstating them in traditional roles.

ISSUES OF GENDER AND RACE IN THE MEDIA ENTERTAINMENT CULTURE

The popularity of the crime drama genre during primetime television, as well as in the Internet age is undeniable.[30] Crime formats have proliferated on US television and other international television systems, including Greece's,[31] crossing factual and fictional modes, adopting various aesthetic styles, and exploiting a long-standing cultural fascination with criminality, violence, and policing.[32]

Crime television deals at a basic level with crime and its investigation, with the pursuit of criminals, the policing of society and the legal systems, which either successfully or unsuccessfully govern investigation and policing.[33] Crime is frequently characterized as a conservative genre, in part due to its adaptation of grotesque violence for mainstream audiences,[34] in part due to its typical insistence that crime can be solved, violence explained and justice done.[35] In more recent years, though, storylines increasingly feature crimes that were previously considered taboo, such as rape and sexual assault.[36]

Crime television negotiates a difficult terrain of taste and cultural values while exploiting topics such as sexuality, violence, death, and social inequalities.[37] The understanding that crime is a television genre particularly concerned with men and masculinity has influenced the relevant academic approaches. Various writings exploring action and adventure television place gender issues at the epicenter of their scrutiny.[38] These writings approach those TV "texts" from a feminist perspective. Both as a social movement and an academic field, feminism has a long history, has undergone different stages, and is characterized by internal pluralism. Its focus has diachronically been the inferior position of women compared to men in terms of civil and individual rights within the social structure, and a constant effort to overcome this discrimination.[39] The struggle for women's rights extends beyond the right to own property or vote. It is the fight for a woman to be considered an individual in her own right, defined on her own terms, by her own intellect and accomplishments, and afforded the same opportunities as her male peers. Feminism encompasses the victories secured by two centuries of activism: the recognition of women as legal and political entities separate from their fathers or husbands; the rights to own property in their own name, to secure an education, to vote and hold office, to enter the workforce, and to plan their families and control their reproductive lives.[40]

The media, according to Marxist critical approaches, are considered mechanisms, which reproduce power relations, as well as relations of political, social, and cultural hegemony,[41] and, as such, they have been at the epicenter of feminist studies. The media, according to feminist studies, form the prevalent social representations on the image of women and contribute to the preservation of the patriarchal power relations and the undermining of the social position of women.[42] These power relations take on many forms, from the sexual division of labor to the internalized norms of femininity by which we live. Patriarchal power rests on social meaning given to biological sexual differences.[43]

Early cinema feminist studies pointed out the prevalent depiction of women as sex objects and victims, placed at evidently inferior (professional) positions compared to male actors.[44] Women, in contrast to men, function as erotic spectacle,[45] sometimes even interrupting rather than advancing the narrative of a film.[46] The female representations, though, are not static or uniform. In the last fifty years, the depiction of women in the media has changed dramatically. Once featured almost exclusively in the home setting, women are now featured in a variety of roles and settings. Like their real-life counterparts, female characters are doctors, housewives, lawyers, domestic workers, and writers. They are single, married, partnered, lesbian, or heterosexual.[47] Additionally, there is an increasing depiction of "tough" independent women, who "challenge" the patriarchal social structure through their outlooks and character or their direct fight against male characters. These tough women, though, are still presented to appeal to a male audience, being feminine, attractive, and heterosexually appealing.[48]

Even though things have moved forward in terms of the representation of women, gender remains a key constructor and differentiator of character in workplace dramas.[49] Previous research focused on *CSI* has shown that female characters participate as fully in the workplace as their male colleagues but, according to the culture's construction of femininity, family plays a far more important role in the lives of female characters compared to their male coactors. In addition, the boundary between the female characters' public and private lives is blurred to a far greater extent than for the male characters and sometimes causes the personal to impact negatively upon the professional.[50]

Other interesting findings related to specific representations of female characters include the relationships developed between two or more female characters and female and male characters. Competitiveness, backbiting, deep mistrust, and guardedness define female relationships. Divided and contested, women may place their trust in men, often at considerable personal risk, but not each other, and if they are not working under male supervision and/or with men, then they are invariably up to no good.[51]

The abovementioned parameters of female representations articulated in different media texts form a universe of diverse archetypes, in which various models of femininity and female subjectivity operating in the text contribute to a particular ideological construction of what constitutes and "defines" women.[52] These ideological constructions may resemble or differ between various cultural artifacts.

Apart from gender, another field of representation that seems to be placed at the epicenter of media texts' analysis is race, since race is also a key constructor and differentiator of character.[53] There is a significant corpus of research seeking to assess the representation of nonwhites (mostly black people) in popular culture.[54] Initial research focused on quantitative aspects of nonwhite representations in media content, showing a prevalence of white characters, both male and female.[55]

In addition, black characters are usually coded within cultural tropes of black masculinity, through the projection of a problematic past with criminality, corruption, and gambling issues, from which they have been saved with the help of other people (relatives, mentors).[56] In the same vein with the white female characters, the black male characters perform the same roles as the white male characters, but the blurring of the boundaries between their public and private lives often causes the personal to impact negatively upon the professional.[57]

For black feminists, femininity within Western culture has been predominantly defined as white femininity. White feminists have been preoccupied by women's reduction to image and spectacle. It is the invisibility of black women within the category "woman," which has been the issue for black feminists. If white women in television have served as signifiers of male desire, black women, when present at all, have served quite different functions. Most frequently, they have served as an embodiment of either female sexuality or maternity. Elsewhere, as unfeminine women, they seem to be coded as not really women at all.[58]

RESEARCH QUESTIONS AND METHODOLOGY

Based on our theoretical background, our primary research question is: how are the main characters of the three most popular series aired on Greek free-to-view TV channels during November 2017 (*Criminal Minds, NCIS, Hannibal*) represented? Under this rationale, we will examine (among others):

1. Whether the female or nonwhite characters are represented as inferior in qualitative terms to white male characters.
2. Whether female or nonwhite characters are being equally represented in quantitative terms to white characters.
3. Whether women characters follow the historical pattern of being attractive to a male audience.
4. Whether female characters are being represented as more "sensitive" and if the boundaries between their personal and professional lives are blurrier than the male characters.
5. Whether female characters are more often represented as victims.
6. Whether nonwhite characters are being connected more frequently to crime, compared to white ones, or if noncriminal black characters are connected to an illegal past.

The research method implemented for the scope of the current research is textual analysis, a method that allows researchers to collect information on the ways in which individuals make sense of the world.[59] According to McKee, when someone implements textual analysis, she actually forms an academic assumption about the prevalent interpretations of a given "text." The term "text" includes a multiplicity of different texts or artifacts, such as movies, television programs, advertisements, magazines, clothes, etc. According to social constructivism, we understand the world according to the culture of the specific social context we live in. "Texts" are the traces left behind, the various efforts to understand reality, the only empirical evidence we have of how people make sense of the world.[60]

Although textual analysis has been criticized as simplistic and deterministic, since it claims to offer an "appropriate" analysis of a text and does not conduct research on the production and consumption of the text,[61] the knowledge produced through the use of this method offers an understanding of the most likely interpretations of a text, given that the researcher is familiar with its production context and content.[62] Like every research methodology, textual analysis has its own limits, but it can develop several parameters of possible readings of a text and sketch perspectives, which shed light on the cultural and ideological directions of the text.[63]

TEXTUAL ANALYSIS

NCIS (Season 13)

NCIS' main characters are Special Agent Leroy Jethro Gibbs, (Gibbs), leader of the group, special agent Anthony DiNozzo, forensics specialist Abby Sciuto, special agent Timothy McGee, and Dr. Donald "Ducky" Mallard, a charismatic doctor and medical examiner of the team. The characters are mainly male and Caucasian; the only character of color is the director Vance, but his appearances are limited and he actually supports the decisions and actions of Gibbs. As for the two female characters, while Sciuto is integral to discovering the guilty parties, her screen time is limited and, as we will show below, her portrayal problematic.[64]

The different style of portrayal between protagonist male and secondary characters is evident from the credit scenes in the beginning of every episode; we notice that Gibbs, DiNozzo, and McGee have action sequences that project power as they are holding their guns extended toward the viewer, while the rest of the characters are portrayed in nonaction sequences. Additionally, both Gibbs and Ducky, the older males, are portrayed as strong, experienced and "wise" characters. High intelligence is attributed to Sciuto and McGee, but the former is also socially awkward. Sciuto is often portrayed as unable to extrapolate the solution from the data she produces in her lab and has to present them to Gibbs in order to extract meaning, promoting a solution to the case.

Gibbs is portrayed as a strong silent character; he is perceptive and able to sense lies and inconsistencies. Despite his personal drama occurring from the death of his wife and daughter, as a result of his work, he has no regrets, keeps his feelings to himself, and puts his duty above all. Gibbs dedication to his duties is made clear from the first episode of the season, when he returns to active duty before his nearly deadly bodily wounds heal. In his spare time, Gibbs either eats at a diner or works on building a boat. Both activities are "manly" and support the archetype of the strong male hero. In the episode "Double Trouble," Gibbs partners up with his superior director Vance. It is the only episode in which the non-Caucasian character has enough screen time. We notice that Vance accepts Gibbs as his superior in the field and he is regretful of his decision to stop being a field agent. During the same episode, Gibbs' sense of duty and his dedication to active duty is glorified, while Vance is called "just a politician."

Special agent DiNozzo works very closely with Gibbs. Both Gibbs and DiNozzo are the strong characters that protect the team. The theme of the male protector is recurring in the series. In the episode "Homefront," we watch a young boy being assigned the role of the protector of his mother and sister by the Marine father who is leaving for the front, with the mother present in the scene. On the one hand, it speaks to the patriarchal traditions embedded in war and army-related settings. On the other, it highlights the irony of asking a minor to protect the adult, his mother, who is actually the one working to raise him and his baby sister while the father is absent. In the same episode, the boy's mother can no longer work as a lawyer due to her husband's transfer. It is interesting that even though Bishop, a female character, first notices the problem, instead of taking action, she asks Gibbs for help. The archetype of "damsel in distress"[65] is thus reinforced, as now two women need Gibbs as a savior.

While Gibbs' superiority is apparent in rank, DiNozzo constantly needs to refer to himself as "very special agent" in order to differentiate himself from the rest of the "plain" special agents. His character is portrayed as the "player." He has a strong role in the group, he is handsome, and has a number of romantic partners. We watch him in his "game" as he prepares his bachelor pad to entertain and impress a date in the episode "After Hours," building a whole illusion of himself; expensive wine that he does not actually like, a music sheet of "Strangers in the Night" so he can demonstrate his piano skills, and fake photos of himself with pets in order to convince his date of their compatibility.

The duty toward family is another recurring theme in *NCIS*, as previously mentioned, where the male is the protector and the female is the nurturer, if we see the whole team as a family, with Gibbs as the Father and DiNozzo as the eldest son. The title of "very special agent" is passed on to McGee in the season finale when DiNozzo quits in order to take care of a daughter he did not know he had. This is an important twist in the gender roles attributed so far, since family-related issues usually seem to affect the work decisions of the female characters rather than the male ones.[66]

McGee is not a typical male character; he likes theatre, he has been tap dancing, he is in a steady relationship, and he is always ready to listen to the advice of a secondary female character, Bishop. McGee is both intelligent and an action-driven character but above all he is portrayed as dutiful. His worth is finally validated when DiNozzo, by leaving the force, names him "very special agent."

The fourth main character is a female one, forensic expert Abby Sciuto. Sciuto is a brilliant and very capable scientist; she runs the whole forensic lab on her own and her ability to identify critical clues is highly praised. She can extrapolate evidence from the most intricate crime scenes to move the plot along. The way the show portrays her, though, is caricature-like. She is quirky, she drinks copious amounts of energy drinks, she appears socially awkward, and whenever we see her in her lab, the soundtrack suddenly becomes a loud electronic beat. This is reminiscent of the "mad scientists" in kids' animation series who are in their own, different world. At the same time, and because of the loud music, the audience cannot quite make out what she says, but it does not really matter, since Gibbs or someone else from the investigating team will contextualize the data she extracts and move the plot forward. Her appearance follows her caricature-like portrayal, with extravagant hairstyles, Goth-style clothes, platform boots[67] and bright make-up. Given all the above, and despite her importance for the team,[68] she is striped of her authority as a genius. Sciuto, even though we learn she has been part of the team for sixteen years, is portrayed as an ageless woman, since we do not see changes in her appearance and clothing choices nor can we perceive a hierarchical progress.

The last main character is Donald Mallard or Ducky. Ducky is over seventy years old and a doctor. He is portrayed as extremely capable and smart. His value is such that in the first episode, the doctor operating on Gibbs, and saving him, is compared to Ducky as an assurance of his capabilities. Also in episode "Spinning Wheel," we see Ducky's talents as a military doctor and his dedication to family, since we learn of his missing half-brother, whom he has been searching for all his life. It is interesting that both Ducky and Gibbs are older and their age signifies wisdom and authority.

Criminal Minds (Season 8)

This show's team consists of seven members, four male—one of color—and three white females, and each member has special characteristics that contribute to the action. While the supervisor of the team is male, the unit has a female director and even though her screen time is limited—like the supervisor in *NCIS*—she is a more robust character who helps and protects the team, her authority is never questioned and no negative comments are made about her. In *Criminal Minds*, the opening credits present all members equally, giving the same action sequences to both male and female characters.

The leader of the unit is Aaron Hotchner, "Hotch." Hotch is a middle-aged white male, whose authority is made apparent from his dress code and deeper voice. Subordinates and supervisors respect him since he acts as an excellent delegate, who can take advantage of each member's special attributes. He also remains calm under pressure, promoting a confident image. Despite the fact that he is not constantly in the field, he is always in control and provides valuable insights that prove his abilities as team leader. In previous seasons, he appeared to be married and have a son, but, due to the hectic nature of his work, he cannot maintain his family, embodying the archetype of the dedicated to work man who sacrifices his personal life and his family. In Season 8, during the episode "Brothers Hotchner," we see Hotch's personal issues with his brother and we see him with his girlfriend, Beth, a recurring character who is very supportive to him.

The senior agent of the team is David Rossi, also a white middle-aged male character. He is Italian, has a military background with distinguished service, and is portrayed as an honorable and wise agent, since he is usually the narrator of the show. He has a troubled family past with a number of divorces and at the end of the season we learn of his special bond with the female director. His advice is always well received from the rest of the team members thereby promoting his "wise" attributes. Again, we note that while *Criminal Minds* has older female characters, their age is never actually seen as the asset it is for the male characters to whom (similarly to *NCIS*) experience, wisdom, and respect are always attributed. However, Rossi is the only male character that suffers from personal loss. In the season finale, stressed by the death of the director (secondary female character), he turns against the only nonwhite male character, Derek Morgan. The crisis is resolved by Hotch who has the ability to see through the episode's villain's plan. Rossi manages to compose himself and ends up saving the whole team and killing the villain.

Derek Morgan is a supervisory special agent. He is African American and more casually dressed in order to promote his physical stature. He is young and strong but with a dark past. Not only has he been a part of gangs as a boy, he has also suffered abuse at the hands of a community center coach after losing his father. His trauma, though, does not seem to create issues with his character. However, in episode "Restoration," he is forced to reveal his secret and that revelation is integral to solving the case. Surprisingly, the abuser is not referred to as homosexual, nor do we see any attacks to the masculinity of the male victims because of the abuse. Therefore, the writers chose to identify the abuser as a violent criminal and portray abuse as a violent, but not sexual, crime.[69] Derek is a rather interesting character because of his excellent relationships with the female members. He encourages them, talks nicely to them and compliments them on their work.

Penelope Garcia is another important character. She is the sole female analyst, always working on her computer finding clues and connections. Just as in *NCIS*, the female computer genius in *Criminal Minds* has some "quirks." Penelope is portrayed as very lively; we see her dating while also exchanging sexual comments with Morgan. She is curvy, always dresses in colorful, short (over the knee) body-conscious dresses, and her style is generally eye-catching. Garcia is the one female character with a sexy appearance despite not conforming to typical white beauty standards. After the first episode and her sudden jealousy of a new female team member (Blake)—which Penelope resolves by speaking directly with Blake—there are no more occurrences of woman versus woman and the whole team works together without any issues. We must note though, that from time to time Penelope admonishes herself for not being able to assist the team, showing some self-doubt. In addition, she occasionally praises other team members for guiding her on how to seek clues, but she is never in need of rescuing like Sciuto in *NCIS*. Finally, we see Garcia having a minor panic attack when a villain infiltrates her computer. The panic is not attributed to her femininity though, but to the seriousness of the attack. This is the only instance that Penelope needs to rely on a male coworker to assist her.

Before proceeding to the rest of the female characters we should analyze the youngest male character, Dr. Spencer Reid. He is a highly intelligent person, the "genius," with multiple degrees and an eidetic memory. As a genius, he is portrayed as slightly socially awkward and tormented by headaches. In Season 8, we witness him trying to build a relationship with a female doctor, a relationship doomed by a stalker and a villain. The failure to save his romantic interest marks a turning point in Reid's character. At first, he mourns and seems ready to withdraw from the team, but with the support of his fellow team members, who offer varying advice, he returns to action. Reid's character is complimentary to Garcia as both of them are a constant stream of information that the rest of team uses to solve the case. His outfits are also casual, and he has long hair. He is the youngest member of the team and the least rugged.

In Season 8, Dr. Alex Blake is introduced as a new female member of the team to replace a character who decided to step into Interpol. Blake is a linguistics expert with many years in the FBI, but she just manages to join the team. Blake's career has suffered due to the director's past mistakes. In the first episode, Blake receives the proper recognition from her coworkers especially from the female ones who seem to support her in her comeback to duty, but Hotch seems to be more careful about accepting the new team member. We can attribute his reluctance to her past and not to her femininity, since after the first episode she is considered an equal partner. Notably, Blake, in two cases, as an older female, acts as a mother figure toward "unsubs" or "unknown subject of an investigation" in an attempt to de-escalate the situation. An interesting character evolution could be the appearance of her husband, who quit his job in "Doctors without Borders" to be back with his wife, and proposes to enact an older agreement they have in order to veto each other's career and live a peaceful life together. While she considers it during that episode, finally Blake explains how hard she worked to be a part of the unit and refuses, putting her career first at the expense of her personal life.

The last but equally important member of the team is Jennifer Jareau, called "JJ." She is the most active of the female members. We see her often on the field, inspecting crime scenes and arresting perpetrators. While young, thin and blonde, she is not oversexualized, neither by other characters, nor through her appearance. JJ is the only character that is in a happy marriage. Her husband has no issue with her work and she is never criticized for having a nanny. Even during the episode "Nanny Dearest," where nannies and children are targeted by the "unsub," we notice no internal struggle for her choices, but instead she uses her own experiences to connect with a victim and get information. She is portrayed as a balanced character, who has an active and dangerous job, but manages to keep a family in which she finds refuge.

Besides the more diverse cast and the progressive portrayal of female _characters we also notice a balanced portrayal of the unsubs. While mostly white males are portrayed as serial killers, there are a number of women and persons of color on this show. One recurring myth is that serial killers are white males; however, statistics from Radford University[70] show that even though the majority of serial killers are white (51.7 percent in overall instances 1900–2010) and mainly male (88.6 percent in overall instances 1900–2010[71]). That myth is also being debunked by Scott Bonn who also points that despite Black serial killers being active only white males get the major media attention.[72] Of course it is ironic that only the diversity of criminals is part of the pop culture. The first episode portrays a serial killer with disabilities, but his crimes are not attributed to his disability, but rather to his social surroundings. We notice a balance in the language concerning unsubs, as there are no racial or gender stereotypes around the trauma or the triggers of the perpetrators. In addition, in episode "Broken," where the perpetrator is a homosexual young boy who has suffered trauma in "therapy" camps, the show takes a stand against institutions that perceive homosexuals as persons in need of therapy.

Hannibal

The full cast of *Hannibal* consists of eight characters, five of whom are male and three who are female. The cast is mainly Caucasian, with only one male character being African American (Jack Crawford) and one female main character being Asian (Beverly Katz). Even though the supervisor is not Caucasian, the actual heroes of the show are white. While the two main characters work for the FBI trying to profile and stop serial killers, their antagonist is not hidden from the audience. The criminal is the third main male character, Dr. Hannibal Lecter, who is both a serial cannibalistic killer and a psychiatrist.

The plot moves forward mainly through the evolving relationship of a character named Graham with his psychiatrist Dr. Lecter. The emphasis is on the dynamics between protagonist and antagonist and the shadow games that Lecter employs to manipulate Graham, hence the plot line is based on the two male Caucasian characters.

Graham is called back into action because of his special ability to put himself, mentally, in the shoes of killers and understand their motives and actions. He attributes this ability to his self-declared autism and his choice to be a loner. He suffers from psychological problems like PTSD and sleepwalking. That is why he previously left the FBI and why his supervisor Crawford employs Dr. Lecter to act as Graham's therapist and assist him in maintaining his mental stability. Unfortunately, for Graham, Lecter, being fascinated with the way Graham's mind works, is manipulating him in an attempt to push Graham to become a killer.

Crawford is portrayed as a strict powerful character, though his screen time is considerably less than the other two main characters. He is well dressed, mostly in dark colors, promoting a serious image and has a deep, steady voice. He is not letting his emotions show, but he aggressively commands his team in order to achieve positive results. Graham, on the other hand, dresses casually and due to his tormented psyche, is uncertain of himself. He lives alone with a pack of dogs that he has found as strays.

Dr. Lecter is portrayed as a gentle educated person, very well dressed with expensive-looking clothes. He speaks slowly and peacefully, as his authority comes from his stature and thus he does not need to be aggressive like Crawford, but rather makes his suggestions calmly, as a manipulator. He is also portrayed as a wealthy person living in a mansion that is always well maintained, which serves as both his office and his residence.

Hannibal features three women characters, two of whom are main characters: Alana Bloom and Beverly Katz. Alana Bloom has many connections with the main male characters. She is a former student of Dr. Lecter, she is a psychology professor, and she works as an FBI consultant. Therefore, she has personal and professional relationships with all the male protagonists. Bloom is a very dynamic character; she respects Lecter and does not fear Crawford. Graham expresses his admiration that she is able to shout at Crawford, something he cannot do. We also watch her as she actively confronts Lecter because he "stole" her patient. As the show evolves, Bloom develops romantic feelings for Graham, but because of her understanding of his fragile psychological state, she avoids making a move toward a relationship. Bloom is well dressed but not oversexualized; she has an attractive appearance, but the series focuses on her professional abilities, rather than her looks.

The second main female character is an Asian one; Beverly Katz is a crime scene investigator but her role is more important than her male counterparts'.

We are introduced to Katz when she decisively shoots a female serial killer in a standoff. An active character, Katz is good at both field and laboratory work. Katz is a perceptive character, honest, and trustworthy and so is able to connect with Graham and set ground rules for successful communication with him, despite his autism. The rest of the cast seems to rely on her honorable intentions and her abilities. In Season 2, while Graham is imprisoned after being framed, Katz is the one character that manages to find clues about the real killer and as a result, Katz is murdered (Season 2, episode 5). According to Mulvey's theory on the punishment of strong female characters,[73] we could conclude that Katz was punished for being more productive than the male characters and/or that her death is a plot point to promote determination for male characters.

Hannibal focuses on male serial killers. Most killers are not driven by sexual motives and their victims are both male and female. Even though the first serial killer we witness on the show is a man who has managed to slay eight women, and his copycat killer continues to prefer female victims, the series portrays a number of male victims and a fair number of female serial killers.

DISCUSSION

Wrapping up the findings of our textual analysis, in terms of the characters depicted in the protagonist roles, one can easily observe the predominance of white male characters in the of the three series under scrutiny. The white male characters are in most cases carriers of masculine heroic connotations (especially in *NCIS*), and enriched with leadership capabilities and wisdom. There is definite underrepresentation of men of color (only two as major factors in the development of the plot and one in a less "active" protagonist role) and female characters (no blacks, only one Asian). In addition, the more "active" black male character (Morgan on *Criminal Minds*) has a stereotypical troubled past.

As far as the white female characters are concerned, they are being presented as rather dynamic or even career oriented individuals, but still, with only one exception, under the supervision or even the protection of male characters. Additionally, the female characters are mainly represented as "ageless," and in the cases where they are a bit older than the mainstream mid-twenties to mid-thirties age range, their abilities are not attributed to their increased age, in contrast to the (significantly) older male characters.

Quite interestingly, the male and female characters who possess some special mental capabilities are sketched as having behavioral peculiarities. These peculiarities are a bit more evident in the case of the female characters, since they are also materialized in their nonmainstream appearances (e.g., Sciuto and Garcia).

Overall, *Criminal Minds, NCIS,* and *Hannibal* demonstrate that though significant progress has been made in the depiction of nonmale/nonwhite characters, especially in qualitative terms, there are still several quantitative and qualitative aspects that need to be addressed. Popular culture, as expressed by these three crime series, remains a fruitful domain for critical feminist and race analysis.

The current chapter is not enough to support a causality between the overall patriarchy in Greece and the high viewership of police dramas. We can however assume that the problems of the country (crises, migration, rise of crime, etc.) that create a need for escapism, allow crime dramas to achieve higher ratings. At the same time, the sexist notions of those shows support the already established patriarchy.

NOTES

1. Myrtou, Poulakidakos, Nakou (2016).
2. Apart from the relevant sources cited in the previous chapter dedicated to Greek television in 2016, one can find a very comprehensive and solid periodization and approach of the US originated television content under the rationale of cultural studies in the edited volume: Vamvakas V., Gazi A. (eds.) (2017) "American series in the Greek television" (in Greek). Athens: Papazisis (especially chapters 1–7).
3. The reference period of the previous quantitative research was November 2014.
4. Fiske and Hartley (2003); Gamble (2006); Kellner (2011).
5. The current research includes only the free-to-view TV channels, since there are no audience ratings on the different programs broadcast by the subscription platforms of NOVA and COSMOTE TV. Until mid-2017 the total number of subscribers in these two platforms in Greece was calculated at about one million (500,000 for COSMOTE TV and 450,000 for NOVA). The overall penetration of subscription TV is at about 25 percent of the total number of the Greek households. See Skoumpouris (2017).
6. The audience measurements come from the daily audience-ship ratings for November 2017 measured by AGB-Nielsen Greece that were obtained for the scopes of the current research.
7. Moreno et al. (2011), 167.
8. Papageorgiou and Tsironis (2013), 101; Angeli, Dimitriadi, and Triandafyllidou (2014).
9. European Asylum Support Office (2017).
10. Tramountanis (2016).
11. Afouxenidis et al. (2017), 17.
12. Antonopoulos, Tierney, and Webster (2008), 353.

13. Moschopoulou (2005); Kountouri (2009).
14. Dalakoglou (2013), 520.
15. Moschopoulou (2005); Constantinidou (1999), 130–37.
16. Kountouri (2009), 46, 55.
17. Kountouri (2009), 60.
18. Kountouri (2009), 47.
19. Lawrence (2005).
20. Dalakoglou (2013); Wodak and Angouri (2014).
21. Dimitrakopoulou (2012), 8; Poulakidakos (2018).
22. Stratigaki (2007), 125.
23. Stratigaki (2014), 84, 124.
24. Panagiotopoulou (2012), 172.
25. Karamessini and Ruberty (2014).
26. Karamessini (2014), 84.
27. Delphy and Leonard (1992).
28. Delphy and Leonard (1992).
29. Payton (2015), 114.
30. Stacey et al (2015), 1369; Tasker (2016), 304; Logotheti (2017).
31. Paschalidis (2017); Pappas (2017).
32. Tasker (2016), 304.
33. Tasker (2016), 305.
34. Stacey et al. (2015), 1369.
35. Tasker (2016), 312.
36. Stacey et al. (2015), 1369.
37. Tasker (2016), 312.
38. Tasker (2016), 308.
39. Kakavoulia, Kappa, Liapi (2001); Athanasiou (2006); Gamble (2006); Gill (2007).
40. Lee-Lerner, Wilmoth-Lerner, and Wilmoth-Lerner (2006), 65.
41. Van Dijk (1993); Kakavoulia, Kappa, and Liapi (2001), 4; Kellner (2011), 7.
42. Kakavoulia, Kappa, and Liapi (2001), 4.
43. Gamble (2006), 3.
44. Mulvey (1975); Fiske and Hartley (2003); Mulvey (2003).
45. Asa-Berger (2015), 122. Contemporary sexualization is not limited only to women, but includes men as well. In the field of cultural studies this trend is named after the term "sexualization of culture" (see also McNair [2002]).
46. McCabe (2007).
47. Lee-Lerner, Wilmoth-Lerner, and Wilmoth-Lerner (2006), 353, Brunsdon (2012), 375.
48. Inness (2004), 14.
49. Pearson (2007), 48.
50. Pearson (2007), 48–49; Weissmann and Boyle (2007).
51. McCabe (2007), 151.
52. McCabe (2007), 161.
53. Pearson (2007), 48.
54. Fiske and Hartley (2003).

55. This finding also came up in the quantitative research of Myrtou, Pouakidakos, and Nakou (2016).

56. See for example the black male CSI team member Warrick Brown. Pearson (2007), 48–49.

57. Pearson (2007), 48–49.

58. Gamble (2006), 81.

59. McKee (2003), 4.

60. McKee (2003), 6–15.

61. Creeber (2006), 83; Philo (2007), 194.

62. McKee (2003), 137.

63. Kellner, (2011), 14.

64. Please see "Canada: Women, People of Colour & Diversity on Top Law Shows" in this volume for a different interpretation of Abby Sciuto.

65. Peacock (2007), 149–62.

66. Pearson (2007).

67. There is one episode where Sciuto is barefoot and has broken fingers on both hands because, as she explains, she *miscalculated the height of new shoes while dancing;* the whole situation diminishes her character.

68. There is one episode, entitled "Lockdown," which aired in November 2017 in Greece, wherein all the action revolves around Agent Sciuto and her importance to the entire team is therefore highlighted.

69. However, the abuser, while serving his prison sentence for other crimes, is left facing prison rape as punishment for his abuse.

70. Aamodt, M. G. (2016, September 4). "Serial Killer Statistics." Retrieved (June 2017) from http://maamodt.asp.radford.edu/serial killer information center/project description.htm.

71. For a better idea on the fluctuation by decade please check "Serial Killer Statistics" (see n. 70) the analysis of data per decade, e.g., the rise of female serial killers until the 1950s do not fall on the scope of this chapter.

72. Bonn (2014).

73. Mulvey (1975).

BIBLIOGRAPHY

Afouxenidis, A., Petrou, M., Kandylis, G., Tramountanis, A., and Giannaki, D., "Dealing with a Humanitarian Crisis: Refugees on the Eastern EU Border of the Island of Lesvos," (2017) *Journal of Applied Security Research*, 12(1), 7–39.

Angeli, D., Dimitriadi, A., and Triandafyllidou, A., *Evaluating the Cost-Effectiveness of the Irregular Migration Control Policies in Greece* (Athens: Midas, 2014).

Antonopoulos, G. A., Tierney, J., and Webster, C., "Police Perception of Migration and Migrants in Greece," (2008), *European Journal of Crime Criminal Law and Criminal Justice,* 16(4), 353–378.

Asa-Berger, A., *Ads, Fads and Consumer Culture: Advertising's Impact on American Character and Society* (5th edition, Lanham, Boulder, New York, and London: Rowman & Littlefield, 2015).

Athanasiou, A., (ed.) *Feminist Theory and Cultural Criticism* (in Greek) (Athens: Nisos, 2006).

Bonn, Scott., *Why We Love Serial Killers: The Curious Appeal of the World's Most Savage Murderers* (New York: Skyhorse Publishing, 2014).

Brunsdon, C., "Television Crime Series, Women Police and Fuddy-Duddy Feminism," (2012) *Feminist Media Studies*, 13(3), 375–394.

Constantinidou, C., "Social Representations of Crime: The Criminality of Albanian Immigrants in the Athenian press." In A. Koukoutsaki (ed.) *Images of Crime* (Athens: Plethron, 1999).

Creeber, G., "The Joy of Text?: Television and Textual Analysis," (2006) *Critical Studies in Television: The International Journal of Television Studies*, 1(1), 81–88.

Dalakoglou, D., "From the Bottom of the Aegean Sea to Golden Dawn: Security, Xenophobia, and the Politics of Hate in Greece," (2013) *Studies in Ethnicity and Nationalism,* 13(3), 514–522.

Delphy, C., *Familiar Exploitation: A New Analysis of Marriage in Contemporary Western Societies* (Cambridge: Polity Press, 1992).

Dimitrakopoulou, F., "The Factor of Religion in the Integration of Immigrants: The Case of Europe's Muslims," (2012) *Migration Quarterly*, 4, 5–9.

EASO, *Latest Asylum Trends – May 2017* (2017), European Asylum Support Office Report.

Fiske, J., and Hartley, J., *Reading Television* (2nd edition, London and New York: Routledge, 2003).

Gamble, S., *The Routledge Companion to Feminism and Postfeminism* (2nd edition, London and New York: Routledge, 2006).

Gill, R., "Postfeminist Media Culture: Elements of a Sensibility," (2007) *European Journal of Cultural Studies,* 10, 147–166.

Inness, S. A., "'Boxing Gloves and Bustiers': New Images of Tough Women.'" In S. A. Inness (ed.) *Action Chicks: New Images of Tough Women in Popular Culture* (New York and Houndmills: Palgrave Macmillan, 2004).

Kakavoulia, M., Kappa, V., and Liapi, M., *Gender and Mass media: A Field Research* (in Greek) (Panteion University, DIOTIMA Centre for Research on Women's Issues, 2001).

Karamessini, M. and Rubery, J., *Women and Austerity: The Economic Crisis and the Future for Gender Equality* (New York: Routledge, 2014).

Kellner, D., "Cultural Studies, Multiculturalism, and Media Culture." In G. Dines and J. M. Humez (eds.), *Gender, Race and Class in Media: A Critical Reader* (London, Thousand Oaks, and New Delhi: Sage Publications, 2011).

Kountouri, F., "The Financial Migrant in the Political Agenda: The Public Constitution of the Migration Issue in Metapolitefsi (in Greek)," (2009) *The Greek Review of Social Research*, 128, 39–76.

Lawrence, C., "Re-bordering the Nation: Neoliberalism and Racism in Rural Greece," (2005) *Dialectical Anthropology*, 29, 315–334.

Lee-Lerner, K., Wilmoth-Lerner, B., and Wilmoth-Lerner, A., (eds.) *Gender Issues and Sexuality: Essential Primary Sources* (Farmington Hills: Thompson Gale, 2006).

Logotheti, I., "'Out of TV': American Television Series in the Internet (2004–2015)." In V. Vamvakas and A. Gazi (eds.), *American Series in Greek Television: Popular Culture and Psychosocial Dynamics* (in Greek) (Athens: Papazisis, 2017), 259–310.

McCabe, J., "Damsels in Distress: Female Narrative, Authority and Knowledge in 24." In S. Peacock (ed.) *Reading 24: TV against the clock* (London and New York: I. B. Tauris, 2007), 149–161.

McKee, A., *Textual Analysis: The Beginner's Guide* (London, Thousand Oaks, and New Delhi: Sage Publications, 2003).

McNair, B., *Striptease Culture: Sex, Media and the Democratization of Desire* (London and New York: Routledge, 2002).

Moreno, E., Rodríguez, N., Stavropoulou, U., Mousmouti, M., Zavos, A., Katsas, T., Pentafronimos, G., Karantjias, T., Papanikas, D., Ntouskas, T., Polemi, N., Krobisch, V., Wacker, M., Bosswick, W., Donda, A., Branchetti, S., Angiò, M., Matteucci, C., and Solinas, L., *State-of-the-Art and Advances in European Migration Policies* (Brussels: Immigration Policy 2.0, 2011).

Moschopoulou, A., *The Criminality of Migrants: Representation of the Phenomenon in the Afternoon Press 1990–1999* (in Greek) (Athens-Komotini: Sakkoulas, 2005).

Mulvey, L., "Visual Pleasure and Narrative Cinema," (1975) *Screen*, 16(3), 14–26.

Mulvey, L., "Visual Pleasure and Narrative Cinema," In A. Jones (ed.) *The Feminism and Visual Culture Reader* (London and New York: Routledge, 2003), 44–52.

Panagiotopoulou, R., "Social Cohesion in the Greek Society of the Economic Crisis." *Journal of Social Survey* (Athens: Politeia Press, 2012).

Papageorgiou, N. and Tsironis, C., "Gender, Migration and the Economic Crisis in Greece: The Current Debate," (2013) *Culture and Research*, 2, 101–120.

Pappas, F., "First Post-junta Period (1974–81): Attack of Television, Consolidation of American Television Entertainment and an Attempt for Native Qualitative Counterbalance," In V. Vamvakas and A. Gazi (eds.), *American Series in Greek Television: Popular Culture and Psychosocial Dynamics* (in Greek) (Athens: Papazisis, 2017), 103–140.

Paschalidis, G., "Television Entertainment 1967–74: The American Narrative Series." In V. Vamvakas and A. Gazi (eds.), *American Series in Greek Television: Popular Culture and Psychosocial Dynamics* (in Greek) (Athens: Papazisis, 2017), 41–102.

Payton J., "Familiar Exploitation: A New Analysis of Marriage in Contemporary Western Societies," (2013) *Gender and Education*, 25(1), 113–115.

Pearson, R., "Anatomising Gilbert Grissom: The Structure and Function of the Televisual Character." In M. Allen (ed.) *Reading CSI: Television under the Microscope* (London and New York: I. B. Tauris, 2007), 39–56.

Philo, G., "Can Discourse Analysis Successfully Explain the Content of Media and Journalistic Practice?" (2007) *Journalism studies*, 8(2), 175–196.

Skoumpouris, A., *The 10 New Channels of Cosmote TV and the "Fatigue" of Subscription TV* (in Greek), http://www.liberal.gr/arthro/169357/oikonomia/epicheiriseis/ta-10-nea-kanalia-tis-Cosmote-TV-kai-i-isonkoposisin-tis-sundromitikis.html.

Stacey, J., Hust, T., Garrigues-Marett, E., Ming, L., Chunbo, R., and Weina, R., "*Law & Order*, *CSI*, and *NCIS*: The Association between Exposure to Crime Drama Franchises, Rape Myth Acceptance, and Sexual Consent Negotiation among College Students," (2015) *Journal of Health Communication*, 20(12), 1369–1381.

Stratigaki, M. *The Gender of Social Policy* (Athens: Metaixmio, 2006).

Tasker, Y., "Sensation/Investigation: Crime Television and the Action Aesthetic," (2016) *New Review of Film and Television Studies*, 14(3), 304–323.

Tramountanis, A., *Defining National Belonging and Exclusion: The Case of Greek Immigration and Refugee Policy* (Athens: Greek National Centre for Social Research, EKKE, 2016).

Vamvakas, V. and Gazi, A. (eds.), *American Series in Greek Television: Popular Culture and Psychosocial Dynamics* (in Greek) (Athens: Papazisis, 2017).

Van Dijk, T. A., "Stories and Racism." In D. K Mumby (ed.) *Narrative and Social Control: Critical Perspectives* (Newbury Park: Sage, 1993), 121–142.

Weissmann, E. and Boyle, K., "Evidence of Things Unseen: The Pornographic Aesthetic and the Search for Truth in CSI." In M. Allen (ed.) *Reading CSI: Television under the Microscope* (London and New York: I. B. Tauris, 2007), 90–102.

Wodak, R. and Angouri, J., "They Became Big in the Shadow of the Crisis: The Greek Success Story and the Rise of the Far-Right," (2014) *Discourse & Society*, 25(4), 540–565.

Chapter 7

Poland

Polish Productions about Polish Problems

Zofia Zawadzka

POLISH PUBLIC MEDIA

On January 7, 2016, the amendment of the Radio and Television Act of December 29, 1992 was signed into law, enabling the conservative government to control the state media. Under the new law, the public radio and television chiefs, members of public media supervisory boards, and civil service directors are appointed and dismissed by the Treasury Minister, instead of through elections organized by the National Broadcasting Council (*Krajowa Rada Radiofonii i Telewizji*). Current managers were fired with immediate effect.[1] In response to the new media bill, a coalition of freedom of the press groups started protesting it, suggesting it facilitates restrictions on media freedom, censorship, and the dispersal of biased information. Since the bill's signing into law in January 2016, several thousand demonstrations and "free media" protests have been held in various Polish cities.[2]

The European Union Commission has voiced its concern that Poland may be jeopardizing European Union values by approving a law which gives the government direct control over recruitment in television and radio broadcasting.[3] The EU Commission has launched, for the first time, a formal investigation into the rule of law framework in a Member State. The Commission is concerned that the changes Poland's government is making to public broadcasting are damaging the rule of law and interfering with the right to freedom of expression and freedom of information.

The new Radio and Television Act gives the current conservative government sufficient room to control state run television and radio and promote biased agendas. State media nowadays are engaged in the political fight, supporting the ruling conservative Law and Justice party (*Prawo i*

Sprawiedliwość) by disseminating propaganda and stating that any opposition to its propaganda is anti-Polish and hurts Poland's interests.[4]

GENDER, ETHNICITY, AND DIVERSITY IN POLAND

A survey of Polish public opinion conducted in Poland recently demonstrates quite a negative picture of Polish society when it comes to matters such as gender equality, attitudes toward refugees and same sex relationships.[5]

The April 1997 *Constitution of the Republic of Poland* ensures equal rights to both women and men.[6] Article 32 introduces the equality before the law rule and provides that no one shall be discriminated against in political, social or economic life for any reason whatsoever. Furthermore, article 33 states that men and women shall have equal rights in family, political, social and economic life in the Republic of Poland. Men and women shall have equal rights, in particular, regarding education, employment and promotion, and shall have the right to equal compensation for work of similar value, to social security, to hold offices, and to receive public honors and decorations. Anyone whose right to be treated equally has been violated can seek redress for such infringement. The Constitution, civil, criminal and labor law directly guarantee protection against discrimination.

Although the above-mentioned legal guarantees exist, the reality in Poland is not equal treatment. It is most visible while comparing men's and women's professional lives. The main factor that contributed to increasing female participation in the labor force was the economic growth that followed the end of The Second World War. In 1950 women comprised about 31 percent of the workforce, at the beginning of the 1970s they were close to 40 percent, and in 2014 women were almost 49 percent of the Polish work force.[7]

Women's occupational status in Poland is limited by many barriers and stereotypes that hinder equal access to work and promotion. Particularly relevant is the mental barrier, which has its roots in stereotypical approaches to the roles that men and women play in society. From an early age children inculcate specific models of male and female behavior. Later this process is continued in school. Throughout existing educational programs, a traditional view of men's and women's place in society is solidified. Subsequently, this can affects the course of study young people decide to choose for their careers. In the end we face the case of feminization of particular jobs, mostly ones that are less valued and lower paid.[8] Attempts to change the negative effects of such sex stereotyping on the labor market are being undertaken. One example is an action called "Girls to Polytechnics" that was under the honorary patronage of the Minister of Science and Higher

Education.[9] The published report results suggest that since the action begun in 2007, the percentage of women that attend polytechnics and technical universities is systematically growing. In 2007/2008 the share of female students in technical universities was 30.7 percent. In 2017/2018 this number rose to 37 percent.[10]

The Central Statistics Office Report shows that the average salary of a female worker is lower than of a male worker.[11] In October 2014, men were paid 9.1 percent more than the average remuneration in the country. During the same period women received 9.5 percent less money than the country's average. This means that the average salary of a female employee was 17 percent lower than the average salary of a male employee.[12] The average earnings of the 10 percent of women with the highest incomes was equal to 77 percent of the average earnings of men with the highest incomes. In the case of the 5 percent of women with the highest incomes, the ratio was even more unfavorable, amounting to 73 percent.[13]

The Polish people's attitude toward admitting refugees seeking shelter has not changed significantly in recent years. More than half of people surveyed (52 percent) questioned generally whether refugees should or should not be admitted, are opposed to accepting asylum requests Only 4 percent of questioned persons think that resettlement within Polish boarders should be allowed.[14] Regarding the matter of Middle East and Africa refugees' relocation within European Union countries, the vast majority of respondents (68 percent) are against admitting refugees fleeing those regions, whereas only little more than a quarter (27 percent) support admission.[15] Not all the refugees who seek asylum in the European Union come from the Middle East and Africa—although they are the ones that dominate in public discussions. Some refugees are from Eastern Ukraine. Most Polish people lean toward assisting immigrants from this region; more than half (57 percent) of questioned people believe that Poland should accommodate refugees from the areas of armed conflict in the eastern Ukraine.[16]

Relatively few Polish people (12 percent) share the opinion that being homosexual is normal. The majority (83 percent) believe that homosexuality should be treated as a deviation from the norm. This includes more than half (57 percent) who think homosexuals should be tolerated, whereas one quarter (26 percent) disagree, saying homosexuality should not be accepted.[17] Most of Polish society is reluctant to grant rights to same sex couples: almost two-thirds (63 percent) take the view that same-sex couples should not be granted the right to publicly show their lifestyle, more than two-thirds (68 percent) do not accept legalization of homosexual marriage, and nearly nine out of ten people (87 percent) agree that they should not be able to adopt children.[18]

TV SERIES WITH THE HIGHEST VIEWERSHIP IN NOVEMBER 2017

Based on ratings provided by the website wirtualnemedia.pl, the three legally themed TV series with the highest viewership in November 2017 were *Ojciec Mateusz* (Season 18, episodes 235–238) with over 3,000,000 viewers,[19] *Belfer* (Season 2) with 306,000 viewers,[20] and *Wataha* (Season 2) with 208,000 viewers.[21] *Ojciec Mateusz* is produced on commission public television Channel TVP1, while *Belfer* and *Wataha* are productions of Canal+ Poland and HBO Poland, respectively, which are paid, not public, TV stations.

The high viewership of *Ojciec Mateusz* follows from the fact that it is broadcast on public television. It airs on Thursdays when in general there are no other alternatives to be watched. The huge gap between the viewership of *Ojciec Mateusz* and *Belfer* and *Wataha*, despite the tremendous success of the two latter TV shows, is a result of the limited access to those series as both Canal+ and HBO are paid TV stations.

Ojciec Mateusz, which translates to Father Matthew, is a Polish television series produced by the public television Channel TVP1, starring Artur Żmijewski and Kinga Preis. The pilot episode aired on November 11, 2008. It series is the Polish version of the cult Italian detective series, *Don Matteo*, broadcast in Italy by Rai Uno.[22] The series presents the adventures of a Roman Catholic Priest, Father Mateusz Żmigrodzki, who takes a job in a small parish in Sandomierz, Poland. As a priest, Father Mateusz solves mysteries and helps to investigate local crimes thanks to his intelligence, impressive insight into human nature and remarkable talent of finding links between seemingly unrelated events. Father Mateusz is wise and respected in the local community and is willing to help. These qualities help him to convince criminals to confess to their crimes.

The second TV series with the highest viewership in November 2017, *Belfer* (The Teacher) is a Polish television crime-mystery-thriller series starring Maciej Stuhr, broadcast by Canal+ Poland. The first ten-episode season that premiered on October 2, 2016 won two awards: Best TV Series Award at the Polish Film Awards Orły 2017 and the Special Prize at Telekamera 2017.[23] It was a ratings success for Canal+ with an average audience rating of 254,000 viewers per episode.[24] (The finale of the first season attracted over 461,000 viewers).[25] *Belfer* tells the story of a high school Polish language teacher from Warsaw, Paweł Zawadzki (Maciej Stuhr), who arrives in the small town of Dobrowice to teach in the local school. As he acclimatizes to his new reality he starts to investigate the recent murder of one of the school's students. His private investigation reveals corruption and fraud among local entities.[26]

The second season that premiered a year later on October 22, 2017 also won the Best TV Series Award at the Polish Film Awards Orły 2018.[27] The premiere episode of the second season averaged 423,000 viewers.[28] In the second season, the title character, teacher Paweł Zawadzki, is forced by the Polish Central Bureau of Investigation to take a job in one of the prestigious high schools in Wrocław to find out more about the mystery of the missing three students.[29] When he arrives, the three students are back in class claiming that they skipped school to visit Paris. Later, on Saturday, during the rehearsals for the school play led by Zawadzki, one of the students who was missing comes to school with a gun. He kills one student, and another student and one teacher are seriously injured. The investigation is led by the Polish Central Bureau of Investigation (*Centralne Biuro Śledcze—CBŚ*), which is one of the elite, best equipped and trained Police Special Units and as a rule, takes action to combat international organized crime, drugs, terrorist acts and economic crimes. An officer of CBŚ cooperates with Paweł Zawadzki hoping he will be able to penetrate the students' environment to solve the high school's tragedy. The teacher, while getting closer to a group of students, discovers some ambiguities in their testimony about their alleged trip to Paris. He tries to discover where have they been and why are they lying about it.

The third most viewed TV series in November 2017 was Season 2 of the drama series *Wataha*. The original Polish title literally translates as "the Pack" or "Wolfpack," but Channel 4's foreign-language online demand service, Walter Presents, translated it as "The Border" as it is set at the border.[30] The first season, consisting of six episodes, earned great reviews.[31] There was praise for the acting, the believable characters, an interesting, clever, and intelligent plot with various twists, Nordic Noir character, and the feel of authenticity. *Wataha* was said to provide an overview of life in a distant Polish border area. But the most acclaimed part of *Wataha* was the cinematography—stunning landscapes of the heavily wooded Bieszczady Mountains with its wilderness, wolves, and bears.

The first season aired in October 2014 and was meant to be a one-off miniseries. However, due to high viewership, HBO Poland decided to produce a second season. The second season premiered on October 15, 2017. The average audience ratings of all six episodes of Season 2 were 208,000 (as a comparison, the average audience of first season was 335,000 viewers).[32] These results do not include viewers of HBO GO and HBO OD services, which are much higher, Three times more viewers watched Season 2 on HBO GO than Season 1. The high score of viewership of *Wataha* beat even *Game of Thrones* broadcast on HBO Poland. HBO decided to premiere Season two simultaneously in nineteen different countries (Sweden, Denmark, Norway, and Finland on HBO Nordic, Spain on HBO España, Central Europe on HBO

Go platform, and Czech Republic, Slovakia, Hungary, Romania, Bulgaria, Croatia, Serbia, Slovenia, Macedonia, Bosnia and Herzegovina, Montenegro, Moldavia, and Kosovo on HBO Go).[33]

Wataha tells the story of a Polish border patrol unit that operates and monitors the heavily wooded border between Poland and Ukraine in the Bieszczady Mountains. Border guards try to stop traffickers from smuggling alcohol, weapons, refugees, and illegal immigrants across the border. The first season of *Wataha* focused mostly on solving the mystery of a bomb attack on a guard post, which kills all but one member of the border guard team. The only survivor is captain Wiktor Rebrow (Leszek Lichota). Investigators and relentless public prosecutor Iga Dobosz (Aleksandra Popławska) turn their suspicions toward the sole survivor, suggesting he may have been involved in the explosion due to the cryptic text message he received moments before the blast. However, there are plenty of suspects, including one of the guards. The crime remains unsolved, making an opening for the next season.

In the second season, the situation is turbulent as more and more migrants illegally cross the border. The border patrol unit targets Ukrainian gangs trafficking illegal migrants from Eastern Europe and refugees from Syria. The strong, confident, and determined prosecutor Iga Dobosz returns after four years to Bieszczady Mountains to investigate the gruesome murder of over twenty illegal immigrants. The unsolved killing of the border guards' unit still haunts her. Wiktor Rebrow, still pursued as the main suspect, stays in a hideout in the mountains on the Ukrainian side of the border.[34] His only contact and help are two old friends—Łuczak, a former border guard expelled from duty due to his contacts with smugglers, and Marta, who works in refugee center. The situation changes when Marta disappears and an illegal female immigrant named Alsu appears in Rebrow's shelter with her son.

GENDER

The issue of gender is not directly brought up in any of the three legally themed TV series most viewed in November 2017. It is however strongly noticeable in *Ojciec Mateusz*. One of the main characters in this series is Natalia Borowik (Kinga Preis), who is a housekeeper at Father Mateusz's rectory. The character of priest's housekeeper presents many gender stereotypes and generalizations about female attributes. She is hard-working and diligent, loyal, and devoted to the priest. She does the housework, washes dishes, folds laundry, wonders what to cook for dinner and serves food to the priest. In one episode, Father Mateusz announces he is going to cook dinner and the housekeeper understands this as a great joke and she bursts into laughter. While cooking, Father Mateusz mixes up the spice jars causing the dinner to be inedible. This situation perfectly reflects gender stereotypes of male priest and his female housekeeper.

AGE

The issue of age generally does not play a role in the plot of the three legally themed Polish TV series. The issue of age was however important in the TV series *Ojciec Mateusz*. Due to the age difference, a female police inspector was not sure whether to get emotionally involved with a younger surgeon. The age difference between the two is approximately ten years. This is perceived to be a cumbersome age difference for women, yet it is not perceived to be problematic when the genders are reversed. The police inspector wonders whether the relationship with the younger surgeon can succeed or should even be started at all. The police inspector's concerns illustrate that these views are common in Polish society. In one episode, the police inspector comes late for a meeting, enters the restaurant and does not find her date. She asks her acquaintances, who happen to be in the restaurant, if they have seen a man waiting for her. In response she hears that there was "a boy" waiting for someone but he could not have been waiting for her, because by implication, she is too old for him.

ABILITY

The issue of ability and disability is not brought up as a main subject in any of the three TV series watched in November 2017. Criminals, investigators and the victims of crimes are not disabled or handicapped. However, a secondary motif of disability is presented in one of the episodes of *Ojciec Mateusz*. A brother of a boy in a coma, alive due to a life-support machine, steals a car to get money to pay the costs of treatment and rehabilitation. He commits a crime guided by good motives and makes an effort to give back to Ojciec Mateusz the relics of a saint found in a bag in the stolen car. Meanwhile, in *Wataha* the writers give us a glimpse of the private life of relentless and strong public prosecutor Iga Dobosz, whose mother was diagnosed with Alzheimer's disease. Dobosz feels morally responsible to take care of her sick mother, but this obligation affects her job. On the one hand, she needs to be available at any time when she is on duty; on the other hand, not personally taking care of her mother is the subject of continuous societal judgment.

ETHNICITY

The subject of illegal migration and border crossing is brought up from the very beginning on *Wataha*. But during the first season (October 2014), this topic was not as vivid and dramatic as it is today. Within a couple of years, the issue of refugees rose to being one of the biggest struggles in Europe. Issues of war in Syria, terrorism, refugees, illegal migration, and human trafficking are the most current topics depicted in *Wataha*. They are not a media creation; they represent real life problems faced by Polish society and government.[35] The 2017 season of *Wataha* could not avoid the ideological discourse which takes place in Poland. Ethnicity is a live topic in Poland, especially if one considers the daily news reports and 2017 headlines,[36] which focus on refugees escaping conflict and risking their lives seeking a safe haven on European shores. The series however does not take a stand on the European migration crisis. *Wataha* finds a golden mean, not imposing any views or opinions on relocating asylum seekers, and not sanctifying or demonizing migrants and refugees.

The show presents human tragedies that take place when migrants attempt to illegally breach borders, both at home, in their country of origin, and from Polish traffickers, who treat them as a booty. The traffickers exploit the vulnerability of migrants as an opportunity for abuse and harassment of women and children.

The series tackles the problem of growing racism and xenophobia. It presents Poland, truthfully, as an unwilling host for whom illegal migrants and refugees are a political issue and a propaganda opportunity. *Wataha* depicts a harrowing scene of an attack by a radical nationalist group against a refugee center, which ends when the entire center is burned down.

Recently in Poland there has been a noticeable growth of xenophobia. Right-wing extremists present an ideology based on a belief that members of ethnic and religious minorities cannot be truly Polish as "real" Poles have to be Caucasian Catholic. The nationalist movement is anti-Semitic. Radical nationalist groups are using violence, hate speech and often committing hate crimes. The majority of the victims of those radical nationalist groups belong to ethnic minorities as well as small religious groups or are homosexual.[37] On November 11, 2017 (Polish Independence Day), the so-called independence marches were organized by the members of radical nationalist groups, including far-right hooligans supporting various Polish football clubs. These marches are an opportunity for extreme-right groups to demonstrate strength and power.[38] The marches often trigger riots in the streets between radical nationalist groups who throw rocks at police officers and anti-fascist counter-demonstrators. The hooligans also cause damage to police cars, TV vans, bus stops, and random vehicles. They chant slogans such as "Poland for Polish people, foreigners out!," "whole Poland, all white," "beat red scum!," or "neither red, nor rainbow."[39] This climate of racism, xenophobic populist mentality and hostility toward refugees is reflected in *Wataha*.

CLASS

The story presented in episode 237 of *Ojciec Mateusz* concerns the issue of class. It is about a family with two sons from the dregs of society. The mother was cleaning houses; the father was an employee on a construction site, struggling with a drinking problem. The mother, being afraid of her husband who was abusing the whole family, took the excruciating decision to send the younger son to her distant relatives in another city, cutting all contact with him. The older son stayed at home in this dysfunctional family. This choice caused the future of both boys to be completely different. The younger one, although still underage, was learning in high school, played football professionally and was offered a transfer to a football club abroad. The older one, on the other hand, never finished school, did not get the matriculation examination in secondary school, had no education and no profession. This situation of two brothers from one family, brought up in different environments reflects how class and one's background affect one's future life.

SEXUAL ORIENTATION

The subject of sexual orientation appears in two of three legally-themed TV series watched in November 2017: *Belfer* and *Wataha*. However, it is depicted completely differently. In *Belfer,* two students in high school, where the main character Paweł Zawadzki (Maciej Stuhr) works, are lesbians. This is not presented as a problem, there is no hostility against the girls, and they are not discriminated against. In larger cities such as Wrocław, where the show is set, the acceptance of LGBTQ people is increasing, mainly among younger people. However, opinion polls conducted in Poland throughout the years find that the majority of the population considers homosexuality an unnatural activity, are overwhelmingly opposed to same-sex marriage or civil unions, and to adoption of children by same-sex couples. Most Poles also oppose equality or pride parades and are against gays and lesbians publicly showing their way of life.[40] These beliefs are depicted in *Wataha*. One of the border guards, Piotr "Rambo" Wójcik (Maciej Mikołajczyk) who is gay tries to keep this fact a secret, choosing to stay in the closet. The smuggler Wiśniak discovers his secret and starts to blackmail him. In return for not revealing photos of Rambo kissing another man, the smuggler demands information about the locations of border guard patrols. Rambo discloses this information because he is embarrassed and ashamed of his homosexuality and afraid of discrimination and social exclusion.

RELIGION

Religion is, for obvious reasons, a common topic in *Ojciec Mateusz*. Father Mateusz helps criminals on their way to redemption, convincing them, by appealing to God and the Bible, to confess their crimes and take legal responsibility for their actions. Two of the four episodes of *Ojciec Mateusz* broadcast in November 2017 are directly connected with religion. The story presented in episode 236 was about young priest (acolyte) who came for his apprenticeship to Father Mateusz's parish. He explained that his calling caused him to cut ties with his family. His father could not come to terms with him going to theological seminary as he failed to meet his father's expectations of taking over the family business. During the conversation between Father Mateusz and the young acolyte quotations from the Bible are often used.

Another episode of *Ojciec Mateusz*, episode 238, dealt with the crime of theft of a bishop's car, which contained the relics of a saint. The police were trying to find the stolen car, while local priests were more focused on finding the holy relics. While hidden in the house of a thief, the relics manage to work miracles. Thanks to their presence, the robber's comatose brother woke up. In the end, the relics are safely returned to Ojciec Mateusz.

CONCLUSION

It is important to emphasize that all three legally-themed TV series with the highest viewership in November 2017, *Ojciec Mateusz, Belfer* and *Wataha*, are series produced in Poland. If the research was not conducted in November 2017, the results would have been different, because *Belfer* and *Wataha* are mini-series that were only broadcast in October and November 2017. However, the fact that the series in question are Polish productions makes it even more interesting considering the outcome of the survey and significance of emerging themes.

The task of television in Poland includes spreading civil education. Legislation provides guidance on the content of broadcasts, demanding that they cannot advocate breaking the law, immorality, or any actions against public interest. Hate speech, incitement to hatred, or discrimination on the grounds of race, disability, sex, religion, or nationality are prohibited.[41] Public television was additionally tasked with a particular responsibility to accomplish public service goals. Thus, public television is expected to provide impartial, balanced and independent news, culture, entertainment, education and sport. It should also be of high quality and ethical. Public television should create and disseminate programs which meet the democratic, social and cultural needs of local communities.[42] In addition, programs of public television should respect the Christian system of values, which are assumed to be the foundation of universal principles of ethics, strengthen the family and combat antisocial activities.[43] *Ojciec Mateusz* is a model example of fulfilling the objectives and responsibilities set for public television. This series illustrates the implementation of the public service goals of conducting media education and forming public opinion imposed on public television through creating. The title character, Father Mateusz who, thanks to his remarkable abilities, reads the miseries of the human soul, together with references to religion and quotations from the Bible, propagate the Christian system of values.[44] That is the reason why issues such as same-sex marriage do not emerge in the series.

The analysis of the content of the three legally themed TV series with the highest viewership in November 2017 suggests that the series, especially those on public channels, tend to avoid tackling the highly controversial, social, and ethical problems of the present. However, from time to time, in single episodes, problems of importance are touched upon, these being, for example, religious or ethnic discrimination. In the episodes of *Ojciec Mateusz* broadcast in November 2017, the issue of ethnicity was not presented. It does not however mean that this TV series refrains entirely from speaking out about ethnicity, nationality, or migration. For example, the first episode of the new season, episode 240 broadcast on January 25, 2018, is about four Arabian families that are supposed to come to Sandomierz—the small town where Father Mateusz is a priest. This fact causes anxiety and deep concerns among the local community. The topic of migration, ethnicity, and refugees is not however brought up as openly as it is in *Wataha. Wataha* gives a hard-hitting look at the growing xenophobia and racism in Poland. *Wataha* perfectly depicts a social climate of hostility and fear of refugees.

The content of the three series in November 2017 does not present an imbalance between male and female roles. The characters of police officers, border guards, victims, or perpetrators are both men and women. The role of public prosecutor Iga Dobosz on *Wataha* is an example of the evolution of female figures in legally themed series. She is strong, confident, fearless, and good at her job. On the other hand, being on duty and not being able to look after her sick mother makes her feel guilty. Not personally taking care of her mother is also a subject of social judgment. This assumption that a daughter/woman is supposed to look after her mother is a stereotypical gender approach which is not required of men. Gender stereotypes are also vividly presented in the character of the priest's housekeeper in the series *Ojciec Mateusz*.

The theme of homosexual relationships is not often undertaken in Polish productions and tends to be avoided. That is why it is worth noting that during November 2017, homosexual relations were brought up in two of the three series in question. In *Belfer* the presence of lesbian students was treated as an every-day reality, not marked negatively. More common in Poland is the approach to homosexual relationships presented in *Wataha*, where homosexuality is shown as something to be ashamed of and embarrassed about.

NOTES

1. *The Guardian* (January 7, 2016): https://www.theguardian.com/world/2016/jan/07/poland-president-signs-bill-putting-state-media-under-government-control.

2. E. Rutkowska, W całym kraju manifestacje pod hasłem "wolne media," https://www.press.pl/tresc/42379,w-calym-kraju-manifestacje-pod-haslem-wolne-media; "Wolna Polska, wolne media," Tysiące ludzi na manifestacjach KOD, https://www.tvn24.pl/wiadomosci-z-kraju,3/zmiany-w-mediach-publicznych-manifestacje-kod,609345.html.

3. M. Khan, The Polish media law controversy: national protests and European discontent, http://www.youthpress.org/polish-media-law-controversy.

4. C. Turp, Regional News Outlets: The Real Target of Poland's New Media Law?, http://emerging-europe.com/intelligence/regional-news-outlets-the-real-target-of-polands-new-media-law.

5. *Kobiety i mężczyźni na rynku pracy*, opracowanie Departamentu Badań Demograficznych i Rynku Pracy, Warszawa 2016, Zakład Wydawnictw Statystycznych, https://stat.gov.pl/files/gfx/portalinformacyjny/pl/defaultaktualnosci/5821/1/6/1/kobiety_i_mezczyzni_2016.pdf; A. Głowacki, *Stosunek Polaków do przyjmowania uchodźców*, Komunikat z badań nr 1/2017, Centrum Badania Opinii Społecznej; M. Feliksiak, *Stosunek do praw gejów i lesbijek oraz związków partnerskich*, Centrum Badań Opinii Społecznej. Komunikat Badań, Warszawa, luty 2013, https://www.cbos.pl/SPISKOM.POL/2013/K_024_13.PDF.

6. Konstytucja Rzeczpospolitej Polskiej of April 2nd, 1997, Dz.U. Nr 78, poz. 483 with amendments.

7. *Kobiety i mężczyźni na rynku pracy*, opracowanie Departamentu Badań Demograficznych i Rynku Pracy, Warszawa 2016, Zakład Wydawnictw Statystycznych, https://stat.gov.pl/files/gfx/portalinformacyjny/pl/defaultaktualnosci/5821/1/6/1/kobiety_i_mezczyzni_2016.pdf, p. 2.

8. Marzena Hapioniuk, *Sytuacja kobiet na rynku pracy w Polsce*, Analiza 2014/2, Instytut Obywatelski, http://www.instytutobywatelski.pl/wp-content/uploads/2014/03/analiza_sytuacja_kobiet_na_rynku_pracy_w_polsce.pdf, p. 11.

9. http://www.dziewczynynapolitechniki.pl.

10. Raport Kobiety na politechnikach 2007–2017, Fundacja Edukacyjna Perspektywy, marzec 2017, http://www.dziewczynynapolitechniki.pl/pdfy/Raport_Kobiety_na_politechnikach_2017.pdf, p. 3.

11. *Kobiety i mężczyźni na rynku pracy*, opracowanie Departamentu Badań Demograficznych i Rynku Pracy, Warszawa 2016, Zakład Wydawnictw Statystycznych, https://stat.gov.pl/files/gfx/portalinformacyjny/pl/defaultaktualnosci/5821/1/6/1/kobiety_i_mezczyzni_2016.pdf, p. 15.

12. *Kobiety i mężczyźni na rynku pracy*, opracowanie Departamentu Badań Demograficznych i Rynku Pracy, Warszawa 2016, Zakład Wydawnictw Statystycznych, https://stat.gov.pl/files/gfx/portalinformacyjny/pl/defaultaktualnosci/5821/1/6/1/kobiety_i_mezczyzni_2016.pdf, p. 15.

13. *Kobiety i mężczyźni na rynku pracy*, opracowanie Departamentu Badań Demograficznych i Rynku Pracy, Warszawa 2016, Zakład Wydawnictw Statystycznych, https://stat.gov.pl/files/gfx/portalinformacyjny/pl/defaultaktualnosci/5821/1/6/1/kobiety_i_mezczyzni_2016.pdf, p. 15.

14. A. Głowacki, *Stosunek Polaków do przyjmowania uchodźców*, Komunikat z badań nr 1/2017, Centrum Badania Opinii Społecznej, p. 5.

15. A. Głowacki, *Stosunek Polaków do przyjmowania uchodźców*, Komunikat z badań nr 1/2017, Centrum Badania Opinii Społecznej, p. 7.

16. A. Głowacki, *Stosunek Polaków do przyjmowania uchodźców*, Komunikat z badań nr 1/2017, Centrum Badania Opinii Społecznej, p. 11.

17. M. Feliksiak, *Stosunek do praw gejów i lesbijek oraz związków partnerskich*, Centrum Badań Opinii Społecznej. Komunikat Badań, Warszawa, luty 2013, https://www.cbos.pl/SPISKOM.POL/2013/K_024_13.PDF, p. 2.

18. M. Feliksiak, *Stosunek do praw gejów i lesbijek oraz związków partnerskich*, Centrum Badań Opinii Społecznej. Komunikat Badań, Warszawa, luty 2013, https://www.cbos.pl/SPISKOM.POL/2013/K_024_13.PDF, p. 4.

19. http://www.wirtualnemedia.pl/artykul/ojciec-mateusz-stracil-1-02-mln-widzow-9-63-mln-zl-z-reklam.

20. http://www.wirtualnemedia.pl/artykul/belfer-2-hitem-canal-wyniki-ogladalnosci.

21. http://www.wirtualnemedia.pl/artykul/208-tys-widzow-watahy-2-wzgledem-pierwszego-sezonu-premiery-serialu-stracily-127-tys-ogladajacych.

22. http://ojciecmateusz.vod.tvp.pl/184918/o-serialu#.

23. http://www.filmweb.pl/serial/Belfer-2016-746188/awards.

24. http://www.wirtualnemedia.pl/artykul/belfer-2-hitem-canal-wyniki-ogladalnosci.

25. https://fdb.pl/wiadomosci/28590-belfer-z-rekordem-ogladalnosci-w-calej-historii-canal.

26. https://belfer.canalplus.pl/sezon-1#o-serialu.

27. http://www.filmweb.pl/serial/Belfer-2016-746188/awards.

28. http://www.wirtualnemedia.pl/artykul/belfer-2-hitem-canal-wyniki-ogladalnosci.

29. https://belfer.canalplus.pl/#o-serialu.

30. https://www.theguardian.com/tv-and-radio/2016/jun/21/the-border-walter-presents-no-one-in-britain-would-dare-to-make-this-tv-show.

31. Mateusz Cyra, Wreszcie coś dobrego – Michał Gazda – „Wataha", sezon 1. Recenzja, Głos Kultury, http://www.gloskultury.pl/wreszcie-cos-dobrego-michal-gazda-wataha-sezon-1-recenzja.

32. http://www.wirtualnemedia.pl/artykul/208-tys-widzow-watahy-2-wzgledem-pierwszego-sezonu-premiery-serialu-stracily-127-tys-ogladajacych.

33. https://wpolityce.pl/kultura/361211-drugi-sezon-watahy-z-jednoczesna-premiera-w-19-krajach.

34. http://www.hbo.pl/wataha/index.html.

35. M. Czarnecki, M. Jałoszewski, T. Kwaśniewski, Boisz się uchodźców? Oto 16 faktów, http://www.newsweek.pl/polska/wszystko-co-musisz-wiedziec-o-uchodzcach-i-imigrantach,artykuly,370682,1.html.

36. https://wiadomosci.wp.pl/uchodzcy-6028863260541569c.

37. Oskar Górzyński, Polska coraz mniej przyjazna obcokrajowcom. Rośnie liczba rasistowskich napaści, https://wiadomosci.wp.pl/uchodzcy-6028863260541569c.

38. Aleksandra Gersz, Marsz Niepodległości 2017, http://www.nto.pl/polska-i-swiat/a/marsz-niepodleglosci-2017-swiatowe-media-o-marszu-pokaz-nacjonalizmu-faszyzmu-i-rasizmu,12669490.

39. http://wyborcza.pl/7,75399,22634943,marsz-niepodleglosci-w-zagranicznych-mediach-tysiace-nacjonalistow.html.

40. M. Feliksiak, *Stosunek do praw gejów i lesbijek oraz związków partnerskich*, Centrum Badań Opinii Społecznej. Komunikat Badań, Warszawa, luty 2013, https://www.cbos.pl/SPISKOM.POL/2013/K_024_13.PDF, p. 2, 4.

41. Art. 18 of the Radio and Television Act of 29 December 1992.

42. Art. 21 of the Radio and Television Act of 29 December 1992.

43. Art. 18 of the Radio and Television Act of 29 December 1992.

44. Art. 21 of the Radio and Television Act of 29 December 1992.

Chapter 8

Switzerland

Diversity as a Means of Seduction

Lukas Musumeci and Fabian Odermatt

CHOICE AND LIMITATION OF THE OBJECT OF INVESTIGATION

The editors asked us to analyze the three most popular legally themed TV shows in our country, Switzerland, in November 2017. However, due to the following considerations, we restrict ourselves to one show only, a Swiss series called *Wilder*, which was shown weekly on Swiss television from November 7 until December 12, 2017:

1. The Swiss TV market is divided by three of the four national languages: German, French, and Italian. Hence, there are three submarkets at the linguistic-regional level, each of which competes with a considerably bigger foreign market. Due to the lack of comparability between the linguistic regions, we focus on the German-speaking part.[1]
2. *Wilder* and *Tatort* are the two most popular legally themed shows in November 2017 in Swiss TV.
3. We exclude streaming services for two reasons. First, we lack the necessary data to include them. Neither Netflix, the most popular streaming service in Switzerland, nor its competitors, such as Amazon Prime, publish user numbers or audience figures for their shows by country (even less by domestic linguistic regions). Second, we exclude Netflix because a recent survey suggests there are only about 647,000 Netflix subscribers in German-speaking Switzerland.[2] Comparing this number with the aforementioned audience figures, we can reasonably assume that audience-wise, streaming services do not compete with TV.
4. We can easily determine the two most popular TV shows, but it is not possible to identify a third show from the data available. There are no further

Table 8.1 Viewers and Market share *Wilder* and *Tatort*

Show	*Date (program service)*	*Audience Figures*	*Market Share %*
Wilder (Episode 1)[1]	7.11. (SRF 1)	681,000	41.9
	8.11. (SRF 2)	35,000	8.7
Wilder (Episode 4)	28.11. (SRF 1)	622,000	38.7
	29.11. (SRF 2)	27,000	5.2
Wilder (Episode 2)	14.11. (SRF 1)	613,000	38.0
	15.11. (SRF 2)	16,000	4.5
Wilder (Episode 3)	21.11. (SRF 1)	570,000	35.9
	22.11. (SRF 2)	32,000	11.7
Tatort (Der Fall Holdt)	5.11. (SRF 1)	481,000	25.2
Tatort (Gott ist auch nur ein Mensch)	19.11. (SRF 1)	440,000	21.6
Tatort (Auge um Auge)	12.11. (SRF 1)	352,000	17.9

[1]SRF made *Wilder* available as a stream on their website until the end of December 2017. Streaming figures are not available.
Source: www.srf.ch/medien/publikumszahlen.

legally themed prime-time shows on TV, but a couple of afternoon and late-night fillers, mostly older police shows from Germany (*SOKO Leipzig* and *Kommissar Rex*) or the United States (*Monk*). Their audience numbers oscillate between 1,000 and 20,000 viewers, their market share between 2 and 5 percent.

5. Show number 2, *Tatort* is covered in the Germany chapter of this book, so we focus on the one Swiss show, *Wilder*.
6. *Wilder* has been an event in Switzerland. The audience figures and market shares are extraordinary. Episodes 1, 2, and 6 are among the SRF Top 100 (since 2013) and received critical acclaim. There was broad media coverage even ahead of the broadcasting: background stories, reports from the shooting, interviews with cast and directors, reviews of each episode in every major newspaper. For six weeks, *Wilder* has been the talk of the day: at work and at home, people would puzzle over the crimes and discuss the events and characters in the series. In short, *Wilder* dominated the investigation period, if not the whole year. It is little wonder that the SRG already announced season two.
7. In 2016's *A Transnational Study of Law & Justice on TV*, we noted the lack of Swiss shows with a law and justice theme and regretted the consequence that "depictions of the Swiss legal system are very rare and they are strikingly underrepresented as compared with depictions of foreign legal systems."[3] Now we have *Wilder*, which took inspiration from various well-known and internationally acclaimed series such as *Broadchurch* or *The Killing*. *Wilder* is an original Swiss series: produced by Swiss Television, engaging Swiss directors and screenwriters, starring Swiss actors,

referring to Swiss mythology, reproducing Swiss clichés, and addressing Swiss debates and social policy issues.

For these reasons, we hold it justified, if not even necessary, to limit ourselves to this one production. Before we turn to the series' plot, we will briefly outline seduction theory and establish why we hold this theory suitable for the analysis of filmic depictions of diversity.

SEDUCTION THEORY AND DIVERSITY

We submit the thesis that the filmic representation of diversity themes has the power to deceive and seduce the viewer. This idea is based on seduction theory, a poststructuralist approach in film theory, developed by the German film Scholar Marcus Stiglegger.[4] With recourse to Dianne Hunter[5] and Patrick Fuery,[6] Stiglegger understands film as a medium of seduction at three levels. First, a film seduces to itself, meaning that it must awake and attract the interest of the potential viewer. Strategies on this level include marketing, trailers, cast, budget; they all stimulate expectations. Second, a film can convey a specific, explicit message, such as in ideological propaganda films. Third, much more subtlety, a film seduces to catch hidden, implicit (ideological) subtexts, found on the meta-level. Seduction in this third way lies on the level of performance (e.g., movements, sensuality, sexuality, etc.), narration (e.g., epic narration), and ethics, for example, if the movie exposes the viewer to an ambivalent experience.

Seduction theory normally applies to movies, and so far, no specific theory on seduction by TV series has been developed. We do not attempt to do so in this paper, but we submit that while seduction in TV series might not be genuinely different from seduction in movies, serial narration offers specific seduction techniques. Further, series have a different need to seduce; above all, series have to seduce the viewer after each episode anew. Think for example of cliffhangers at the end of an episode, seducing the viewer to continue watching. In contrast, series regularly lack the uniqueness of the screening as part of a visit to the cinema or overwhelming audiovisual effects often associated with cinematic screenings.

Based on Stiglegger's findings, we claim that depicting diversity in movies and TV series amounts to an ambivalence experience and thus has the power to deceive and seduce the viewer. Showing diversity creates an ambivalent experience, because it exposes the viewer to different, probably contradictory or even irreconcilable realities that nevertheless exist synchronously and thus raise questions and doubts and challenge the viewers' worldviews. Hence, filmic reproduction of diversity is a means of seduction on the third level, seducing the viewer to capture a hidden subtext, ultimately shaping and influencing the viewer's perception of the law. Seduction theory thus is a helpful approach for establishing the influence of filmic representations on the viewer as well as on our culture. In his seminal essay "Law, Lawyers and Popular Culture", Lawrence M. Friedman has carved out the mutual interference between popular culture on the on hand and social issues and legal culture on the other hand. Popular culture is influenced to a considerable degree by social issues and our legal culture, while it has the power to shape our culture and ultimately the law. (FN: Friedman)[7] Whereas it is relatively easy to demonstrate the influence of law on works of pop culture, it is much more challenging to examine how filmic representations of law effectively influence our legal culture. In this context, seduction theory is a helpful approach and instrument, as can be shown through the example of *Wilder*.

BRIEF OUTLINE OF THE SERIES' PLOT

Oberwies, a small alpine village somewhere in the Bernese Oberland, Switzerland, has a dark past and a promising future. Thirty years ago, a landslide buried a school bus, leaving twelve children dead. Now, Karim Al-Baroudi, a rich investor from Egypt, plans to build a luxury holiday resort. An endeavor brings money, work, and hope to Oberwies, a prospect to heal the wounds from the past. However, not everyone profits equally and discord breeds within the village community. The appearance of the investor brings up various conflicts smoldering beneath the surface in the village, conflicts between those who stayed and those who left, between rich and poor, and conflicts within families.[8] While wealthy people, especially Mayor Robert Räber, sense big business opportunities with the upcoming investments, others—especially farmers—are rebelling and refuse to sell their land. Past and future collide: on the 30th anniversary of the catastrophe, Baroudi and his daughter Amina arrive for the ground-breaking ceremony. An event that brings people back who left Oberwies and made impressive careers: Barbara Rossi, Attorney General of Switzerland and designated prosecutor at the International Criminal Court, as well as internationally acclaimed artist Armon Todt.

The morning after the ceremony, Todt is found slain and Amina Baroudi has disappeared without a trace. Did she kill Todt or was she kidnapped, probably by the murderer? Did opponents of the construction project commit the crimes? Is the motive to be found in the village's dark past or is it a rather profane personal one such as envy, hatred, or disappointed love? Almost everyone has a motive for the alleged crime.

The investigation is carried out by cantonal policewoman Rosa Wilder and Federal Criminal Investigator Manfred Kägi. Wilder grew up in Oberwies and is therefore familiar with the local conditions, but has left the village. She is about to leave for California for further training but decide to stay in Switzerland in order to solve this case. Kägi, a loner, broken since the loss of his boyfriend, is initially rather discontentedly involved in the investigation. In the course of their investigation, the two are increasingly caught up with the events personally. When Wilder was less than sixteen years old (Swiss age of consent), she had a romantic affair with Todt, whereas Kägi recognizes in the bodyguard of Baroudi a participant in his former boyfriend's murder. Finally, both Wilder and Kägi are confronted with the question of whether the law offers a sufficient basis to reduce certain ambivalences, or whether it is necessary in individual cases to exceed the limit of legality in pursuit of a fairer result.

Fictitious Oberwies appears as a symbolic microcosm of Switzerland, if not the world, where cultural, religious, sexuality-related, age-related diversity exists. Moreover, it should be noted that certain diversity-related conflicts have always existed within the village community (socioeconomic differences, gender roles, different moral concepts, etc.), while others arise only with the arrival of Al-Baroudi (especially cultural conflicts) or intensify as a result (increasing gap between rich and poor). This very image of Oberwies corresponds to the idea of Switzerland as a nation of diversity, which in this sense is even explicitly enshrined in the constitution.[9] We will show that precisely these differences, and the tensions resulting therefrom, form the motives for potentially criminal actions. The seduction lies in the spectator's desire to resolve the differences, which in part is only possible within the framework of crossing boundaries, as discussed. First of all, however, it is necessary to clarify our concept of diversity, and to explain to what extent the legal reality of Switzerland is reproduced by TV's representation of diversity.

DIVERSITY ISSUES IN *WILDER*

We understand diversity as a sociological concept that is used in the academic context, for the distinction and recognition of group characteristics and characteristics of individuals.[10] Diversity of persons—if also legally relevant—is considered in the context of the present work in particular with reference to the following dimensions: diversity is culture (ethnicity), age, gender, sexual orientation, or religion and worldview. Then there are other socialization-related and cultural differences such as working style, patterns of perception, dialect, etc., which further increase the diversity of a group as its cultural diversity and, depending on the context, also require attention and, if necessary, social recognition.[11]

In *Wilder*, we identified the following specific diversity-related structure features, some of which correspond to current social hot buttons in Switzerland.

ETHNICITY AND RELIGION

The Oberwies village community is ethnically homogenous: there are no foreigners; everyone living there was born and raised there. Enter the Al-Baroudi family, the potential savior, flown into the village by helicopter. Mayor Räber welcomes Al-Baroudi with a remarkably submissive attitude, also revealing some stereotypical views in his attempt not to make any mistakes. Thus, he welcomes Amina nervously saying, "Salem Aleikum," the Arabic greeting which means "peace be unto you." The worldly investor's daughter, noticeably puzzled, answers, "Nice to meet you." Those opposing the construction project do not instrumentalize xenophobic fears for their cause. There is only one "Arabs go home" graffito, hidden in the gas station's bathroom.

The character Karim Al-Baraoudi has an obvious real-life counterpart: Samih Sawiris, an Egyptian entrepreneur who is currently building a large holiday resort in Andermatt. Al-Baroudi is presented as a stereotype of foreign benefactor. The submissive way the village community treats him, except those opposing the project, is stereotypical, pointing to an ambivalence in Swiss politics and the political debate. There seems to be a distinction between the good and the bad foreigner. On the one hand, the Swiss People's Party became the strongest political force in the country by sticking to national conservative course directed against migrants and the European Union. The Federal Act on Foreign Nationals[12] and the Federal Act on Asylum[13] have been made more restrictive several times in recent years, culminating in new constitutional provisions on the expulsion of criminal foreign nationals and on the restriction of immigration. On the other hand, wealthy foreign nationals are more than welcome; some cantons grant them privileged fiscal treatment. An initiative to end this cantonal practice was defeated at the ballots.

In contrast to Karim Al-Baraoudi, is his bodyguard Rashad Rahmani who obviously has connections to terrorist networks and thus appears to pose a real threat to Switzerland's security interests. In this respect, the social cliché of dangerous foreigners is completely fulfilled. As a suspected Islamist, Rashad Rashami is the only character who is thus related to religion, albeit in a fundamentalist context. However, this is a marginal theme of the series.

SOCIOECONOMIC STATUS

There is a divide between rich and poor in the village itself, symbolized in the characters of farmer Paul Wilder and wealthy Mayor Robert Räber. The upcoming investment increases this divide. Räber, the richest inhabitant and owner of a construction company, profits the most, while others, such as Wilder or gas station owner Glutz, fear losing their livelihood. Above them all stands Baroudi who nevertheless attempts to position himself close to the village community. Paul Wilder sabotages the ground-breaking ceremony, sending a billy-goat on to the stage, shouting "a goat will not be enough this time."[14] As a reaction, Baroudi pets the goat, saying it reminds him of the goats his grandfather used to have. He addresses the village: "We have more in common than you think. We all descend from simple peasants and herders. And we are proud of it." However, when his daughter Amina disappears, the most powerful character in the story shrinks down, becoming the most vulnerable person in the village.

The ever-increasing gap between the super-rich and the increasing impoverishment of the lower class, as depicted in the series, is by no means a fiction but a living reality.[15] While Switzerland is still considered the second richest country in the world after the United States, many inhabitants are still affected by poverty. According to the latest figures from the Federal Statistical Office, 7.5 percent of the permanent resident population in private households was affected by income poverty in Switzerland in 2016. This corresponds to around 615,000 people. The most affected groups included people living alone or in single-parent households with underage children, people without secondary education and people in households without participation in the labor market.[16]

GENDER AND MORAL VALUES OF THE MAJORITY

Armon Todt and Rosa Wilder had a relationship when she was less than sixteen years old, which is the Swiss age of consent. From a legal point of view, therefore, Wilder is the victim of a sexual offence. In recent years there has been an increasing tightening of criminal law governing sexual offenses in Switzerland, for example, by adopting the statute of limitations initiative. This means that sexual acts with children are no longer subject to a statute of limitations. People who commit sexual crimes with children are probably the criminals who attract the most contempt and the least sympathy. No one ever wants to take side with a sex offender. The portrayal of Armon Todt as the perpetrator and Wilder as the alleged victim completely opposes this perception. Rosa Wilder is not harmed by the sexual act with an adult per se, but by society's reaction. Finally, her mother forced her to have an abortion. The series creates a courageous image of a suspected sex offender, avoiding clear assignments of victim and perpetrator roles. Thus, the representation is implicitly also a plea for the criminal law to grant more judicial discretion in such cases. Rosa Wilder and Armon Todt seem more open-minded and flexible in their moral concepts than the villagers imprisoned in their rigid, patriarchal and conservative structures. In this respect, both Rosa Wilder and Armon Todt are outsiders in the village community.

GENDER

The series juxtaposes the patriarchal village community and two strong female characters who have left the village and now compete successfully in male dominated professions: policewoman Rosa Wilder and Attorney General Barbara Rossi. Given that so far in Switzerland only one woman has been Attorney General, *Wilder* adopts a progressive position. The reference to reality regarding Attorney General Rossi, who functions here as a filmic image of Carla del Ponte,[17] is obvious. Thus, Wilder and Rossi stand for emancipated, contemporary women who break out of patriarchal structures and realize themselves. This is a development that is as real in Switzerland as is the neo-conservative backlash calling for women to refrain from professional careers and sacrifice themselves entirely to their family responsibilities. Women are still underrepresented in top positions, be it in economics, in public authorities, in politics or in academia.[18] There is a gender pay gap. A German study shows that women are also underrepresented on TV: only a third of all protagonists are female.[19] In this sense, strong female figures, as shown in *Wilder*, are still not a matter of course, not in real life, nor on television.

SEXUAL ORIENTATION

A homosexual policeman, coming from a liberal city to a conservative village, carries a tempting potential to construct diversity-related tension, both individual and social. This is a temptation the show resists. Avoiding any gay stereotypes, the show neither problematizes nor even thematizes Kägi's sexual orientation, but accepts it. He comes out implicitly to the viewer, a framed picture of his boyfriend gives a first hint, later he tells Wilder about his late boyfriend. Kägi is a character who, among other things, happens to be gay rather than a gay character.

That being said, Wilder and Kägi form a remarkable investigation team in an environment where straight men and a rather traditional image of masculinity prevail. However, a short scene shows the subtle way discrimination within the police force works. In the course of a disciplinary investigation against Kägi, the investigator stands out with an arbitrary remark asking Wilder whether she found anything disturbing about Kägi, apart from his being gay. Thus, only when being confronted with other problems, is the "gay card" played against him. This is an example of a mechanism that forces members of minorities to be better and to behave with more integrity than their majoritarian counterparts.

DIVERSITY AS A SEDUCTIVE MOTIF

All the previously described diversity-related characteristics—be it the cultural differences between the family of the investor and the peasants in the village, the gap between rich and poor, the different ideas between patriarchal villagers and strong female roles—are important for the dramaturgy of the series. Diversity always creates conflicts and conflicts are accompanied by tension. The filmic representation of such conflicts is *per se* seductive, as far as it arouses the viewer's desire to reduce these tensions and to search for a possible solution. In this respect, the series seduces the viewer to go on—in the hope of experiencing such a solution as the story progresses. Will the murder ever be solved? Does the disappearance of the investor's daughter have a racist background? Can the hotel project be realized despite cultural and ideological differences within the village community? Can Wilder and Federal Prosecutor Rossi assert themselves in a patriarchal environment? The audience can join in the mysteries and the characters' personal issues and, participate emotionally in the performances. Thus, viewers can energize themselves about the village's backwardness regarding the prevailing sexual morality, they can be afraid of the Arab investor family, or they can get upset about the increasing globalization and economization of tranquil village life. Viewers can participate in cultural conflicts without having to get directly and concretely involved. The viewer is never directly affected by the conflicts shown, but can still judge them and take a position on social matters. It is precisely in this interrelation between TV presentation and audience that seduction can be found.[20] In this respect, diversity in *Wilder* is a seductive motif that addresses the viewer's desires and interacts with them at various levels.

THE SEDUCTION OF BREAKING TABOOS AND CROSSING BOUNDARIES

The character of Armon Todt combines most of the aforementioned diversity-related characteristics. Being one of the few Oberwies born who managed to leave the village, he travelled the world making career as a freelance artist, achieving worldwide fame. Accordingly, he speaks different languages fluently and, due to his cosmopolitan attitude, his ideas and standards regarding morality and culture differ from those of the village community. In this respect, the seduction in the character of Armon Todt seems to be most concrete and obvious. He is himself a seducer in that he obviously exerts a great fascination on young women. Not only Armina Baroudi seems to be attracted to him, also Wilder had a sexual relationship with Armon at a young age. At that time Wilder was not yet sixteen years old. In this respect, Armon is, at least from a legal point of view, a sex offender. Nevertheless, he is not portrayed as a sex-driven monster, contrary to expectation of the viewer. Rather, he appears at the beginning of the series as a jovial, intelligent, sensitive, worldly free spirit that arouses sympathy in the viewer. Furthermore, Wilder does not seem to have been harmed or in any way negatively influenced by her earlier sexual relationship with Armon. It only seems to trouble the villagers, because they cannot reconcile it with their values and morals. In this context Wilder was also forced to have an abortion by her own mother. The aforementioned depiction of Armon breaks not only with the ideas of the villagers, but also with the spectators' image of a criminal, in particular a sex offender. The viewers' expectations are denied recognition in this respect. Therefore, the series requires its viewers to question their ideas, prejudices and desires for filmic representation. Why am I suddenly sympathetic to a child molester? Am I envying this person? If the televisual representation succeeds in moving viewers away from their fixed positions, then seduction has been effective.[21] Here, the series seduces at the third level of seduction: it exposes viewers to an ambivalent experience[22] and leads them away from their original, supposedly consolidated positions. Here, seduction is achieved by forcing viewers to deal with their own sexual morality and desire for the forbidden. In *Wilder*, the viewer is repeatedly forced to deal with various socially anchored taboos resulting from the aforementioned social, religious, cultural or sexuality-related differences, to question his or her existing ideas. In such a breach of taboos lies the special fascination of the series and thus also the seduction. Whenever diversity-related social conflicts are particularly pronounced, the breaking of taboos is also the greatest. The game of crossing borders is a leitmotif of *Wilder* and can be found at several occasions within the plot. Thus, the series repeatedly raises the idea that a satisfying solution to certain social or even personal conflicts is not always possible within the current legal system.

Manfred Kägi realizes that the bodyguard of investor Al-Baroudi, Rashad Ramani, is apparently the murderer of his former life partner. However, Kägi is unable to convict Rashad Ramani of his actions, as too many other interests are at stake—in particular the future hotel project in Oberwies. Rashad Ramani is also protected by the investor family and, ultimately, the Federal Prosecutor's Office, due to both money and influence. Since Manfred Kägi cannot achieve much against the alleged offender with the law, he finally takes the law into his own hands and kills Rashad Ramani himself. It is only through normative border crossing that justice is finally established. Rosa Wilder also has to adopt self-help to achieve a fairer result when she tries to withdraw her own father from prosecution and conceals corresponding evidence. Her father, being a poor farmer, has no other way of evading prosecution, unlike Rashad Ramani. Both Kägi and Wilder therefore break taboos and cross legal boundaries to achieve greater justice. Like Armon Todt, Kägi and Wilder also breach standards, forcing viewers to question and revise their values: is objective law always fair? Is it okay to breach the limits of the law in order to achieve higher objectives? Are we sympathizing and fraternizing with criminals here? This examination of the breach of taboos allows the viewer to participate in the breach of the norm. Thus, the taboo of taboo-breaking also passes over viewers and becomes part of them without viewers having to expose themselves to the risk of facing the legal consequences of their mental experiment.[23] The question of exceeding the norm is a legal matter. In this respect, corresponding representations within the *Wilder* series are all reflections of law. With respect to crossing borders, the viewer is seduced and indirectly stimulated to think, which provides evidence of how and why legal representations in *Wilder* influence viewers. Such an influence is not only found in the context of crossing borders, but also in seduction through the search for truth.

SEDUCTION OF THE SEARCH FOR TRUTH

As already mentioned, *Wilder* tells the story of various social conflicts that need to be resolved. Some of these conflicts have, as shown, a diversity-related background, while others refer to the personal characteristics of the protagonists. The representation arouses in the viewer the desire to find a possible solution for these conflicts. The greatest tension is the crime of murder, which the investigator Wilder tries to solve as the series progresses. Moreover, the act in question seems to be directly linked to the village's other dark secret, the mysterious landslide that took place years ago. The viewer is encouraged to act as a detective, solve the case, and assign one of the possible motives to the crime in question. Thus seduction appears here as a kind of challenge, which lies primarily in the mystery itself.[24] The seduction plays with the secret of the murdered artist and appeals to the urgent need of the observer to have an encounter with the truth in uncovering the mystery. The seduction provokes in this sense the hope for the truthfulness that seems to be hidden behind the mystery. This is the greatest seductive potential of the series: the search for truth.[25] The viewer can speculate, exchange hypotheses and long for the final resolution together with other viewers. In this sense, *Wilder* appears as an event, as a collective search for the truth and the desire for salvation. Here, in turn, parallels with law, and in particular with criminal procedure law, can be drawn. After all, the search for truth is ultimately an intrinsic part of any criminal procedure.[26] In this respect, every crime film, every crime series, is ultimately a reflection of the law. Since seduction is based on the secret itself, the dissolution of the secret can only be a disappointment, indeed it must be a disappointment. The dissolution in *Wilder* disappoints in several respects. Rosa Wilder's own father turns out to be a murderer: a personal disappointment, if not a personal defeat, for the ambitious investigator, seducing her to cover for her father. She tries to undo the exposure of the mystery and to make any evidence that points to the truth disappear, a desperate attempt to push the unwanted truth back into mystery. Once the truth is exposed, however, there is no turning back. Ultimately, the investigator must also understand this. She comes to terms with the disappointment of truth. The dissolution of the mystery, however much Wilder insisted on it, gives her no redemption, no liberation, and also no satisfaction, but only pain and grief. The question remains whether the truth is really better or more desirable than the secret or the moment of deception. At this moment, the viewer thinks back to Prosecutor Rossi's words: "Better a lie that heals, than a truth that hurts." This sentence is the overriding theme of the whole series. Suddenly the truth no longer seems to be as desirable as lies and deception. Thus the seductive power lies always in what is currently unattainable.[27] The disappointment of the main character is also immediately felt by the viewer. The unmasking of the father of Rosa Wilder as the murderer can hardly be surpassed in its banality. It is more banal and disappointing than all the hypotheses the viewer has prepared in the run-up to the final dissolution. The dissolution is an insult to the personal investigation and efforts of the viewer. What remains is the disillusionment of the viewers and the ultimate realization that the seductive power of what is shown lies only in their imagination. Nothing else, moreover, must apply to criminal proceedings, because any judgment is a disappointment in the sense that it can never fully satisfy all the previous evidence and requests of the parties, it can never undo what has happened, never heal the wounds of the past.[28] Legal truth is ultimately a construct[29] that cannot claim truthfulness or absolute justice. At the end of *Wilder* we see a broken policewoman turning her back on the village and leaving it for the city. It is ultimately an escape from the unpleasant truth. At the same time, however, this flight is accompanied by hope for something new. Here we find it again: the seduction, in the form of the spectator's hope for another season of the series and for more mysteries to be solved.

CONCLUSIONS

We have shown that diversity-related features in *Wilder*, some of which refer to real legal problems, expose the viewer to an experience of ambivalence. The greater the experienced ambivalence, the greater the respective need of the viewer to reduce and solve these conflicts and ambivalences. Diversity-related conflicts are therefore a seductive legal feature within the series. However, it is not always possible to resolve televisually depicted ambivalences within the framework of existing legal boundaries, making it unavoidable to exceed the law. The question whether the occasional transgression of boundaries should be allowed in order to achieve a higher level of justice is again a legal question. The exceeding of the norm forces viewers to deal with and question their own value systems. Finally, we have discovered that the search for legal reflection can also be tempting for viewers. Legal representations within the framework of the *Wilder* series—be they those with a direct connection to diversity, those that refer to the violation of legal norms, or those regarding the search for truth—are fundamentally suitable for seducing, manipulating and thus influencing viewers' perceptions of the law. Of course, this influence is not always causal, and undoubtedly depends on various individual characteristics and the socialization of viewers. Not every viewer sympathizes with Armon Todt or actually deals with the various questions of justice that have been raised. Not every viewer participates in the solution of the posed mysteries. In this respect, seduction theory can only be used to determine staging intentions that aim to create an ideal-typical effect in a hypothetical, gender-neutral viewer.[30] The theory does not address whether the intended effect actually occurs in the individual viewer. Therefore, seduction theory refers to an ideal synthesis of a media-competent viewer on the one hand, and self-confident seductive filmic staging on the other.[31] Seduction theory offers a theoretical foundation for establishing the influence of TV representation on our legal culture. It is upon empirically based media impact research to determine how and to what extent the influence occurs.

NOTES

1. For a detailed outline of the Swiss TV market see Musumeci and Odermatt (2016), 195–196.
2. https://www.moneyland.ch/de/streaming-schweiz-studie-2018.
3. Musumeci and Odermatt (2016), 209–210.
4. Stiglegger (2006, 2012, 2014); for a good introduction to the theory in English see Stiglegger (2007).
5. Fuery (2000).
6. Hunter (1989).
7. Friedman (1989).
8. The opening credits introduce this motif of conflicts breaking open: a crack forms in the ice, growing continuously, until it reaches the village.
9. Art. 2 (1) "The Swiss Confederation shall protect the liberty and rights of the people and safeguard the independence and security of the country. (2) It shall promote the common welfare, sustainable development, internal cohesion and cultural diversity of the country."
10. Salzbrunn (2014), 5–6.
11. Ibid.
12. Federal Act on Foreign Nationals of December 16, 2005.
13. Asylum Act of June 26, 1998.
14. This is a reference to a Swiss legend. The people needed the devil's help in order to build a bridge. In return the devil claimed the first soul who passes the bridge. The people then outsmarted the devil and sent a goat instead of a human being.
15. Fluder et al. (2017).
16. https://www.bfs.admin.ch/bfs/de/home/statistiken/wirtschaftliche-soziale-situation-bevoelkerung/soziale-situation-wohlbefinden-und-armut/armut-und-materielle-entbehrungen/armut.html.
17. Carla del Ponte was the Swiss Attorney General from 1994 to 1999. Subsequently she was a Prosecutor at the International Criminal Tribunal for the former Yugoslavia.

18 On the underrepresentation of woman amongst legal academics, see Schultz and Böning (2018).

19. Prommer and Linke (2017). We can observe a similar misrepresentation of gender in legal education materials, see Valentiner (2017).
20. Stiglegger (2006), 23.
21. Ibid.
22. Ibid., 33–35.
23. Sigmund Freud also recognized this seductive aspect of the taboo model by recording that the taboo breaker is infectious for imitation, see Freud (1913), 36.
24. Cf. Stiglegger (2006), 45.
25. Cf. also the thesis of the French poststructuralist Jean Baudrillard in Baudrillard (1983), 130.
26. Their (2014), 252–253.
27. Cf. Stiglegger (2006), 45.

28. Müller-Dietz (1971), 266; Kunz (2009), 578.
29. Damaska (1998), 291.
30. Stiglegger (2012), 89.
31. Ibid.

BIBLIOGRAPHY

Baudillard, J. (1983) *Lasst euch nicht verführen!* (Berlin: Merve).

Baumann, H., Gallusser, M., Herzog, R., Klotz, U., Michel, C., Ringger, B., and Schatz, H. (eds.) (2017) *Technisierte Gesellschaft* (Zürich: edition 8).

Damaska, M. R. (1998) "Truth in Adjudication," *Hastings Law Journal* 49, 289–306.

Feury, P. (2000) *New Developments in Film Theory* (New York: Palgrave Macmillan).

Fluder, R., Farys, R., Hümbelin, O., and Jann, B. (2017) "Die Verteilung der Vermögen in der Schweiz," in Baumann, H., Gallusser, M., Herzog, R., Klotz, U., Michel, C., Ringger, B. and Schatz, H. (eds.).

Freud, S. (1913) [1956] *Totem und Tabu* (Frankfurt a. M.: Fischer).

Friedman, L. M. (1989) "Law, Lawyers, and Popular Culture," *Yale Law Journal* 98, 1579–1606.

Hunter, D. (ed.) (1989) *Seduction and Theory: Readings of Gender, Representation, and Rhetoric* (Champaign: University of Illinois Press).

Kleiner, M. S. and Rappe, M. (eds.) (2012) *Methoden der Populärkulturforschung* (Berlin: LIT).

Kunz, K. L. (2009) "Tatbeweis jenseits eines vernünftigen Zweifels – Zur Rationalität der Beweiswürdigung bei der Tatsachenfeststellung," in 121 *Zeitschrift für die gesamte Strafrechtswissenschaft* 572–606.

Lange-Kirchheim, A. and Pfeiffer, J. (eds.) (2014) *Film und Filmtheorie* (Freiburg: Königshausen und Neumann).

Müller-Dietz, H. (1971) "Der Wahrheitsbegriff im Strafverfahren," *Zeitschrift für evangelische Ethik* 15, 257–272.

Musumeci, L. and Odermatt, F. (2016) "Switzerland," in Robson, P. and Schulz, J. L. (eds.) 195–210.

Prommer, E. and Linke, C. (2017) *Audiovisuelle Diversität. Geschlechterdarstellungen in Film und Fernsehen in Deutschland* (Rostock: Universität Rostock) available at www.imf.uni-rostock.de/forschung/kommunikations-und-medienwissenschaft/audiovisuelle-diversitaet.

Robson, P. and Schulz, J. L. (eds.) (2016) *A Transnational Study of Law and Justice on TV* (Oxford: Hart).

Schultz, U. and Böning, A. (2018) *De jure und de facto: Professorinnen in der Rechtswissenschaft: Geschlecht und Wissenschaftskarriere im Recht* (Baden-Baden: Nomos)

Salzbrunn, M. (2014), *Vielfalt/Diversität* (Bielefeld: Transcript).

Stiglegger, M. (2006) *Ritual und Verführung. Schaulust, Spektakel und Sinnlichkeit im Film* (Berlin: Bertz + Fischer).

Stiglegger, M. (2007), "Rituals of Seduction: Seductive Strategies of the Cinema," available at www.ikonenmagazin.de/artikel/Rituals_of_Seduction.htm.

Stiglegger, M. (2012) "Die Seduktionstheorie des Films, Verführungsstrategien filmischer Inszenierung," in Kleiner, M. S. and Rappe, M. (eds.) 85–114.

Stiglegger, M. (2014) "Verführung – Wunsch – Begehren, die Seduktionstheorie des Films am Beispiel von Darren Aronofskys Black Swan," in Lange-Kirchheim, A. and Pfeiffer, J. (eds.) 49–64.

Thier, A. (2014) "Die Wahrheit und nichts als die Wahrheit, Wirklichkeitskonstruktion und Wahrheitsanspruch im Recht," in *Zeitschrift für Kulturphilosophie*, 8(2), 247–260.

Valentiner, D. (2017) *(Geschlechter)rollenstereotype in juristischen Ausbildungsfällen* (Hamburg: Universität Hamburg) available at www.uni-hamburg.de/gleichstellung/download/studie-rollenstereotypen-geschlechterforschung-1.pdf.

Chapter 9

United States

Some Representations of Ethnicity, Gender, and Diversity on Law-Related TV Series

Christine A. Corcos

BACKGROUND

In this essay, I continue and extend the examination of US legal and law-related television shows, which I began in my chapter included in 2016's *A Transnational Study of Law and Justice on TV*.[1,2] My first essay focused on the image of law, justice, and policing generally on legal and law-related shows broadcast on US television. In addition, I included a short explanation of the development and current state of US broadcasting and the landscape of US media law. In this chapter, I examine three US television shows more closely with regard to their depiction of women and minorities.

In keeping with the methodology of the 2016 project, I examined Nielsen ratings for various parts of the country and various legal and law related television series for the 2016/2017 broadcast year.[3] As I noted in the 2016 book, no overall reporting system exists for the entire country that can identify the "top ten" shows in any particular subject area because US households can subscribe to one of a number of different cable services as well as streaming services, and those services offer different combinations of shows. Households might also opt to receive shows over the air rather than through a cable service or via streaming. In addition, depending on the part of the country one examines, various audiences tend to favor different shows. While no three legal or law-related shows as a group consistently ranked at the top of any list of reported "top shows" for the period, the three shows that ranked generally highest on all lists were *Bull, How to Get Away with Murder* (*HTGAWM*), and *Law & Order: SVU*.[4]

After identifying these three shows, I watched the episodes for each one broadcast during the month of November 2017. Because November is a month in which over the air networks broadcast a number of sports events, these networks generally preempt several episodes in favor of sporting events, and they did so in November, 2017. Thus, I examined fewer than twelve episodes in total.

GENDER, ETHNICITY, AND DIVERSITY IN THE UNITED STATES

All female US citizens received the right to vote through an amendment to the United States Constitution ratified in 1920.[5] Male African American citizens had received the right to vote in 1870 under the Fifteenth Amendment.[6] In 1965, President Lyndon Baines Johnson signed the Voting Rights Act, intended to prohibit state and local barriers to the right to vote.[7] Congress passed the Equal Rights Amendment (ERA) in 1972 but the required number of states (38) failed to ratify it by the extended 1982 deadline.[8] The ERA would provide that "equality of rights under the law shall not be denied or abridged by the United States or any state on account of sex."[9]

Over the years, the United States Congress has enacted a number of laws to protect the civil rights of women and minorities. The best known include the Equal Pay Act of 1963, prohibiting employers from paying their male and female employees differently if those employees are performing "substantially equal work,"[10] Title VII of the Civil Rights Act of 1964 (Title VII),[11] prohibiting employment discrimination based on race, religion, sex, or national origin, and the Americans With Disabilities Act of 1990 (ADA),[12] which prohibits discrimination against the disabled in employment, public services and accommodations, and the provision of telecommunications. The Age Discrimination in Employment Act of 1967 (ADEA) prohibits employment discrimination against those forty years of age or older.[13] In addition, a number of federal, state, and municipal agencies protect the rights of women and minorities in the United States.[14]

WOMEN AND MINORITIES IN THE LEGAL PROFESSION

Margaret Brent was the first woman to practice law in the American colonies, as early as the 1640s.[15] Myra Bradwell attempted, but failed, to be admitted to practice law in Illinois in 1869; the US Supreme Court affirmed the state's right to deny that admission in 1873 on the grounds that the right to practice law is not one of the "privileges and immunities" protected under the Fourteenth Amendment.[16] However, other states, including Iowa in 1869, Missouri in 1870, and Illinois in 1873 admitted women to practice.[17] African American males began to be admitted to the bar much earlier; Maine admitted Marcus Bolling Allen in 1844.[18]

That women and minorities have been admitted to practice for over a century does not mean that discrimination against them has disappeared. Many reports attesting that female lawyers face bias in their chosen profession exist and proliferate.[19] Their complaints about poor treatment concern law firm management, in particular, more and more minority women are choosing to leave practice.[20] A 2014 report indicates that implicit bias among law firm partners can result in unequal evaluations which impact the careers of African American and white associates at those firms.[21]

The American Bar Association provides an annual report on women in the legal profession, breaking down the number of female lawyers in private practice, corporations, legal academia, and the judiciary (at both the federal and state levels).[22] It also provides some information on the gender wage gap for female lawyers. According to the 2017 survey, which reports information from the Bureau of Labor Statistics, female lawyers in 2015 (the most recent data then available) earned less than 90 percent of the salary of male lawyers.[23] Another source notes that in 2014, of the 1,132,000 lawyers in the United States, 5.7 percent were black or African American, 32.9 percent were female, 4.4 percent were Asian, and 5.6 percent were Hispanic.[24] The National Association for Law Placement (NALP) reports that in 2017 the number of self-reporting LGBTQ lawyers rose to 2.64 percent, up from 2.48 percent in 2016.[25]

Legal dramas present tension between minority lawyers (female lawyers, disabled lawyers, LGBTQ lawyers, lawyers of any ethnicity) and the norm (white male heterosexual middle- or upper-middle-class lawyers) in ways that demonstrate that the lawyers who fall outside the norm must fight for acceptance and against discrimination. That discrimination may come from the law itself or it may come from society, including other lawyers.

AN EXAMINATION OF THREE POPULAR US LEGAL DRAMAS

The most popular legal shows in the United States during the 2017 season were *Bull* (CBS),[26] *Law & Order: SVU* (*SVU*) (NBC), and *How to Get Away with Murder* (*HTGAWM*) (ABC).[27] Each of the series presents a fair amount of diversity in its characters and storylines.[28] However, they differ in the ways they approach questions of ethnicity, diversity, and gender, and in the ways they suggest that ethnicity, diversity, and gender interrogate the legal system.

Bull, which features a forty-something Caucasian male trial consultant Dr. Jason Bull, played by Michael Weatherly, offers the audience the least-exposure to diverse characters and storylines. The other two shows have female leads: Viola Davis as Annalise Keating, the African American criminal law professor and practicing lawyer on *HTGAWM* and Mariska Hargitay as Olivia Benson, the Caucasian police officer on *SVU*. *SVU* and *HTGAWM* are more specifically interested in the interaction of legal issues and ethnicity, diversity, and the law.

Bull is a formulaic legal drama and has at its center a fairly traditional white male character who dominates the action. While he is not a lawyer, Jason Bull participates in the legal process in ways familiar to the US television audience. *SVU* is also formulaic to the extent that it mimics the traditional format that *Law & Order* creator Dick Wolf has developed over the years for the franchise. But it places at its heart a female police officer to drive the action, and it takes as its subject a contentious legal issue, that of sexual violence in contemporary US society. *HTGAWM* also includes a number of minority characters: Oliver Hampton and Connor Walsh who are gay, African American detective Nate Lahey, Annaliese's sometime boyfriend who eventually begins to work against her,[29] and African American law student Michaela Pratt. In all three series, the female characters who exhibit assertive behavior must contend with attacks on their characters and ethics in ways that the male characters do not suffer. Double standards abound.

BULL

Set in Manhattan, the series *Bull* stars Michael Weatherly as the founder of Trial Analysis Corporation (TAC), a company that provides trial consulting assistance for lawyers in need of guidance in the selection of jurors for their cases. Dr. Jason Bull is the consultant, a man with three PhDs.[30] As the show's website notes, Dr. Phil McGraw's early career[31] is the inspiration for the show, which places the consultant, rather than a lawyer, at the center of the action.

The show is primarily focused on the lead character, whose purpose is to select winning jurors for the lawyers who hire him. He is not interested in the causes of the clients those lawyers represent. The fact that Jason Bull has so little interest in morality emphasizes the "game" aspect of the law. He and his team employ technology that reinforces that notion of the legal process, from the continuous computer searching that they seem addicted to, to the "mirror juries" that they use and the monitoring of the reactions of the real life juries in the courtroom throughout the trials.

From the beginning, we know that Jason Bull is an outsized character, smarter and more capable than anyone else, including any lawyer he encounters. Indeed, he must outthink both lawyers and judges in order to prevail in every case. Bull's self-confidence and self-importance overwhelm every other character in every episode. Although in some scenes another character may "one-up" him temporarily, as Arti Cander, another trial consultant, does in the episode "The Devil, the Detail,"[32] Bull always triumphs. He often lectures the lawyers on his team, including his ex-brother-in-law Benny Colón, about trial tactics and strategy. He may sit in on a client interview, even before he is part of the case, as in the episode "No Good Deed."[33] He continually puts himself or others who perform the same function he does in the place of the lawyer, as in "The Devil, the Detail."[34] When a question to a witness results in an admission that does not go his client's way, he mutters that "she" (the trial consultant on the opposing side) is "representing" her client "like a bulldog." Normally, the "bulldog" characterization attaches to lawyers, not to others on a client's team, as does the verb "to represent" in the legal context. In "The Devil, the Detail," the trial consultant on the opposing side, Arti Cander, is female and Indian American, and Bull finds her disturbingly challenging as well as very attractive.[35] That she does not prevail at trial is not her fault. The client is not forthcoming to the lawyer or to her and fails to disclose crucial information. The parties end by settling the case. Otherwise, her skills are certainly equal to Bull's, as he concedes in the final scene of the episode. Bull's "win" in this episode is not truly his; the writers hand it to him. Benny Colón forces the witness in this case, who is the strong and confident female CEO of a drug company, to come close to admitting on the stand that she has committed at least an ethical breach, if not a crime. Her testimony forces her lawyer to ask Benny to discuss a settlement, which ends the trial. The episode must show the female CEO as a failure in order for Bull to succeed. The trial consultant must also "fail" in order for Bull to prevail, even though trial consultants, as we know from Bull's business model, take cases as they find them and work for the lawyers who hire them, regardless of the moral worth of the client's argument. The depiction of the women in this episode is quite alarming. Cander is capable, attractive, and intelligent. She and Bull share a career and educational attainments, and certainly some interests. Indeed, we see them having a drink together at the end of the episode. They could at a minimum be friends. They do not have to have an intimate relationship. Yet he is abusive and rude to her. Why? Because he misreads her at the beginning, he thinks she is a lawyer when they meet and discovers that she is, like him, a psychologist. He wants revenge. His reaction is swift. He begins to harass her, suggesting that she has mimicked his career. Because he is the central figure of the show, we must see him as the hero, but his behavior is hardly heroic here. He is petty and vindictive. She, on the other hand, is never nasty to him. Arti Cander is calm, pointing out that in fact she does not actually use his methods, noting that she does not use "mirror juries."

When the client in "No Good Deed" makes a decision about a plea deal offered to her, Bull, not the defense lawyer handling the case, says he will call the assistant district attorney (ADA).[36] When the lawyer eventually withdraws from the case, Bull takes charge.[37] Bull is not a lawyer, and a lawyer should be performing these functions. This particular series sends the audience the explicit and, for a legal drama, unusual message that someone other than the lawyer or judge (or perhaps the police officer) can be the most significant individual in the legal system.[38] It also suggests that someone other than the lawyer knows the law, often better than the lawyer.[39] As an early review of the show suggests, "[A]pparently the kind of game-playing depicted actually goes on, but it sure isn't pleasant to think about . . . . The principle of being judged by an impartial jury of peers is a myth?"[40]

Bull does present a number of diverse characters. Among the permanent cast members are Bull's ex-brother-in-law, a Latinx lawyer, a white female psychologist, an African American female investigator, and a white female computer expert. However, because of Bull's dominance as a character, the show tends to marginalize these other individuals. In particular, the female characters refer to Bull constantly as "Dr. Bull" and tend to cater to him, taking very traditional female "helper" roles, even though all of these individuals are part of the same team.[41] In traditional lawyer dramas, the lawyer would be the dominant figure, and the other characters would assist him, but ultimately in support of a client. On *Bull*, the characters appear to be supporting players concerned about Bull's well-being. Women in particular are more likely to play these roles.

Jason Bull's brother-in-law Benny Colón (played by Freddy Rodriguez) is one of a handful of Latinx lawyer characters on television, but we rarely see him in action independently, either in court or behind the scenes in trial preparation. One might expect that because of his background and his role as a defense attorney, Benny would show some sympathy and indeed empathy toward particular defendants or marginalized groups. Indeed, one might hope for that message from the show.

As the lawyer who is sometimes in charge of the case, and certainly the expert on legal procedures, Benny should be leading the team's approach to proceedings, but Bull's dominant personality and over-the-top approach (three PhDs and a seemingly unbeatable track record) forces Benny into the background. Similarly, Danielle ("Danny") James, the African American investigator (played by Jaime Lee Kirchner), Marissa, the Caucasian psychologist, and Cable, the Caucasian female computer expert, all of whom we assume Bull employs because they are more than competent in their fields, have relatively little to do until Bull orders them to produce results. Again and again, we see a white male in a position of authority over minority and female characters. Further, the male is the manipulator, rather than the characters we would normally expect to see as manipulators—the females. Interestingly, in the episode "The Devil, the Detail," Cable encourages the parents of a friend to ask Bull to involve the team in finding out why the young man killed himself while participating in a series of drug trials. The resulting proceeding becomes extremely complicated; Cable becomes despondent, blames herself, and apologizes to Bull. Her reaction is typical for a self-doubting young woman. Bull could have declined to take the case. He has much more experience than she and anyone else on the team and makes it a point to remind them of that. Indeed, he builds his entire business model on his ability to manipulate people and obtain desired objectives. He also makes it clear that he makes the rules. Instead, however, he responds snarkily, "Well, that's why I normally make it a point not to work on behalf of immature slackers who quit without notice, lie without giving it a second thought, and jump off rooftops without any regard for people they leave behind. But that's just me." Cable is crushed, and the rest of the team is understandably downcast.

Similarly, the female lawyer in "No Good Deed" is competent and presents a trial strategy for the client that has a fair chance of success. She wants to argue that standardized school testing is inherently unfair. Bull, who is not an attorney, wants to use a trial strategy based on Machiavelli, a "fourteenth-century philosopher" and present a necessity defense.[42] As the lawyer notes, one presents a necessity defense in criminal cases, not in fraud cases. When she goes "off-script," during voir dire, he says to her, "I thought we had a strategy," and she replies, "*You* thought we had a strategy. . . . You thought I was working for *you*." The exchange presents the lawyer as argumentative and nasty, unwilling to follow Bull's advice, and Bull as competent. Yet, she is correct about the law. Later, Bull encourages the client to proceed to trial even though the prosecutor offers an attractive plea deal. The lawyer, who actually represents the teacher's union, and thus the teacher, withdraws from the case, leaving the teacher without representation. Still, we are invited to see Bull's actions as heroic and advisable, even though he admits that he did not anticipate the lawyer's reaction, although he is an experienced psychologist. Eventually, the jury convicts the client. The episode presents the female lawyer who does not cooperate wholeheartedly with Bull as disagreeable, even though her assessment of the situation is accurate.

In "Thanksgiving,"[43] Bull sends his team off to enjoy the holidays and finds himself alone to handle a case. Leaving aside the high unlikelihood that such a thing would happen (a lawyer might have to see a client on Thanksgiving, but a trial consultant would not be called upon in this way on a holiday), Bull meets with an African American lawyer on his own and heroically begins to deal with a very difficult situation, that of an African American boxer accused of murdering his neighbor, an African American drug dealer. (The lawyer is also African American.) The reason for the emergency is risible—jury selection begins the day after Thanksgiving. Only an incompetent trial lawyer would wait until Thanksgiving Day to contact a trial consultant for a trial that begins the day after, and this lawyer is obviously not incompetent.

Additionally, this particular episode presents Bull's presumably competent female employees Marissa and Cable as incompetent to make good choices in their personal lives. Marissa becomes romantically involved with a man who tells her someone mugged him and stole his passport. She helps him replace it through her connections and provides him with financial assistance, only to discover that he has stolen from her. The inference is that smart women make foolish romantic choices. In the same episode, Benny impulsively gives his airplane ticket to an attractive young woman he meets in the airport departure lounge. We are meant to understand that although he has only known her for a few hours, his choice is both romantic and ethically good. Marissa's choice, to assist her boyfriend, whom she has known for weeks if not months, is also romantic and ethically good, but incorrect, because her boyfriend is a criminal. Benny is a more effective judge of character than she is. *Bull* is essentially a traditional legal drama. It tends to pose no ethical or moral questions that it cannot answer in the forty to forty-five minutes that it has to tell its story.

LAW & ORDER: SPECIAL VICTIMS UNIT (SVU)

Law & Order: SVU is one of the many series in the Dick Wolf *Law & Order* franchise, and currently the only *Law & Order* series still on the air.[44] The show, set in New York City, highlights cases specifically involving sexual assault, rather than cases that involve all types of crime, as did the original *Law & Order*.[45] Because of the subject matter, the episodes tend to focus on female characters, young women of varying social classes and ethnicities.[46] They do not necessarily end with the incarceration of the evildoers. Instead, the show concentrates on presenting the audience with the difficulty of creating a viable case that the district attorney can take to trial, and the pain that the victims, the accused, and society all suffer. The regular cast on the show includes Lt. Olivia Benson, a white woman in her late forties, played by Mariska Hargitay, Detective Amanda Rollins, a white female detective in her twenties, played by Kelli Giddish, Detective Odafin Tutuola, an African American male detective, played by Ice-T,[47] Rafael Barba, a Latinx prosecutor in his forties, played by Raúl Esparza, Dr. Melina Warner, an African

American female medical examiner, played by Tamara Tunie, and Alexandra Cabot, a white female prosecutor in her forties, played by Stephanie March.[48] The show emphasizes three dimensional characters, in particular women, as they face the impact and the result of sexual violence, noting that such violence has lasting effects on families and friends as well as victims. In this series, the legal system tries but does not always succeed in addressing many or some of the harms that sexual assault causes. One study notes that with regard to interactions among diverse characters, police procedurals such as *Law & Order: SVU* tend to represent relatively high percentages of such interactions.[49] The study suggests that an explanation for this result might be that:

> many police procedurals take place in urban city environments . . . where one might expect to find more Racial/Ethnic/Identities living close to one another. Moreover, due to the tendency for these shows to routinely bring in a number of new characters for the primary case in each non-serial episode, there is more potential to introduce individuals of different REIs. As a result . . . , the depiction of characters as victims and perpetrators may be more diverse in this genre.[50]

The episode "Unintended Consequences"[51] presents the *SVU* team investigating the mysterious drug death of a white "Jane Doe" teenager. The unit discovers that the teen had escaped from a residential drug treatment center, and further, that the treatment center and a series of halfway houses are engaged in a scheme to overbill insurance companies, ensure that the patients become re-addicted, and thus make certain that the treatment center and the halfway houses have a never-ending supply of patients and endless income stream. The *SVU* team enlists the assistance of Rosemary Taylor, the center's manager, to try to obtain some financial records to expose the scheme. Taylor becomes so angry at the center's owner that she kills him with an overdose of Fentanyl before the officers can arrest him. She then surrenders. This particular episode presents us with an Asian American female lawyer as the legal representative for the treatment center. The prosecutor points out that bringing charges in the case is difficult because no clear link exists between the center and the halfway houses. Thus the District Attorney's office would have trouble demonstrating causation. The employee in this episode is highly moral. That is, she understands both the illegal act she commits (murder) and the necessity that she admit to it. She also understands if she does not act, the center's director will probably go free and will not alter his behavior. She is willing to go to prison, to sacrifice the rest of her life, and to prevent him from creating future drug addicts. The lawyer for the treatment center is singularly unappetizing to the viewer. She seems rather cold and unwilling to cooperate with the police, but of course she is defending her client. Viewers confronted with a male lawyer in the role would have a different perception of such an attorney. They might not like him, but they would understand that he is doing his job. Because this lawyer is female, the audience is likely to find her distant and unfeeling. I would also suggest that because she is Asian American, an overwhelmingly white audience may find her reserved and "difficult to read,"[52] particularly because people expect women in general to be more overtly emotional than men.

The episode "Something Happened"[53] centers on Lt. Benson's investigation and reconstruction of a rape victim's account. Initially, the survivor, Laurel a white female in her late thirties, can remember nothing, but Lt. Benson is patient and soon the woman reveals a grim story that includes not just rape but child abuse. Laurel also admits that she might have stabbed her rapist with a pair of scissors. The woman's sister, Leah, a lawyer, has arrived; she now agrees to provide her sister with legal advice. This decision is not wise. The two sisters begin to quarrel as the interview continues. Laurel reveals that Leah was also a victim of child abuse. Leah insists that she drop the subject and accept her counsel. Laurel refuses. Leah finally storms out of the interview room. This episode presents the attorney in a very poor light. We have no reason to believe she has any expertise in criminal law, and she should probably not have agreed to provide her sister with representation beyond advising her not to speak to the police. She should have sought out competent counsel for her sister. The two have a difficult relationship based on their shared experience of child abuse at the hands of their father.

The emphasis in this episode is on the victim's credibility. Only slowly do we begin to consider that the victim, while she might have undergone a horrific event, might also be misremembering what happened. Here the episode presents what is a common theme in this show. While some individuals are nearly completely evil (like the director of the drug treatment center in "Unintended Consequences"), most are not. Most people are complex. Laurel is remembering a terrible event, but she is also a perpetrator. She actually killed an innocent person. What is a difficult issue for this series to handle is presenting stories that present victims as perpetrators as well. In cases of rape, domestic violence, and child abuse, those who typically bring the charges are women and children. They are also the ones who are the least likely to be believed. When "Something Happened" suggests that female victims are not being completely truthful, it opens the door to allegations that we should not believe women victims.[54]

Both of these episodes illustrate the difficulty of reconciling the letter of the law with the spirit of justice. In neither case does the law seem adequate to address the actual wrong that the center director in "Unintended Consequences" or the abuse that the dead father in "Something Happened" actually committed. In "Unintended Consequences" the killer understands that she is committing murder, but she makes a calculation that the justice system will never hold her victim fully accountable for his actions (in her case, the death of her son from a drug overdose). In "Something Happened," the victim makes the mistake of becoming involved with a mentally ill woman, who kills him.[55] He certainly deserves justice. But should society imprison an individual who does not fully understand the nature and quality of her act because of the wrongs a family member has committed against her?

HOW TO GET AWAY WITH MURDER (*HTGAWM*)[56]

HTGAWM is set at fictional Philadelphia (Pennsylvania's) Middleton University's law school. It centers on criminal law professor Annalise Keating and several of her most promising students. The show's title encapsulates its approach. In particular, the idea that an individual can manipulate the legal system to obtain a favorable outcome is not one that the show supports, particularly if the character is female, poor, gay, or nonwhite. These characters must know the system better than wealthy and privileged white males, but they must also be honest. If they are not, the workings of the legal system will ultimately destroy them, either because honest lawyers and judges will bring them down, or because other, more corrupt individuals will intervene to vanquish them in some way. Actually trying to get away with murder is ultimately doomed to failure; such an enterprise dooms those who try it to destruction. One should also note that of all the crimes humanity condemns, murder is one of the most heinous because it is irreversible. We cannot restore the victim to life. Thus, "getting away with murder" implies the ultimate commission of an act without regard for the consequences. The characters in this drama discover that such a thing is simply not possible.

HTGAWM takes many liberties with real-life legal education, from the notion that a law school would allow its first year students to participate in a professor's current cases, to the novel (and completely unacceptable) idea that a professor would abandon teaching case law in favor of teaching her own cases to the exclusion of all else.[57] In addition, Keating is teaching criminal law, a required first-year course in the law school curriculum, although she is an adjunct professor. The American Bar Association, one of the legal academy's accrediting agencies, generally requires that full-time faculty teach such courses.[58] While a school might, out of necessity, recruit a practitioner to teach such an important course for one year (perhaps because the designated faculty member is for some reason unavailable), it would certainly mount an effort to find a permanent member of the faculty to teach it in the future.

Keating's imperious approach in the first season of the show eventually leads to disaster in later seasons as her marriage implodes and her unethical behavior comes to the attention of the disciplinary board. The "murder" in the first season is her husband's untimely death. Her students decide to cover it up to help her. What happens afterward is a series of events unrolling from the cover-up that leads all of the characters in the show down a very dangerous path. Each of the November 2017 episodes illustrates ways in which the *HTGAWM* characters confront ethical problems and several succumb to ambitions or weakness hinted at in the first season of the show.

The "Stay Strong, Mama"[59] episode centers on the two female attorneys, recurring character Caucasian Bonnie Winterbottom, who now works as a prosecutor, and Annalise Keating. Annalise, having lost her position at Middleton and working hard to keep her law license, is trying to push ahead with a class action lawsuit against the city. She confronts the district attorney and in particular his young assistant district attorneys, urging them to think about the victims of the district attorney's wrong-headed policies. The judge in the class action suit tells Annalise that she might not be an appropriate lawyer to pursue the case because she is politically vulnerable. However, Annalise perseveres, both because of ambition and because of her need to vindicate herself. The episode also presents Annalise in a tense interaction with her Hispanic therapist, as she reveals feelings about the death of her child years before and complains about Bonnie. Meanwhile, Michaela and Tegan, both ambitious, female, African American attorneys at a prestigious law firm, discuss the difficulties that women face in law practice in life and love. Michaela comes to like and admire Tegan, causing difficulties amongst the other law students.

In particular, this episode highlights the difficulties that various characters have in making decisions concerning personal and professional choices. Annalise should probably turn the class action lawsuit over to another attorney, but refuses. Michaela should be loyal to Tegan, the attorney who believes she could be Michaela's mentor. Certainly, none of the law students should be planning to set one of their colleagues up for theft.

The episode "Live. Live. Live"[60] illustrates how the main characters continue to develop their relationships, generally in destructive ways, even as various events sound the opposing themes of life and death. The episode also further expands several of the themes the series introduced beginning in its first season. Bonnie visits Annalise's house and declares her feelings, but Annalise asks her to leave. At an office party, Simon admits he has feelings for Connor. Meanwhile, he also overhears a plan to plant Tegan's access card on him. He becomes furious, seizing Laurel's purse. The gun in her purse discharges, striking him. Laurel runs off, going into premature labor, and seeks help by going to Annalise's building. With a 911 operator's assistance, Annalise delivers Laurel's baby.

While many of the characters in *HTGAWM* are African American, little of the interaction among the characters deals overtly with race. Annalise does take cases that have overt racial aspects, as does the class action lawsuit, but the students relate easily to one another without much mention of racial difference. However, the female law students seem to gravitate more easily to female mentors than to males, and the female lawyers and law students have much stronger presences than do the males. None of them seem to consider the rules of legal ethics or the law itself to be any sort of constraint on their behavior. Among the law students, the brooding Laurel is particularly dominant, leading the group to create a plan to frame her father for murder, at the same time that she seems reluctant to confront her father for his evil deeds. The ambitious Michaela befriends attorney Tegan as part of the plan to frame Laurel's father. These depictions of women, either in the workplace or preparing for professional careers, are really unfortunate. The images of their personal relationships are also rather sad. Laurel, awaiting the birth of her child (which comes in "Live. Live. Live.") does so without the father, who died in Season 3 as a result of the events set in motion in Season 1—the first death.[61] She eventually has to do battle with her father over custody of the child. Michaela doesn't understand her boyfriend's objections to the fact that she keeps a bridal gown from another relationship in her closet. Annalise continues to see a therapist who willingly involves his ex-wife in his professional relationship with her. All of these women seem trapped by men in their pasts.

The only stable personal relationship the show offers is that between Connor and Oliver, whose relationship has steadily intensified. Same-sex partners are still the exception rather than the rule on US television, and shows tend to portray gay men, particularly ambitious and good-looking ones, as less than faithful, but this particular relationship is increasingly solid and based on shared interests and values.

CONCLUSION

Bull is a relatively traditional legal drama, except for the fact that the protagonist is not a lawyer. It tends to take few chances in terms of presentation of ethnicity, gender, or diversity, because its interest is in presenting a formulaic story in which the main character "rides to the rescue" and presents a winning solution. *Law & Order: SVU* follows a less-used but still recognizable formula. The emphasis on law enforcement personnel, who receive information about a crime, identify and then pursue suspects, decide on the most likely perpetrator, and then arrest him or her and deliver that person to the district attorney. Because it examines domestic violence and sexual assault as its thematic material, its victims are usually young and female.

However, despite this, the show presents a much wider range of ethnically diverse characters. *How to Get Away with Murder* is the most adventurous of the three shows. It offers a years-long convoluted story arc as well as shorter stories within seasons. It bristles with twists and turns, and viewers know it for its flashbacks and flash forward. It unfolds in serial format, not in the familiar self-contained episodes of traditional dramas. Its timeline is complex, recalling such earlier TV series as *Damages.*[62] Because it is set in a racially diverse city and in a contemporary law school, the writers have the opportunity to present ethnically and racially diverse characters. That television series exhibiting such different approaches rank among the most popular suggests that as American audiences fragment further, networks and content creators will offer material that recalls traditional formats while taking some opportunities to offer viewers characters and situations that reflect changes in US society.

NOTES

1. Richard C. Cadwallader Associate Professor of Law, Louisiana State University Law Center; Associate Professor, Women's and Gender Studies, Louisiana State University, Baton Rouge, LA.

2. Christine A. Corcos, "United States," in *A Transnational Study of Law and Justice on TV 211* (Peter Robson and Jennifer L. Schulz, eds., Hart Publishing, 2016).

3. I examined the following lists: http://www.indiewire.com/2017/05/most-watched-tv-show-2016-2017-season-the-walking-dead-this-is-us-football-1201832878; https://www.ranker.com/list/legal-drama-tv-shows-and-series/reference; https://tvseriesfinale.com/tv-show/suits-season-seven-ratings;https://tvseriesfinale.com/television-ratings/tv-ratings-by-season-channel;http://www.imdb.com/list/ls058489550.

4. NBC, 1999, https://www.nbc.com/law-and-order-special-victims-unit.

5. "The right of citizens of the United States to vote shall not be denied or abridged by the United States or by any state on account of sex." United States Constitution. Nineteenth Amendment. However, a number of states had granted women the right to vote before 1920, including Wyoming (1890), Colorado (1893), Utah and Idaho (both 1896), Washington (1910), California (1911), and Arizona, Kansas, and Oregon (all 1912). See National Constitution Center, Centuries of Citizenship: A Constitutional Timeline, at https://constitutioncenter.org/timeline/html/cw08_12159.html.

6. "The right of citizens of the United States to vote shall not be denied or abridged by the United States or by any State on account of race, color, or previous condition of servitude." United States Constitution. Fifteenth Amendment.

7. See 52 U.S.C. §10101. Voting rights (2018). However, in the 2013 case of *Shelby County v. Holder,* the Supreme Court held (5–4) that two sections of the Act are unconstitutional because the formula the government has been using to apply

them is based on outdated information. Unless Congress replaces the old formula with a new one, the Act loses its ability to address voting rights discrimination. *Shelby County v. Holder,* 570 U.S. 2 (2013).

8. In 2017, Nevada became the latest state to ratify the amendment. See Terry Carter, *Nevada Ratifies Equal Rights Amendment Decades After Deadline,* ABA Journal, March 23, 2017, at http://www.abajournal.com/news/article/nevada_ratifies_equal_rights_amendment_decades_after_deadline. Today, ERA supporters are pursuing a different strategy, that of persuading the states that did not ratify the amendment to adopt their own ERAs. See AAUW, *Let's Ratify the ERA: A Look at Where We Are Now,* at https://www.aauw.org/2015/11/05/ratify-the-era.

9. A member of Congress often introduces a bill to re-introduce the ERA. In the 115th Congress, Representative Carolyn Maloney introduced the bill. See https://www.congress.gov/bill/115th-congress/house-joint-resolution/33/text.

10. The Equal Pay Act and other relevant legislation is available at 29 U.S.C. §201 *passim.* See https://www.gpo.gov/fdsys/pkg/USCODE-2011-title29/html/USCODE-2011-title29-chap8.htm.

11. 47 U.S. C. §2000e et seq.

12. 42 U.S. C. §12101.

13. 29 U.S. C. §631.

14. See for example the Equal Employment Opportunity Commission (EEOC), which handles complaints brought under Title VII, the Equal Pay Act, the ADA, and other laws (https://www.gpo.gov/fdsys/pkg/USCODE-2011-title29/html/USCODE-2011-title29-chap8.htm), the New York State Department of Labor, which investigates complaints brought under state labor laws and regulations (including child labor laws and regulations) (https://www.gpo.gov/fdsys/pkg/USCODE-2011-title29/html/USCODE-2011-title29-chap8.htm), and the Los Angeles Housing and Community Investment Department Agency, which handles housing discrimination complaints under housing laws (http://hcidla.lacity.org/fair-housing).

15. Pamela J. White, *Margaret Brent, Maryland's First Female Lawyer,* 7 RRGC 11 (Spring 2007).

16. *Bradwell v. State*, 83 U.S. 130, 139 (1873).

17. Ellen A. Martin, "Admission of Women to the Bar," *The Chicago Law Times* 76 (1887), available at http://wlh.law.stanford.edu/wp-content/uploads/2011/01/waite-adminssiontobar1887.pdf.

18. Joseph Gordon Hylton, "The African-American Lawyer: The First Generation: Virginia as a Case Study," 56 *University of Pittsburg Law Review* 107, 108 (1994).

19. Joyce S. Sterling and Nancy Reichman, "Overlooked and Undervalued: Women in Private Law Practice," 12 *Annual Review of Law and Social Science* 373 (2016). Also available at https://www.annualreviews.org/doi/abs/10.1146/annurev-lawsocsci-120814-121705.

20. Liane Jackson, "Minority Women Are Disappearing from BigLaw—and Here's Why," *ABA Journal*, March 2016, at http://www.abajournal.com/magazine/article/minority_women_are_disappearing_from_biglaw_and_heres_why?utm_source=Copy+of+Spring+Newsletter+2016&utm_campaign=NJWLA+Newsletter&utm_medium=email.

21. *Written in Black & White: Exploring Confirmation Bias in Racialized Perceptions of Writing Skills, Nextions, (Yellow Paper Series)* at http://nextions.com/wp-content/uploads/2017/05/written-in-black-and-white-yellow-paper-series.pdf.

22. In January 2017, female attorneys were 36 percent of the total number of US attorneys. They were fewer than 25 percent of all law firm partners and fewer than 45 percent of law firm associates. They were fewer than 25 percent of Fortune 500 General Counsel. They were 31 percent of law school deans, fewer than 50 percent of 1L students, fewer than 49 percent of 2L students, and fewer than 48 percent of 3L students. They held 46 percent of leadership positions and 38 percent of the Editor in Chief positions on the law reviews of the top fifty law schools as ranked by US *News & World Report* (according to the 2012–2013 Law Review Diversity Report, *New York Law School Law Review*, and Ms. JD, December 2013 survey). They held three of the eight filled seats on the US Supreme Court (one seat remained unfilled at the time), 35.9 percent of the available appellate federal seats, and 33 percent of the available federal district court seats. See American Bar Association, Commission on Women in the Profession, A Current Glance at Women in the Law, January 2017 at https://www.americanbar.org/content/dam/aba/marketing/women/current_glance_statistics_january2017.authcheckdam.pdf at 2–5.

23. Id. at 6.

24. Pro-Quest Statistical Abstract of the United States 2016, Table 633 (ProQuest, Lanham, MD).

25. "LGBT Representation Among Lawyers in 2017," NALP, at https://www.nalp.org/0118research. See also Institute for Inclusion in the Legal Profession, "IILP Review 2017: The State of Diversity and Inclusion in the Legal Profession" at http://www.theiilp.com/resources/Pictures/IILP_2016_Final_LowRes.pdf.

26. CBS, http://www.cbs.com/shows/bull.

27. ABC, http://abc.go.com/shows/how-to-get-away-with-murder.

28. On LGBTQ diversity in HTGAWM, see Richard Lawson, "Is *How To Get Away With Murder* the Most Progressive Show On Television?" *Vanity Fair*, October 16, 2014 at https://www.vanityfair.com/hollywood/2014/10/how-to-get-away-with-murder-gay-sex. On accuracy in the show, see Alex Rich, "*How to Get Away with Murder* Is Just Wrong," October 8, 2014 at https://abovethelaw.com/2014/10/how-to-get-away-with-murder-is-just-wrong/?rf=1.

29. See Season 4.

30. http://www.cbs.com/shows/bull/about.

31. Anthony D'Alessandro, Dr. Phil McGraw on CBS' Bull: "It's Not Autobiographical, It's Inspired By," *Deadline*, August 10, 2016, at http://deadline.com/2016/08/bull-tca-michaeal-weatherly-cbs-dr-phil-mcgraw-1201801403.

32. CBS, first aired November 14, 2017.

33. *No Good Deed*, CBS, first aired November 7, 2017.

34. Id. at 31.

35. In her chapter in this collection, Jennifer L. Schulz explains how the show marginalizes this character as a woman and as a representative of an ethnic minority.

36. Ibid.

37. Ibid.

38. Law-related TV shows do use as their main characters relatively often, and sometimes place medical examiners at the center of the action. While shows that feature amateur sleuths or private detectives, medical examiners, or even psychics, are not rare, *Bull* features a character who is not an attorney actually taking over some functions that the attorney performs. That is unusual, and sends what I consider an odd message to the audience.

39. Richard Gabriel criticizes the show for its inaccurate portrayal of trial consultants and its effect on audiences in a two-part article. See Richard Gabriel, "Trial Consultants, TV Law, and a Load of Bull," *The Jury Expert*, December 16, 2016, at http://www.thejuryexpert.com/2016/12/trial-consultants-tv-law-and-a-load-of-bull; "What Television Can Teach Us About Trial Narrative," *The Jury Expert*, December 16, 2016, at http://www.thejuryexpert.com/2016/12/what-television-can-teach-us-about-trial-narrative.

40. Neil Genzlinger, "Review: Michael Weatherly, Recast as a Jury-Puppeteer on Bull," *New York Times*, September 19, 2016, at https://www.nytimes.com/2016/09/20/arts/television/review-michael-weatherly-recast-as-a-jury-puppeteer-on-bull.html.

41. See for example the concern they exhibit over *Bull* in the episode "Thanksgiving."

42. Machiavelli lived in the fifteenth century (1469–1527), https://www.biography.com/people/niccol%C3%B2-machiavelli-9392446.

43. CBS, first broadcast November 21, 2017.

44. The *Law & Order: True Crime* mini-series, which also airs on NBC, features dramatizations of high-profile crimes and trials. *Law & Order True Crime: The Menendez Murders* aired in 2017 (https://www.nbc.com/law-and-order-true-crime-menendez). At least one scholar has completed a content analysis of race and ethnicity on *Law & Order* and *NYPD Blue*, concluding that both series underrepresent ethnic populations in New York City, as content analyses of other TV shows have also found. Melissa F. Koski, "The Representations of Race and Ethnicity of *NYPD Blue* and *Law & Order*: An Analysis of the Portrayal of New York City on Crime and Police Drama" (Undergraduate Thesis, Boston College, 2007) at 76–77.

45. NBC, 1990–2010, http://www.imdb.com/title/tt0098844/?ref_=nv_sr_2.

46. At least one scholar has devoted her PhD dissertation to a study of the show. *See* Karla Guevara Corriere, "Depictions of Sex Offenders in the Television Show, *Law and Order: SVU*" (University of Hartford, 2013). A 2007 content analysis of the show argues that most victims are young, female, and white, and that the perpetrators are, at least initially male and black. S. Britto, T. Hughes, K. Saltzman, and C. Stroh, "Does 'Special' Mean Young, White and Female? Deconstructing the Meaning of 'Special' In *Law & Order: Special Victims Unit*," *Journal of Criminal Justice and Popular Culture*, 14(1) (2007), 39–57. It would be interesting to see an updated study.

47. Ice T's birth name is O'Shea Jackson.

48. http://www.imdb.com/title/tt0203259/?ref_=nv_sr_1; https://www.nbc.com/law-and-order-special-victims-unit.

49. J. M. Riles, K. Varava, A. Pilny, and D. Tewksvury, "Representations of Interpersonal Interaction and Race/Ethnicity: An Examination of Prime-Time Network Television Programs," *Journal of Broadcasting & Electronic Media*, 62(2) (2018), 302–319 at 316–317.

50. Riles et ak., "Representations of Interpersonal Interaction and Race/Ethnicity," 302–319 at 316–317. "REI" means racial/ethnic identity.

51. NBC, first aired November 8, 2017.

52. R. E. Jack, O. G. B. Garrod, H. Yu, R. Caldara, and P. G. Schyn, *Facial Expressions of Emotion Are Not Culturally Universal, PNAS*, 109(9) (May 8, 2012), 7241–7244, at http://www.pnas.org/content/109/19/7241. On Asians in film, see Nancy Wang Yuen, *Reel Inequality: Hollywood Actors and Racism* (New Brunswick, NJ: Rutgers University Press, 2016).

53. NBC, first aired November 29, 2017.

54. Attitudes toward the unacceptability existence of domestic violence slowly seem to be changing from the assumption that it does not exist, it happens elsewhere, or women should simply accept it, to recognition that it is unacceptable. See Bernice Yeung, "Domestic Violence Survey Shows Shift in Attitudes, Awareness," *HuffPost*, November 12, 2012, at https://www.huffingtonpost.com/2012/11/12/domestic-violence-survey-_n_2115528.html.

55. For a content analysis of the depiction of mental illness in law-related US TV shows, see Scott Parrott and Caroline T. Parrott, "Law & Disorder: The Portrayal of Mental Illness in US Crime Dramas," *Journal of Broadcasting & Electronic Media* 59 (December 2015), 640–657.

56. ABC, 2014—(http://abc.go.com/shows/how-to-get-away-with-murder).

57. Attorney Nakia D. Hansen takes Keating's approach to legal pedagogy apart in Clover Hope, "Objection: A Real Lawyer Fact Checks *How to Get Away with Murder*," *Jezebel*, October 10, 2014, at https://jezebel.com/objection-a-real-lawyer-fact-checks-how-to-get-away-wi-1644750449. Hansen notes that the show does hit some of the right notes, particularly with regard to the stress and substance abuse that can accompany the law school years.

58. "The full-time faculty shall teach substantially all of the first one-third of each student's coursework." American Bar Association. Standards and Rules of Procedure For Approval of Law Schools 2017-2018. Standard 403. Instructional Role of Faculty. https://www.americanbar.org/content/dam/aba/publications/misc/legal_education/Standards/2017-2018ABAStandardsforApprovalofLawSchools/2017_2018_standards_chapter4.authcheckdam.pdf.

59. ABC, first aired November 2, 2017. A character in each episode speaks the title in one of the scenes.

60. ABC, first aired November 16, 2017.

61. "Who's Dead," aired November 17, 2016.

62. (FX, 2007–2010), (Audience Network, 2011–2012). *Damages* starred a white woman lawyer, played by Glenn Close.

Appendix

TV Shows Mentioned in This Book

13th: A documentary on race in the criminal justice system, which argues that slavery has evolved into modern day mass incarceration.

Acquitted (*Frikjent* original Norwegian title) (2015): Norwegian series focusing on the return to the town of Lifjord of a man twenty years after being acquitted of the murder of his high school sweetheart and the repercussions of his return over eight episodes.

Akte X: Die unheimlichen Fälle des FBI: A very popular crime series originally broadcast under the title *X-Files* from 1993 to 2002. It is an American production and successfully combines elements of crime investigation, science fiction, and horror and is thus regarded as one of the first German mystery series. The series was revived in 2016 and is still being produced and broadcast. Each crime investigated in each episode sooner or later proves to be related to the main plot of the series as a whole, which is a huge conspiracy between aliens and politicians. Main characters Scully and Mulder alternately doubt and believe in this conspiracy, as well as the existence of aliens and the supernatural in general.

Alarm für Cobra 11 ("Alerta Cobra"; original German title: *Alarm für Cobra 11*) (Cuatro, 2014): A long-running successful German export about the highway police: German highways are depicted as a thoroughfare for Europe's organized crime—making the show transnational by definition. Its transnationality can be observed in both content and format. Germany, shown in Spain.

America ("América"): A Brazilian telenovela broadcast in 2005—the story of an illegal Brazilian immigrant to the United States and of those she left behind in Brazil.

Anything Goes ("Vale Tudo"): A Brazilian telenovela broadcast between 1988 and 1989; a divorced woman moves to Rio de Janeiro to make a living and becomes a very successful businesswoman, but witnesses the greed, corruption, and infidelity of the people around her in the Brazilian society.

Babylon ("Babilônia"): A Brazilian telenovela, also known internationally as *Ambitious Women*, which was broadcast in 2015—the story of two childhood friends who become arch-enemies, once one of them becomes rich.

Bad Cop or *Kriminell Gut*: A German television series that premiered in 2017 on RTL Television. Twin brothers *Jesko* and *Jan Starck* lead very different lives. While *Jesko* became a successful detective inspector, *Jan* has taken the career of a criminal and is thus on the other side of the law. But in a fateful moment, everything suddenly changes when *Jesko* is fatally injured in a police operation involving *Jan*. *Jan* then takes on the identity of his deceased brother to save his own life.

Belfer ("The Teach") (2016, 2017): A Polish television crime-mystery-thriller series starring Maciej Stuhr broadcast by Canal+ Poland. It tells the story of a high school Polish language teacher from Warsaw Paweł Zawadzki (Maciej Stuhr), who arrives in the small town of Dobrowice to teach in the local school. As he accommodates into the new reality, he starts to investigate the recent murder of one of the school's students. In the second season, the title character teacher Paweł Zawadzki is forced to take a job in one of the prestigious high schools in Wrocław to penetrate the students' environment and find out more about the mystery that is hidden behind missing of three students. Poland.

Better Call Saul: An American crime drama series. It is a spin-off prequel of *Breaking Bad*. Set in the early 2000s, *Better Call Saul* follows the story of conman turned small-time lawyer, Jimmy McGill, six years before the events of *Breaking Bad*, showing his transformation into the persona of criminal-for-hire Saul Goodman.

Between the Lines (BBC 1992–1994): Followed the work of the fictional Complaints Investigation Bureau looking at claims of police corruption in the Metropolitan Police in London—male lead with a male and female assistants.

Black Silk (BBC 1985): Eight episodes and a single season focusing on a fictionalized version of controversial black barrister Rudy Narayan and his work helping various members of minority ethnic communities.

Blue Bloods (2010–): An American police series that follows the Reagan family of police officers with the New York City Police Department (NYPD). Frank Reagan is the police commissioner. Frank's son Danny is an NYPD detective, his son Jamie is an NYPD police officer, and his daughter is an assistant district attorney.

Bones (FOX, 2005–): A forensic anthropologist Dr. Temperence Brennan (Emily Deschanel) and a FBI Special Agent Seeley Booth (David Boreanaz) team up to solve years-old crimes based on the examination of human remains. USA, shown in Poland.

Breaking Bad (2008–2013): An American crime drama in which Walter White (Bryan Cranston), a struggling and depressed high school chemistry teacher, is diagnosed with lung cancer. Together with his former student, he turns to a life of crime by producing and selling crystallized methamphetamine to secure his family's financial future before he dies.

Broadchurch: Eleven-year-old Dany Latimer is found dead on the beach in his hometown of Broadchurch, a fictitious place in southwest England. More than a murder mystery, the show traces the impact of grief, mutual suspicion and media attention on a village community. Great Britain.

Bull (CBS, 2016–): Protagonist Dr. Jason Bull is a psychologist, jury consultant, and CEO of his company, Trial Analysis Corporation. He His firm, Trial Analysis Corporation. He travels across the United States to consult on behalf of clients, assisting lawyers and legal teams as they select jurors, strategize, and prepare for trial. United States.

Carandiru: Other Stories ("Carandiru: Outras Estórias"): A Brazilian television series inspired by the national best-seller "Estação Carandiru" broadcast in 2005—the routine of the large penitentiary inside the city of São Paulo.

Clone, The ("O Clone"): A Brazilian telenovela broadcast between 2001 and 2002—the story of a prohibited romance between Jade, a Muslim woman, and a nonreligious man, whose premature death becomes an opportunity for experiences with human cloning.

Collateral (BBC, 2018): Police procedural in four parts following the female-led investigation of the murder of a pizza delivery driver with complex interlinked conspiracy-type storylines involving political figures, the Army, sexual harassment and immigration.

Cracker (ITV 1993–2006): Obese, chain-smoking alcoholic gambling criminal psychologist stars in a crime drama set in Manchester solving crimes for the Greater Manchester police involving complex psychological motivations—US version ran for a single season 1997–1998.

Criminal Minds: Police procedural drama about a federal law enforcement unit. The show follows the FBI's Behavioral Analysis Unit—a unit specialized in profiling serial killers or perpetrators that display sociopathic and/or psychopathic tendencies. In each episode, one case is investigated and is usually closed, either by arrest or by death of the criminal. USA.

Crossing Jordan: An American crime drama series that aired on NBC from 2001 to 2007. It starred Canadian actress Jill Hennessy as Dr. Jordan Cavnaugh, a crime-solving forensic pathologist employed in the Massachusetts Office of the Chief Medical Examiner.

CSI: Crime Scene Investigation (CBS 2000–): Horatio Caine (David Caruso) leads a team of police department investigators solving the most odd and ghastly crimes using the most advanced forensic techniques and analysts. Spin offs CSI: Miami (q.v.), CSI: NY (q.v.), and CSI: Cyber. CSI: Miami (CBS, 2002–2012).

Damages (FX, 2007–2010, Direct TV Audience Network, 2011–2012): A legal drama focusing on the law firm of attorney Patty Hewes (Glenn Close) and her associates, and a nemesis, played by a notable guest star (the first season Ted Danson played this character, Arthur Frobisher). The show followed one story arc per season. The series was also famous for its use of parallel narratives and ethical ambiguities.

DCI Banks (ITV 2010–2016): Based on the books by crime writer Peter Robinson, this standard police procedural follows the cases of the eponymous hero and his female assistants in the north of England in two-part episodes over five seasons.

Death in Paradise (BBC 2011–): British-French crime drama with a fish out of water British police detective posted to a fictional Caribbean island, Saint Marie, to assist the local force of three under the oversight of a smooth Commissioner. The detective solves murders in a Poirot style reveal at the end of each episode. Britain.

Dempsey and Makepeace (ITV 1985–1986): Oddball pairing of British aristocratic police detective and working class New Yorker solving crimes for the London Metropolitan Police running for three seasons.

Double Identity ("Dupla Identidade"): A Brazilian television series broadcast in 2014; a serial killer is investigated by a chief police investigator and a forensics psychologist under the pressure of politician afraid that these crimes may ruin his chances of re-election.

Driving Judge ("De Rijdende Rechter"): A Dutch television reality show aired since 1995, in which a judge drives throughout the country to hear local disputes and solve conflicts in a relatively informal way.

Endeavour (2012–): Police detective series set in Oxford, England, following the career of Endeavour Morse (later of Inspector Morse q.v.) when he has just started as a Detective Constable in the mid-1960s with an irascible boss on ITV1 primetime. Britain.

Father Brown (2013–): 1950s English-country village setting for tales of unworldly seeming priest to solve murder cases to the annoyance of a series of local Police Inspectors—based on the GK Chesterton character from the 1920s.

Federal Police: The Law Is Applied to Everyone ("Polícia Federal: A Lei Vale para Todos"): A Brazilian police investigation film directed by Marcelo Antunez and released in 2017—a fictional narrative inspired by the ongoing investigation of corruption in Brazil called "Car Wash Operation."

The Fixer (ITV 2008): Ex-solider recruited by police to act as their assassin for various criminals and rogue police officers over two seasons.

Grantchester (2015–): A young cleric helps his friend, a police detective, solve murders in rural Cambridgeshire. Britain.

Happy Valley (2014–): Catherine Cawood copes with her life as a divorced uniformed Police Sergeant, with a recovering drug-using sister and young child, in the rural North of England. Britain.

Hannibal: Explores the early relationship between the renowned psychiatrist and his patient, a young FBI criminal profiler, who is haunted by his ability to empathize with serial killers. American.

Hawaii Five-0 (CBS, 2010–): Steve McGarrett (Alex O'Loughlin) returns home to Hawaii to catch his father's killer. Meanwhile he is offered by the governor a possibility to build his own task force (Hawaii-Five) as a special police unit. USA.

Hinterland (S4C, 2013–): Detective Tom Mathias (Richard Harrington) moves to Aberystwyth in Wales, where he leads a local investigation unit. Together they solve crime mysteries form the area. Britain.

How to Get Away with Murder (ABC, 2014–): A criminal law professor hires her most promising students to work in her law firm; they are caught up in a baffling murder in which most of the main characters in the series are suspects.

The Hunter ("O caçador"): A Brazilian television series broadcast in 2014; an ex-con police officer tries to demonstrate his innocence after serving his prison time.

Hustle (BBC 2004–2012): Team of five con artists targeting a person whose actions are illegal and/or immoral and making sure that they get their just desserts. Set in London.

India: A Love Story ("Caminho das índias"): A Brazilian telenovela broadcast in 2009—the story of a prohibited romance between Bahuan, an untouchable, and Maya, a woman from a higher caste.

The Indian Detective: A four-hour miniseries/dramedy starring Indo-Canadian Russell Peters, who is a famous stand-up comedian. The show is filmed on location in Cape Town, Mumbai, and Toronto, and stars Peters as a Toronto police officer, Doug D'Mello, who becomes involved solving drug cartel-related crimes while visiting his father in Mumbai.

Inspector Morse (1987–1983 and 5 specials 1995–2000): Police drama set in Oxford. It followed the murder-solving intellectual Inspector Morse and his plodding assistant, Sergeant Lewis and an irascible boss over thirty-three episodes and seven series and specials on ITV1 primetime. Two spin offs: *Lewis* and *Endeavour* (q.v.). Britain.

In the Form of the Law ("Na Forma da Lei"): A Brazilian television series broadcast in 2010; five colleagues from law school reunite a long time after their graduation for the revenge of a colleague brutally murder by the son of a powerful politician.

Irrational Heart ("Insensato Coração"): A Brazilian telenovela broadcast in 2011—the story of two brothers and their personal dramas, including an airplane accident in which one of them becomes paraplegic.

Jessica Jones: An American web television series created for Netflix and based on the Marvel Comics character of the same name. Jessica is a former superhero with superhuman strength who runs her own detective agency. The series has a noir tone, features a strong lesbian, and tackles difficult topics such as rape, assault, and posttraumatic stress disorder (PTSD).

Judge Judy (1996–): Syndicated reality small claims court TV show featuring retired Manhattan trial court judge Judith Sheindlin. Parties agree to Sheindlin's authority before appearing on the show. USA.

Judge Rinder (2014–): Afternoon show with a young gay barrister, Alex Rinder, deciding cases relying on legal principle much more than shows like Judge Judy. Britain.

Killing, The (Fox Television Studios, 2010–2014): US version of the Danish crime series *Commissioner Lund*: In which Mireille Enos embodies the role of criminal policewoman Sarah Linden, who tries to solve the murder of a young girl in Seattle and ends up in a network of lies and corruption. USA.

The Knock (ITV 1994–1997; 1999–2000): British crime drama centered on the actions of customs officers in the south of England mixing running storylines and stand-alone formats.

Kommissar Rex ["Inspector Rex"] (Sat. 1, 1994–2004): A German-Austrian crime-show taking place in Vienna. Police dog Rex and his human partners solve murder mysteries in and around Vienna. Germany-Austria.

LA Law: A television series from the United States broadcast between 1986 and 1994, in which the backstage of a fictional law firm from Los Angeles was revealed for a large audience with discussions of controversial legal topics, such as capital punishment, abortion, gay rights, sexual harassment, and domestic violence.

Law and Order (NBC 1990–2010): A combination of police procedural and legal drama, created by Dick Wolf, which follows a now-familiar pattern. In the first half of the show, detectives investigate a crime, usually a murder, and arrest a suspect, and in the second half, prosecutors and defense attorneys participate in the trial of the accused. This divided show descends from the

"Arrest & Trial" pattern. Wolf updated it by focusing on the prosecution. Most of the episodes derive in part from actual cases but the writers change fact patterns, usually by adding more serious crimes and changing venues. However, the show has been criticized for this "ripped from the headlines" tendency, and at least one person has sued for defamation. *Law & Order* gave rise to a number of spinoffs: *Law & Order: Criminal Intent, Law & Order: LA, Law & Order: Special Victims Unit,* and *Law & Order: Trial by Jury.* USA.

Law and Order: SVU (NBC, 1999–): The longest-running law and order show. Produced by Dick Wolf, the show follows the special victim's unit of the NYPD. as its members investigate some of New York's most heinous offenses. The Special Victims Unit, a specially trained squad of detectives in the NYPD, investigate sexually related crimes.

Law and Order: True Crime (NBC, 2017): An American true crime anthology series that dramatized the trial of Lyle and Erik Menendez, twin brothers who were convicted in 1996 for the murder of their parents, José and Kitty Menendez.

Law and Order: UK (ITV, 2009–2014): British adaptation of the American series with the split between the police apprehension and the forensic adjudication phase. Running for eight seasons.

Life Behind Bars: Visiting Hour (Channel 4, 2017): Intimate look at visiting hour at the maximum security prison Low Moss, Scotland.

Lifers Behind Bars (Channel 4, 2017): A look behind the bars at the experiences and perspectives of long-term prisoners in a maximum security Scottish prison.

Line of Duty (BBC, 2012–): British series focusing in the work of internal anticorruption body, the fictional AC12 of the Central Constabulary with four principal protagonists. Filmed in Birmingham and Northern Ireland but in no clear location.

To Live the Life ("Viver a Vida"): A Brazilian telenovela, also known internationally as *Seize the Day*, which was broadcast between 2009 and 2010—the story of two young top models and their personal dramas, including a bus accident in which one of them becomes paraplegic.

The Love for Life ("Amor à Vida"): A Brazilian telenovela, also known internationally as *Trail of lies*, which was broadcast between 2013 and 2014—the struggle of a wealthy family for control of a hospital in São Paulo.

Lovejoy (BBC, 1986–1994): Light-hearted adventures of a roguish British antique expert in East Anglia as he seeks to ensure that other more nefarious characters get their come-uppance as they try to get an edge in this murky world of fakes and forgeries.

Lucifer: An American fantasy police procedural drama-comedy based on the DC Comics character. The series revolves around Lucifer Morningstar, who is actually the Devil. He abandons Hell for Los Angeles where he runs his own nightclub and becomes a consultant to the Los Angeles Police Department.

Luther (BBC, 2010–): Conflicted black British detective investigates crimes as well as his own psyche over five seasons of serious crime set in London drawing on influences from Holmes and Columbo according to its creator.

Making a Murderer: A docuseries that tells the real story of a man who served almost twenty years in jail for a crime he did not commit, then was released, and arrested again for a different murder.

Marcella (ITV, 2016–): London setting for the return to work of a female detective looking into the unsolved murders committee by an unidentified serial killer eleven years on. In the second series, she continues to investigate another contemporary serial killer. Written by the creator of Scandinoir success *The Bridge*.

Marvel's Luke Cage: An American web TV series created for Netflix based on the Marvel Comics character of the same name. Mike Colter stars as Luke Cage, a former convict with superhuman strength and unbreakable skin who now fights crime and corruption. Luke Cage was in an unsuccessful relationship with fellow superhero Jessica Jones.

Marvel's Daredevil: An American web TV series created for Netflix based on the Marvel Comics character of the same name. Blinded as a young boy, Matt Murdock fights injustice by day as a lawyer, and by night as superhero Daredevil in Hell's Kitchen, New York City.

The Mechanism ("O Mecanismo"): A Brazilian series inspired by the "Car Wash Operation" and produced for streaming by Netflix, whose first season was released in 2018—an ongoing police task force investigates major political corruption in contemporary Brazil.

Mindhunter: An American web TV series created for Netflix about two FBI agents in the late 1970s who expand criminal science by getting in to the minds of murderers. They interview imprisoned serial killers in order to understand how they think, with the hope of applying this knowledge to solving ongoing cases. It is based on the true crime book *Mindhunter: Inside the FBI's Elite Serial Crime Unit* written by John E. Douglas and Mark Olshaker.

Monk (USA, 2002–2009): Former San Francisco detective Adrian Monk becomes a police consultant after his wife is murdered. Monk has extraordinary deductive skills and demonstrates impressive critical thinking and an unwillingness to take what he sees for granted. However, his OCD hampers him in dealing with others. The show's sense of humor tempers otherwise serious subject matter.

Murdoch Mysteries: Set in Toronto during the Victorian Era and based on Maureen Jennings' books, the show features Detective William Murdoch, played by Yannick Bisson, who uses cutting-edge forensic techniques, for that time period, to solve crimes. The coroner, a woman, unusual for that time, struggles for recognition on the show. Aired in Canada and in Greece in November 2017.

Narcos: An American Netflix TV series based upon Colombia's infamously violent and powerful drug cartels. Seasons 1 and 2 are based on the story of Pablo Escobar, who became a billionaire through the production and distribution of cocaine. Season three picks up after the fall of Escobar and continues to follow the Drug Enforcement Administration as it goes up against the rise of other infamous cartels.

NCIS: An American procedural crime drama about a fictional team of special agents. NCIS stands for Naval Criminal Investigative Service. NCIS' primary function is to investigate criminal activities involving the US Navy and US Marine Corps, though its broad mandate includes national security, counterintelligence, counter-terrorism, cyber warfare, and the protection of US naval assets worldwide.

NCIS: New Orleans (2014–): An offshoot of the NCIS franchise centered on the Mississippi River and Texas panhandle looking at crimes, especially murders, connected with the naval military. USA.

News Alert ("Plantão de Polícia"): A Brazilian television series broadcast between 1979 and 1981; an uneducated crime news journalist investigated criminal stories of the underworld in very dangerous situations.

No Offence (Channel 4, 2015–): Manchester-set British police procedural mixing serious murder investigations of a team led by a blunt and dynamic woman with some black humor from the acclaimed writer/producer of social dramas Paul Abbott (*Clocking Off* and *Shameless*—2016 appendix).

Ojciec Mateusz ("Father Mateusz," 2008–): The series presents the adventures of a Roman Catholic Priest Father Mateusz (Artur Żmijewski), who takes a job as a priest in a small parish in Sandomierz. As a pastor, Father Mateusz solves mysteries and helps local police solve criminal cases. It is a Polish version of the cult Italian TV series Don Matteo. Poland.

Open City ("Cidade Aberta"): The first Brazilian television series and was broadcast in 1965 and 1966; a senior crime news journalist investigated crimes with support of a junior colleague and against the opposition of the journal chief-editor.

Orange is the New Black (2013–): A comedy drama set in a women's prison looking at the interactions and past lives of the inmates of the New York federal penitentiary over 2 seasons and 26 episodes thus far. Netflix, USA.

The Other Side of Paradise ("O Outro Lado do Paraíso"): A Brazilian telenovela broadcast between 2017 and 2018; a teacher seeks revenge from the wealth group of people from Tocantins, in central Brazil, who conspired to keep her in an asylum for mentally illness over a long period of time.

Peaky Blinders (BBC, 2013–): Set in Birmingham, England, between the Wars, this follows the exploits and travails of a gangster family, the Shelbys, and their feuds with other gangs and their run-ins with the law.

Perry Mason: A television series from the United States broadcast between 1957 and 1966, in which a criminal defense lawyer would eventually find a witness or any other evidence that would clarify the situation and result in the acquittal of his client.

Police Station for Women ("Delegacia de Mulheres"): A Brazilian television series broadcast in 1990. A special police station was founded to investigate crimes committed against female victims and to deal with domestic violence against women.

Polizeiruf 110 ("Police Call 110," DFF1, 1971–1991 and 1993–present, ARD, 247+ eps.): The East German counterpart of the *Tatort* series became the most successful crime series in the history of the DFF (East German State TV). A variety of officers of the People's Police investigated a sort of crime that officially shouldn't exist in a socialist state. Because of the social background, the realistic locations and cases often inspired by real-life events the older episodes are a fascinating time capsule offering a glimpse into the customs and circumstances of real existing Socialism. It's also the only crime TV show of the GDR that survived the fall of the Berlin Wall and continues to this day, alternating with the *Tatort* entries on Sunday nights, adopting some of *Tatort's* aesthetics as well. Germany.

The Professionals (ITV, 1977–1983): Two agents from Criminal Intelligence 5, Bodie and Doyle, undertake assignments against terrorists, hit-men, racist groups and espionage suspects under the direction of their boss George Cowley.

The Prohibited City ("A Cidade Proibida"): A Brazilian television series broadcast in 2017—a former police officer becomes a private detective and takes cases of adultery, often falling in love for the women he is supposed to be investigating.

The Punisher ("A Justiceira"): A Brazilian television series broadcast in 1997—a former female police officer joined a death squad led by a judge that informally sanctioned criminal suspects that were not punished within the formal justice system.

Raped: My Story (Channel 5, 2017): Documentary looks at the stories behind the statistics recounting the experiences of ten survivors who speak publicly about what happened to them.

Ripper Street (BBC, 2012–2016): Set in London shortly after the Jack the Ripper murders, this series followed the work of H Division in the poor area of Whitechapel covering murder and robbery in the context of the events of the time such as strikes and contemporary political conflicts.

Scott and Bailey (ITV, 2011–2016): Police procedural focusing on the work of two women detectives in Manchester working for the Major Incident Team covering principally murder and rape over five seasons and providing a perspectives on their home lives.

Shetland (BBC, 2013–): Set on the far flung treeless Shetland Islands these short 5 seasons follow the work of Jimmy Perez and his female and male assistants as they investigate murders and are based on the novels of Ann Cleeves.

Silent Witness (BBC, 1996–): Long-running British series centered on the work of various forensic pathologists as they bring their skills to the service of the police. Set mainly in London and in its twenty-first season at the time of writing.

SOKO Leipzig ("Special Commission Leipzig," ZDF, 2001–): The longest-running offshoot of the classic crime series *Soko 5113* reports on the emotionally charged investigations of a special commission of the Leipzig police. The team around chief detective Hans-Joachim Trautzschke regularly deals with explosive capital crimes in exotic locations all over the world. Germany.

Special Branch (ITV, 1969–1974): Police drama series focused on the work of the anti-espionage and anti-terrorist department of the London Metropolitan Police.

Suits (2011–): Smooth, successful corporate lawyer/deal closer who works alongside his hypersmart protégé (who is not actually the Harvard law graduate he pretends to be). Only his boss and an assistant know this, and they all work for a strong African American female boss. The series follows the adventures of the pair as they bend or break ethical rules in order to keep the secret while trying cases. USA.

S.W.A.T. (2017): An American crime drama television series based on the 1975 television series of the same name. The series centers on Sergeant Daniel "Hondo" Harrelson, played by Shemar Moore. Hondo is a Los Angeles native and former Marine. Because he is L.A. born and raised, Hondo feels deeply loyal not only to his "brothers in blue" but also to the people they serve. As such, he tries to build a bridge between the police and the community.

Taggart (ITV, 1983–2010): Glasgow—set police procedural mainly concerned with murder which survived the death of the title character in 1994 but remained imbued with his spirit.

Task Force ("Força-Tarefa"): A Brazilian television series broadcast between 2009 and 2011—the routine of the division of internal affairs of the military police in their investigation of crimes committed by police officers in Rio de Janeiro.

Tatort ("Crime Scene"): The flagship of German crime shows sets standards in almost every department. It is the longest-running series (since 1970) and has the greatest number of investigators in the greatest variety of locales (apparently almost every major city in Germany was at least once the backdrop of a *Tatort* episode), as well as the highest ratings. Moreover, *Tatort* is a transnational show, featuring one investigator team in Austria (Vienna) and one in Switzerland (Lucerne, and from 2020, Zürich), produced by the respective national public broadcasters. The respective regional peculiarities of the city or region of each episode are regularly embedded in the action, as are the personal issues of the commissioners. In addition, socially explosive topics are repeatedly presented in a popular form as part of the series. It is precisely these sociopolitical aspects that have made *Tatort* the subject of various academic studies. Germany, Austria, Switzerland.

Third Watch: Taking place in the fictional fifty-fifth Precinct in New York City, we see the adventures of a group of men and women who serve the City of New York as police officers, firefighters, and paramedics.

Top of the Lake: A brave detective must confront small town secrets and herself as she is trying to find the truth about the disappearance of a twelve-year-old girl near a frozen lake.

Trailer Park Boys: A Canadian mockumentary television series focused on the misadventures of three trailer park residents. The show follows the alcohol-feuled misadventures of three longtime friends and petty criminals who run scams from their fictional Nova Scotia trailer park.

The Tunnel (Sky, 2013–2018): British French collaboration drawing on the concept of *The Bridge* (2016 appendix) with two police forces investigating death in the channel tunnel and emphasizing cultural differences.

Unforgiven (ITV, 2009): Three-part British drama about a woman convicted of the murder of two police officers, searching for her sister after serving fifteen years in prison and avoiding the revenge plans of one of victim's sons.

Vera: Nonglamorous, middle-aged, down to earth Detective Vera Stanhope solves crime in rural and urban North East England. Britain.

Violent Men: Men Behind Bars (Channel 4, 2017): A look behind the bars at the experiences and perspectives of prisoners convicted of violent offences in a maximum security Scottish prison.

Wataha ("The Border," 2014, 2017): The series tells the story of a Polish border patrol unit that operates and monitors the heavily wooded border between Poland and Ukraine in the Bieszczady Mountains. The first season focused mostly on solving the mystery of a bomb rip in a guard post, which killed all but one members of the border guards' team. In the second season, prosecutor

Iga Dobosz returns after four years to Bieszczady Mountains to investigate a gruesome murder of over twenty illegal immigrants.

The Web ("A Teia"): A Brazilian television series broadcast in 2014; a chief police investigator solves an important airport robbery.

Wilder (SRF, November 2017–): A Swiss crime show and one of the most successful TV series in Switzerland. In the small and quite mountain village Oberwies, a world-famous artist is murdered and the daughter of an Egyptian investor disappears. Detective Rosa Wilder and her partner Manfred Kägi investigate both cases and discover a dark secret that lies in the village's past. Switzerland.

WPC 56 (BBC, 2013–2015): A young woman police constable works in the male-dominated British police force of the 1950s over three seasons. Each five-part season is centered on a single case.

Index

About the Contributors

Christine A. Corcos received her law degree from Case Western Reserve Law School and an MA in history from Michigan State University. She is the Richard C. Cadwallader Associate Professor of Law, Louisiana State University Law Center, and associate professor of women's and gender studies at LSU. She teaches media law, entertainment law, theater law, European Union law, gender and the law, privacy law, and law and the humanities. Her research and writing interests include legal history, the First Amendment, media law, and law and popular culture, on which she often speaks to the press. She is the coauthor of several casebooks, including *Theater Law*, *Law and Popular Culture* (2nd ed., with David Papke), and *European Union Law* (2nd ed., with Alain Levasseur, et al.). Her current project is a collection of over twenty essays written by law professors from three countries on how to teach law using the humanities, to be published by Carolina Academic Press in the fall of 2018. She is a member of the board of editors for the *International Journal for the Semiotics of Law* and a member of the board of governors for the Law and Humanities Institute. She blogs for *Media Law Prof Blog*, *Law and Magic Blog*, *Feminist Law Professors*, *Concurring Opinions*, and the *Law and Humanities Blog*. She and several other law professors have recently launched hedgehogsandfoxes.org, an open-access website devoted to law and the humanities.

Olga Derzioti is a graduate of the Department of Mass Media and Communication at the National and Kapodistrian University of Athens. She holds an MSc in gender, media, and culture from the London School of Economics, in which she focuses her research on the representation of gender in exilic/diasporic cinema. Her dissertation, titled "Contested Sites of Gender and Nation: Articulating Gender Politics and Its Representational Treatment in Transnational Feminist Cinema," examines the possibility of alternative routes to the stereotypical cinematic framing of Middle Eastern women as "carriers of tradition" by distinctive filming propensities of the contemporary transnational feminist cinema, regarding both the narrative structure and the visual form. She is interested in issues relating to the crisis of representation, colonial/ postcolonial memory, neoliberalism and cultural dislocations, ethics and queer subjectivities, gendered migration, and gendered violence.

Pedro Fortes is professor of law at FGV Law School (Rio de Janeiro), research associate at the Centre for Socio-Legal Studies at the University of Oxford, and public prosecutor at the Attorney General's Office of Rio de Janeiro, Brazil. He holds a DPhil (Oxford), a JSM (Stanford), a LLM (Harvard), a MBE (COPPE), a LLB (UFRJ), and a BA (PUC-Rio). Recipient of three teaching awards, he has taught complex litigation, constitutional law, and criminal law and procedure. His research interests include law and development, law and popular culture, and law and technology. Between 2012 and 2017, he was the editor-in-chief of the FGV Law School series (Cadernos FGV Direito Rio) and edited two books on law, legal education, and popular culture. Additionally, he edited the special issue of the *Journal of the Oxford Centre for Social Legal Studies* on law and popular culture in 2017, together with coeditor Michael Asimow. In this field, he coined the expression "symbolic affirmative action" and discusses the theme of (un) equal representation in "Affirmative Cinema: When Film-Makers Defend Minorities" in Michael Asimow et al., *Law and Popular Culture: International Perspectives* (2014), "Lights, Camera, Affirmative Action: Does Hollywood Protect Minorities?" (*JOxCSLS*, Special Issue 2017). He has been visiting professor at the WB NUJS (Kolkata), visiting scholar at the Goethe Universität (Frankfurt), and visiting researcher at the MPI (Hamburg and Frankfurt). Fortes currently chairs the WG Law and Development at the RCSL, the CRN Law and Development at the LSA, and the stream Exploring Legal Borderlands at the SLSA.

Lukas Musumeci is researcher, lecturer, and writing consultant at the Writing Centre, University of Hamburg, Germany, and lecturer at the Faculty of Law, University of Basel, Switzerland, where he is also a PhD candidate. Before that, from 2013 to 2015, he was researcher at the Zentrum für rechtswissenschaftliche Fachdidaktik ("Centre for Legal Education") at the University of Hamburg and, from 2008 until 2013, research assistant at the Faculty of Law in Basel. Musumeci teaches courses in academic writing, especially legal writing, constitutional, administrative, and public international law. In 2011, he won the Credit Suisse Teaching Award for Best Teaching (together with Mareike Schmidt). His publications cover the fields of public international law, constitutional law, legal education, and academic writing.

Nickos Myrtou is a specialized Ttaching personnel and a PhD candidate in the Department of Communication and Media Studies of the National and Kapodistrian University of Athens where he teaches television and radio production as well as documentary production. As a member of the department's Audiovisual Media Laboratory, he is in charge of student productions and research on new technologies and practices. He holds a BA and MA degree from the Department of Communication and Media Studies. His MA thesis, "Web Documentary: Multimedia Documentation in the Digital Era," explores the new medium for documentarians and how the basic schools of documentary have transcended in the age of Internet. His PhD examines the transformative extent of digital media on archives and documentaries. He is a guest lecturer on the yearly project "Dialogue of Civilizations: Greece: Then and Now—The Greek Media" of Northeastern University. Also, as a videographer and editor, he was worked in a number of short films and documentaries. He edited the book *Television Production, Video montage, Technology-Art, and Technique* and has authored articles for major technical publications about montage techniques and post-production.

Fabian Odermatt is research assistant and PhD candidate at the Institute for Criminal Law and Criminology at the University of Berne, Switzerland. Fabian's thesis, "The Seduction Through Legal Representations in Film," is a film-scientific approach to the question as to what extent legal films can have a hypothetical effect on their viewers. In addition, Odermatt works as court clerk at the Criminal Court of Baselland and as actuary for the cantonal commission of experts on the supervision of public prosecutors.

Stamatis Poulakidakos is senior research associate and teaching assistant at the Department of Communication and Media Studies of the National and Kapodistrian University of Athens (NKUA). He holds a BA and a PhD from the Department of Communication and Media Studies (NKUA), and an MA degree in new media, information, and society from London School of Economics (LSE). He works at the Laboratory for Social Research in Mass Media at the Department of Communication and Media Studies (NKUA), specializing in media monitoring and quantitative content analysis. At the same time, he is tutor for the BA in Media Production Programme at the Athens Metropolitan College, in collaboration with Queen Margaret University of Edinburgh. He has taken part in many research projects and has participated in various Greek and international conferences. He has authored the book *Propaganda and Public Discourse*: *The presentation of the MoU by the*

Greek Media. In addition, he has published several papers on issues having to do with political communication, propaganda, social media and the public sphere, political advertisements, protests, and other media-related issues.

Peter Robson has an LLB from St. Andrews University and a PhD from Strathclyde University. He is a solicitor and sits as a judge in the Appeals Services dealing with disability issues and is professor of social welfare law at the University of Strathclyde. He has written on law, film, and television in journals and edited collections including coediting *Law and Film* (with Stefan Machura) in 2001. His most recent film work (with Steve Greenfield and Guy Osborn) *Film and the Law: The Cinema of Justice*, was published in 2010 and updates the influential first edition. He is coeditor, with Jessica Silbey, of *Law and Justice on the Small Screen* (2012). He is the author of essays on "British Lawyers on TV," and is coeditor, with Jennifer L. Schulz, of the global TV lawyers project—*A Transnational Study of Law and Justice on TV* (2016). He has recently published essays on law and theater, women lawyers on TV, and law in modern popular fiction.

Jennifer L. Schulz, SJD, is associate professor in the Faculty of Law at the University of Manitoba, Canada, and fellow of the Winkler Institute for Dispute Resolution at Osgoode Hall Law School, Toronto. She has also served as executive director of the Manitoba Legal Research Institute. Schulz is the author of many articles, chapters, and books on mediation and popular culture topics, and she presents her work across North America and Europe. Schulz has won three teaching awards, a national alternative dispute resolution service award, and is a federal and international research grant recipient. She has been a visiting scholar at the Faculty of Law, University of Cambridge; Birkbeck College School of Law, University of London; the Centre for the Legal Profession, Faculty of Law, University of Toronto; the Winkler Institute for Dispute Resolution, Osgoode Hall Law School, Toronto; and the Centre for Feminist Legal Studies, Peter A. Allard School of Law, University of British Columbia. This is her second collaboration with Peter Robson—the first being *A Transnational Study of Law & Justice on TV* (2016).

Germano Schwartz is dean of UniRitter (Brazil). He has an MA from Santa Cruz do Sul University and a PhD from University of Vale do Rio dos Sinos (Brazil). He is a lawyer and professor of social theory of human rights in the Master of Human Rights of UniRitter. He has written on law and arts based on the social systems theory developed by Niklas Luhmann. His work can be seen by his books on this theme: *A Constituição, A Literatura e Direito* (2006) and *Direito & Rock* (2014). He is coeditor of *Another Brick in the*

Law (2016) and of *Direito & Literatura: o encontro entre Themis e Apoio* (2008). He has written eighty papers in numerous languages.

Franziska Stürmer, PhD, is currently working as post-doc at Julius-Maximilians-Universität Würzburg, Germany. She received her PhD in 2014 with a study on Thomas Mann's "Doktor Faustus" and has since done research on law in popular media and on transcultural identity in contemporary literature. She is writing her post-doc thesis on this topic. Stürmer's recent publications on law and media include: *Recht Populär: Populärkulturelle Rechtsdarstellungen in aktuellen Texten und Medien, Nomos* (with Patrick Meier, 2016); "Love and Other Flights—Legal Subtexts and the Law as a Strategy of Reader Guidance in Bernhard Schlink's *Liebesfluchten*" (also with Patrick Meier; *Law and Literature* 2(28): 255–75).

Zofia Zawadzka is a barrister with a civil law and intellectual property law practice in Białystok, Poland. She worked as lecturer in law at the Intellectual Property Law Unit, Faculty of Law, at the University of Białystok from 2011 to 2014, where she taught courses in the areas of intellectual property law and media law. Her doctoral thesis, completed in 2011, examines legal regulation of the rights and conflicts between freedom of the press and privacy and image protection of public figures. Zawadzka's research interests include various areas of intellectual property law. She is the author of the monograph *Press Freedom and Right to Privacy of Public Figures: A Problem of Solving the Conflict of Rules* (2013), coauthor of two textbooks on the subjects of intellectual property rights and media law, and of numerous law review articles concerning aspects of intellectual property and human rights.

www.ingramcontent.com/pod-product-compliance
Lightning Source LLC
LaVergne TN
LVHW090401210926
848480LV00002B/415
* 9 7 8 1 4 9 8 5 7 2 9 2 7 *